a
BENITO
CERENO
handbook

Wadsworth Guides to Literary Study
Maurice Beebe, General Editor

APPROACHES TO *WALDEN*
edited by Lauriat Lane, Jr., University of New Brunswick

A *BENITO CERENO* HANDBOOK
edited by Seymour L. Gross, University of Notre Dame

CONRAD'S *HEART OF DARKNESS* AND THE CRITICS
edited by Bruce Harkness, University of Illinois

CONRAD'S *SECRET SHARER* AND THE CRITICS
edited by Bruce Harkness, University of Illinois

CRIME AND PUNISHMENT AND THE CRITICS
edited by Edward Wasiolek, University of Chicago

DARWIN AND HIS CRITICS: The Darwinian Revolution
edited by Bernard R. Kogan, University of Illinois, Chicago

J. D. SALINGER AND THE CRITICS
edited by William F. Belcher and James W. Lee,
North Texas State University

THE *KING LEAR* PERPLEX
edited by Helmut Bonheim, University of California, Santa Barbara

LITERARY CENSORSHIP: Principles, Cases, Problems
edited by Kingsley Widmer, California State College at San Diego,
and Eleanor Widmer

LITERARY SYMBOLISM: An Introduction to the Interpretation of
Literature
edited by Maurice Beebe, Purdue University

MELVILLE'S *BILLY BUDD* AND THE CRITICS
edited by William T. Stafford, Purdue University

OEDIPUS REX: A MIRROR FOR GREEK DRAMA
edited by Albert Cook, State University of New York at Buffalo

THE RIME OF THE ANCIENT MARINER: A HANDBOOK
edited by Royal A. Gettmann, University of Illinois

SATIRE: THEORY AND PRACTICE
edited by Charles A. Allen and George D. Stephens, California State
College at Long Beach

A *SCARLET LETTER* HANDBOOK
edited by Seymour L. Gross, University of Notre Dame

VOLTAIRE'S *CANDIDE* AND THE CRITICS
edited by Milton P. Foster, Eastern Michigan University

WHITMAN THE POET: Materials for Study
edited by John C. Broderick, Wake Forest College

a
BENITO
CERENO
handbook

edited by
SEYMOUR L. GROSS
University of Notre Dame

WADSWORTH PUBLISHING COMPANY, INC.
Belmont, California

For
The Little Professor
Tommy Linford Gross

L.C. Cat. Card No.: 65–22640

Printed in the United States of America

PREFACE

When George William Curtis read *Benito Cereno* for *Putnam's Monthly Magazine* in April 1855, he decided that despite "the dreary documents at the end" the story was well done and "ought not to be lost."[1] It was accordingly serialized in the last three issues of 1855. The following year, along with "The Piazza," "Bartleby," "The Lightning-Rod Man," "The Encantadas," and "The Bell-Tower," it comprised *The Piazza Tales*, the only collection of stories by Melville published in his lifetime. Whereas such lesser artistic performances as "The Bell-Tower" and "The Lightning-Rod Man" were included in various anthologies of American writing published in the late nineteenth century, *Benito Cereno* was "lost" until 1924, when it once again appeared in print.

Contemporary reviewers of *The Piazza Tales* found *Benito Cereno* (when they singled it out—which most did not) "thrilling" and "powerful," "told with due gravity," "most painfully interesting," or a new but not improved specimen "of his sea romances." Not a single reviewer, however, judged it to be the best piece in the collection.[2] Melville's own estimate of the relative merit of *Benito Cereno* can perhaps be deduced from his original plan to call the book *Benito Cereno & Other Sketches*, in which the other four pieces ("The Piazza" was written specifically for the revised plan) were to follow this leader.[3]

Metaphorically speaking, literary history has agreed with the original plan for *The Piazza Tales*. Ever since 1928, when Edward J. O'Brien placed *Benito Cereno* first in his list of The Fifteen Finest Short Stories, calling it "the noblest short story in American literature," it has evoked more critical response than any other piece of Melville's shorter fiction, with the possible exception of *Billy Budd*. And, from a somewhat different quarter, the continuing viability of the story is evidenced in Ralph Ellison's choosing a quotation from *Benito Cereno* as an epigraph for *Invisible Man* (1952), which has been called the most profound novel about the Negro in America, and in Robert Lowell's recent (1964) verse-drama adaptation of Melville's novella.

The present volume contains the text of *Benito Cereno;* Melville's primary source for the story, Chapter XVIII of Amasa Delano's *Narrative of Voyages* (1817); and a representative selection of criticism. Because so many of the available texts are marred by substantive

---

1 Quoted in Jay Leyda, *The Melville Log* (New York, 1951), II, pp. 500–501.
2 Hugh W. Hetherington, *Melville's Reviewers* (Chapel Hill, 1961), pp. 248–255.
3 Merrell R. Davis and William H. Gilman, eds., *The Letters of Herman Melville* (New Haven, 1960), pp. 178–179.

errors, a special effort has been made to present a text that is as close to what Melville intended as is possible. The inclusion of all textual variants in footnotes, both revisions and accidental errors, should enable the student to study Melville's craft at work and should give him some small idea of the difficulty of preserving texts intact. Since so much of *Benito Cereno* criticism depends to a greater or lesser extent on the critic's evaluation of Melville's use of his source, its inclusion here should facilitate the student's judgment of the validity of the critic's assumptions and conclusions. For the sake of focus, the criticism has been divided into three main but by no means absolutely discrete categories: essays that concentrate on the implications inherent in the narrative point of view, Amasa Delano; essays that assess Melville's attitude toward the Negro and slavery; and essays that set out to explicate Melville's use of the source and various thematic and symbolic motifs. Studies that approach the work from somewhat different angles are listed in the annotated bibliography in Part Five.

The questions in Part Four range from those that can be answered in relatively short papers to those demanding large-scale, extended efforts; every question, however, requires study of both the story and the pertinent criticism. Whenever applicable, the student is directed to additional readings.

This book is designed to serve several purposes. First, with the essays and questions organized around certain critical problems, it may be used when combining research techniques with the study of literature. Second, with inclusion of the materials for a study of Melville's revisions, the primary source, and a variety of critical approaches in the essays, it can serve as an introduction to the study of methods of literary criticism and scholarship. Moreover, the book should stimulate class discussion on all levels of instruction.

Since many of the critical essays included in this anthology are excerpts, I have taken the liberty of giving them my own titles so as to indicate their content. (Original titles are included in the source notes at the bottom of the first page of each selection.) I have transcribed the texts as accurately as possible but have corrected obvious misprints, eliminated footnotes where feasible, and renumbered the remaining ones. The original pagination of the articles is indicated by raised brackets in the text. The amount of material omitted from any essay can be ascertained by checking the original pagination (indicated in the raised brackets) against the complete bibliographical entry in the footnote at the bottom of the first page of each selection. Normal-spaced ellipses (. . .) indicate the editor's omissions; thin-spaced ellipses (. . .) indicate those in the original material.

I would like to express my appreciation to Mr. Lawrence Kelly, Mrs. Mary Ann Domonkos, and especially to Mr. Richard Campolucci, for their efforts on behalf of this book.

CONTENTS

Source, Symbol, and Theme

PART FOUR: QUESTIONS AND TOPICS

PART FIVE: BIBLIOGRAPHY

BENITO CERENO

Herman Melville

In the year 1799, Captain Amasa Delano, of Duxbury, in Massachusetts, commanding a large sealer and general trader, lay at anchor with a valuable cargo, in the harbor of St. Maria—a small, desert, uninhabited island toward the southern extremity of the long coast of Chili. There he had touched for water.

On the second day, not long after dawn, while lying in his berth, his mate came below, informing him that a strange sail was coming into the bay. Ships were then not so plenty in those waters as now. He rose, dressed, and went on deck.

The morning was one peculiar to that coast. Everything was mute and calm; everything gray. The sea, though undulated into long roods of swells, seemed fixed, and was sleeked at the surface like waved lead that has cooled and set in the smelter's mould. The sky seemed a gray [surtout].[1] Flights of troubled gray fowl, kith and kin with flights of troubled gray vapors among which they were mixed, skimmed low and fitfully over the waters, as swallows over meadows before storms. Shadows present, foreshadowing deeper shadows to come.

To Captain Delano's surprise, the stranger, viewed through the glass, showed no colors; though to do so upon entering a haven, however uninhabited in its shores, where but a single other ship might be lying, was the custom among peaceful seamen of all nations. Considering the lawlessness and loneliness of the spot, and the sort of stories, at that day, associated with those seas, Captain Delano's surprise might have deepened into some uneasiness had he not been a person of a singularly undistrustful good nature, not liable, except on extraordi-

---

Benito Cereno was first published in the October, November, and December 1855 issues of *Putnam's Monthly Magazine;* it appeared again, in revised form, the following year in *The Piazza Tales*, which the present text follows. There is no extant manuscript of the story. For the purpose of comparison, textual variants (differences between the two versions) have been indicated by placing the *Piazza* version in brackets in the text and the *Putnam* version in a footnote. Where the editor has occasionally opted for the *Putnam* version or, more rarely, has chosen still another alternative, the choice has also been bracketed and an explanation given in a footnote.

1 mantle

1

nary and repeated [incentives],[2] and hardly then, to indulge in personal alarms, any way involving the imputation of malign evil in man. Whether, in view of what humanity is capable, such a trait implies, along with a benevolent heart, more than ordinary quickness and accuracy of intellectual perception, may be left to the wise to determine.

But whatever misgivings might have obtruded on first seeing the stranger, would almost, in any seaman's mind, have been dissipated by observing that, the ship, in navigating into the harbor, was drawing too near the land[; a sunken reef making out off her bow.][3] This seemed to prove her a stranger, indeed, not only to the sealer, but the island; consequently, she could be no wonted freebooter on that ocean. With no small interest, Captain Delano continued to watch her—a proceeding not much facilitated by the vapors partly mantling the hull, through which the far matin light from her cabin streamed equivocally enough; much like the sun—by this time [hemisphered][4] on the rim of the horizon, and, apparently, in company with the strange ship entering the harbor—which, wimpled by the same low, creeping clouds, showed not unlike a Lima intriguante's one sinister eye peering across the Plaza from the Indian loop-hole of her dusk saya-y-manta.

It might have been but a deception of the vapors, but, the longer the stranger was watched the more singular appeared her manœuvres. Ere long it seemed hard to decide whether she meant to come in or no —what she wanted, or what she was about. The wind, which had breezed up a little during the night, was now extremely light and baffling, which the more increased the apparent uncertainty of her movements.

Surmising, at last, that it might be a ship in distress, Captain Delano ordered his whale-boat to be dropped, and, much to the wary opposition of his mate, prepared to board her, and, at the least, pilot her in. On the night previous, a fishing-party of the seamen had gone a long distance to some detached rocks out of sight from the sealer, and, an hour or two before daybreak, had returned, having met with no small success. Presuming that the stranger might have been long off soundings, the good captain put several baskets of the fish, for presents, into his boat, and so pulled away. From her continuing too near the sunken reef, deeming her in danger, calling to his men, he made all haste to apprise those on board of their situation. But, some time ere the boat came up, the wind, light though it was, having shifted, had headed the vessel off, as well as partly broken the vapors from about her.

---

2 excitement
3 ,for her own safety's sake, owing to a sunken reef making out off her bow.
4 crescented

Upon gaining a less remote view, the ship, when made signally visible on the verge of the leaden-hued swells, with the shreds of fog here and there raggedly furring her, appeared like a white-washed monastery after a thunder-storm, seen perched upon some dun cliff among the Pyrenees. But it was no purely fanciful resemblance which now, for a moment, almost led Captain Delano to think that nothing less than a ship-load of monks was before him. Peering over the bulwarks were what really seemed, in the hazy distance, throngs of dark cowls; while, fitfully revealed through the open port-holes, other dark moving figures were dimly descried as of Black Friars pacing the cloisters.

Upon a still nigher approach, this appearance was modified, and the true character of the vessel was plain—a Spanish merchantman of the first class, carrying negro slaves, amongst other valuable freight, from one colonial port to another. A very large, and, in its time, a very fine vessel, such as in those days were at intervals encountered along that main; sometimes superseded Acapulco treasure-ships, or retired frigates of the Spanish king's navy, which, like superannuated Italian palaces, still, under a decline of masters, preserved signs of former state.

As the whale-boat drew more and more nigh, the cause of the peculiar pipe-clayed aspect of the stranger was seen in the slovenly neglect pervading her. The spars, ropes, and great part of the bulwarks, looked woolly, from long unacquaintance with the scraper, tar, and the brush. Her keel seemed laid, her ribs put together, and she launched, from Ezekiel's Valley of Dry Bones.

In the present business in which she was engaged, the ship's general model and rig appeared to have undergone no material change from their original warlike and Froissart pattern. However, no guns were seen.

The tops were large, and were railed about with what had once been octagonal net-work, all now in sad disrepair. These tops hung overhead like three ruinous aviaries, in one of which was seen perched, on a ratlin, a white noddy, a strange fowl, so called from its lethargic, somnambulistic character, being frequently caught by hand at sea. Battered and mouldy, the castellated forecastle seemed some ancient turret, long ago taken by assault, and then left to decay. Toward the stern, two high-raised quarter galleries—the balustrades here and there covered with dry, tindery sea-moss—opening out from the unoccupied state-cabin, whose dead-lights, for all the mild weather, were hermetically closed and calked—these tenantless balconies hung over the sea as if it were the grand Venetian canal. But the principal relic of faded grandeur was the ample oval of the shield-like stern-piece, intricately carved with the arms of Castile and Leon, medallioned about by groups of mythological or symbolical devices; uppermost and central of which was a dark satyr in a mask, holding his foot on the prostrate neck of a writhing figure, likewise masked.

Whether the ship had a figure-head, or only a plain beak, was not quite certain, owing to canvas wrapped about that part, either to protect it while undergoing a re-furbishing, or else decently to hide its decay. Rudely painted or chalked, as in a sailor freak, along the forward side of a sort of pedestal below the canvas, was the sentence, "*Seguid vuestro jefe,*" (follow your leader); while upon the tarnished headboards, near by, appeared, in stately capitals, once gilt, the ship's name, "SAN DOMINICK," each letter streakingly corroded with tricklings of copper-spike rust; while, like mourning weeds, dark festoons of sea-grass slimily swept to and fro over the name, with every hearse-like roll of the hull.

As, at last, the boat was hooked from the bow along toward the gangway amidship, its keel, while yet some inches separated from the hull, harshly grated as on a sunken coral reef. It proved a huge bunch of conglobated barnacles adhering below the water to the side like a wen—a token of baffling airs and long calms passed somewhere in those seas.

Climbing the side, the visitor was at once surrounded by a clamorous throng of whites and blacks, but the latter outnumbering the former more than could have been expected, negro transportation-ship as the stranger in port was. But, in one language, and as with one voice, all poured out a common tale of suffering; in which the negresses, of whom there were not a few, exceeded the others in their dolorous vehemence. The scurvy, together with the fever, had swept off a great part of their number, more especially the Spaniards. Off Cape Horn they had narrowly escaped shipwreck; then, for days together, they had lain tranced without wind; their provisions were low; their water next to none; their lips that moment were baked.

While Captain Delano was thus made the mark of all eager tongues, his one eager glance took in [all faces],[5] with every other object about him.

Always upon first boarding a large and populous ship at sea, especially a foreign one, with a nondescript crew such as Lascars or Manilla men, the impression varies in a peculiar way from that produced by first entering a strange house with strange inmates in a strange land. Both house and ship—the one by its walls and blinds, the other by its high bulwarks like ramparts—hoard from view their interiors till the last moment: but in the case of the ship there is this addition; that the living spectacle it contains, upon its sudden and complete disclosure, has, in contrast with the blank ocean which zones it, something of the effect of enchantment. The ship seems unreal; these strange costumes, gestures, and faces, but a shadowy tableau just emerged from the deep, which directly must receive back what it gave.

Perhaps it was some such influence, as above is attempted to be

---

[5] all the faces

described, which, in Captain Delano's mind, heightened whatever, upon a staid scrutiny, might have seemed unusual; especially the conspicuous figures of four elderly grizzled negroes, their heads like black, doddered willow tops, who, in venerable contrast to the tumult below them, were couched, sphynx-like, one on the starboard cathead, another on the larboard, and the remaining pair face to face on the opposite bulwarks above the main-chains. They each had bits of unstranded old junk in their hands, and, with a sort of stoical self-content, were picking the junk into oakum, a small heap of which lay by their sides. They accompanied the task with a continuous, low, monotonous chant; droning and druling away like so many gray-headed bag-pipers playing a funeral march.

The quarter-deck rose into an ample elevated poop, upon the forward verge of which, lifted, like the oakum-pickers, some eight feet above the general throng, sat along in a row, separated by regular spaces, the cross-legged figures of six other blacks; each with a rusty hatchet in his hand, which, with a bit of brick and a rag, he was engaged like a scullion in scouring; while between each two was a small stack of hatchets, their rusted edges turned forward awaiting a like operation. Though occasionally the four oakum-pickers would briefly address some person or persons in the crowd below, yet the six hatchet-polishers neither spoke to others, nor breathed a whisper among themselves, but sat intent upon their task, except at intervals, when, with the peculiar love in negroes of uniting industry with pastime, two and two they sideways clashed their hatchets together, like cymbals, with a barbarous din. All six, unlike the generality, had the raw aspect of unsophisticated Africans.

But that first comprehensive glance which took in those ten figures, with scores less conspicuous, rested but an instant upon them, as, impatient of the hubbub of voices, the visitor turned in quest of whomsoever it might be that commanded the ship.

But as if not unwilling to let nature make known her own case among his suffering charge, or else in despair of restraining it for the time, the Spanish captain, a gentlemanly, reserved-looking, and rather young man to a stranger's eye, dressed with singular richness, but bearing plain traces of recent sleepless cares and disquietudes, stood passively by, leaning against the main-mast, at one moment casting a dreary, spiritless look upon his excited people, at the next an unhappy glance toward his visitor. By his side stood a black of small stature, in whose rude face, as occasionally, like a shepherd's dog, he mutely turned it up into the Spaniard's, sorrow and affection were equally blended.

Struggling through the throng, the American advanced to the Spaniard, assuring him of his sympathies, and offering to render whatever assistance might be in his power. To which the Spaniard returned for the present but grave and ceremonious acknowledgments, his national formality dusked by the saturnine mood of ill-health.

But losing no time in mere compliments, Captain Delano, returning to the gangway, had his [baskets][6] of fish brought up; and as the wind still continued light, so that some hours at least must elapse ere the ship could be brought to the anchorage, he bade his men return to the sealer, and fetch back as much water as the whale-boat could carry, with whatever soft bread the steward might have, all the remaining pumpkins on board, with a box of sugar, and a dozen of his private bottles of cider.

Not many minutes after the boat's pushing off, to the vexation of all, the wind entirely died away, and the tide turning, began drifting back the ship helplessly seaward. But trusting this would not long last, Captain Delano sought, with good hopes, to cheer up the strangers, feeling no small satisfaction that, with persons in their condition, he could—thanks to his frequent voyages along the Spanish main—converse with some freedom in their native tongue.

While left alone with them, he was not long in observing some things tending to heighten his first impressions; but surprise was lost in pity, both for the Spaniards and blacks, alike evidently reduced from scarcity of water and provisions; while long-continued suffering seemed to have brought out the less good-natured qualities of the negroes, besides, at the same time, impairing the Spaniard's authority over them. But, under the circumstances, precisely this condition of things was to have been anticipated. In armies, navies, cities, or families, in nature herself, nothing more relaxes good order than misery. Still, Captain Delano was not without the idea, that had Benito Cereno been a man of greater energy, misrule would hardly have come to the present pass. But the debility, constitutional or induced [by hardships],[7] bodily and mental, of the Spanish captain, was too obvious to be overlooked. A prey to settled dejection, as if long mocked with hope he would not now indulge it, even when it had ceased to be a mock, the prospect of that day, or evening at furthest, lying at anchor, with plenty of water for his people, and a brother captain to counsel and befriend, seemed in no perceptible degree to encourage him. His mind appeared unstrung, if not still more seriously affected. Shut up in these oaken walls, chained to one dull round of command, whose unconditionality cloyed him, like some hypochondriac abbot he moved slowly about, at times suddenly pausing, starting, or staring, biting his lip, biting his fingernail, flushing, paling, twitching his beard, with other symptoms of an absent or moody mind. This distempered spirit was lodged, as before hinted,

---

6 "baskets" in the *Putnam* version and not "basket" in the *Piazza* version is clearly what Melville intended (cf. p. 2, l. 36).

7 by the hardships

in as distempered a frame. He was rather tall, but seemed never to have been robust, and now with nervous suffering was almost worn to a skeleton. A tendency to some pulmonary complaint appeared to have been lately confirmed. His voice was like that of one with lungs half gone—hoarsely suppressed, a husky whisper. No wonder that, as in this state he tottered about, his private servant apprehensively followed him. Sometimes the negro gave his master his arm, or took his handkerchief out of his pocket for him; performing these and similar offices with that affectionate zeal which transmutes into something filial or fraternal acts in themselves but menial; and which has gained for the negro the repute of making the most pleasing body-servant in the world; one, too, whom a master need be on no stiffly superior terms with, but may treat with familiar trust; less a servant than a devoted companion.

Marking the noisy indocility of the blacks in general, as well as what seemed the sullen inefficiency of the whites, it was not without humane satisfaction that Captain Delano witnessed the steady good conduct of Babo.

But the good conduct of Babo, hardly more than the ill-behavior of others, seemed to withdraw the half-lunatic Don Benito from his cloudy languor. Not that such precisely was the impression made by the Spaniard on the mind of his visitor. The Spaniard's individual unrest was, for the present, but noted as a conspicuous feature in the ship's general affliction. Still, Captain Delano was not a little concerned at what he could not help taking for the time to be Don Benito's unfriendly indifference towards himself. The Spaniard's manner, too, conveyed a sort of sour and gloomy disdain, which he seemed at no pains to disguise. But this the American in charity ascribed to the harassing effects of sickness, since, in former instances, he had noted that there are peculiar natures on whom prolonged physical suffering seems to cancel every social instinct of kindness; as if, forced to black bread themselves, they deemed it but equity that each person coming nigh them should, indirectly, by some slight or affront, be made to partake of their fare.

But ere long Captain Delano bethought him that, indulgent as he was at the first, in judging the Spaniard, he might not, after all, have exercised charity enough. At bottom it was Don Benito's reserve which displeased him; but the same reserve was shown towards all but his [faithful][8] personal attendant. Even the formal reports which, according to sea-usage, were, at stated times, made to him by some petty underling, either a white, mulatto or black, he hardly had patience enough to listen to, without betraying contemptuous aversion. His manner upon such occasions was, in its degree, not unlike that which might be supposed to have been his imperial countryman's, Charles V.,

---

[8] "faithful" was omitted in the *Putnam* version.

just previous to the anchoritish retirement of that monarch from the throne.

This splenetic disrelish of his place was evinced in almost every function pertaining to it. Proud as he was moody, he condescended to no personal mandate. Whatever special orders were necessary, their delivery was delegated to his body-servant, who in turn transferred them to their ultimate destination, through runners, alert Spanish boys or slave boys, like pages or pilot-fish within easy call continually hovering round Don Benito. So that to have beheld this undemonstrative invalid gliding about, apathetic and mute, no landsman could have dreamed that in him was lodged a dictatorship beyond which, while at sea, there was no earthly appeal.

Thus, the Spaniard, regarded in his reserve, [seemed the][9] involuntary victim of mental disorder. But, in fact, his reserve might, in some degree, have proceeded from design. If so, [then here][10] was evinced the unhealthy climax of that icy though conscientious policy, more or less adopted by all commanders of large ships, which, except in signal emergencies, obliterates alike the manifestation of sway with every trace of sociality; transforming the man into a block, or rather into a loaded cannon, which, until there is call for thunder, has nothing to say.

Viewing him in this light, it seemed but a natural token of the perverse habit induced by a long course of such hard self-restraint, that, notwithstanding the present condition of his ship, the Spaniard should still persist in a demeanor, which, however harmless, or, it may be, appropriate, in a well-appointed vessel, such as the San Dominick might have been at the outset of the voyage, was anything but judicious now. But the Spaniard, perhaps, thought that it was with captains as with gods: reserve, under all events, must still be their cue. But probably this appearance of slumbering dominion might have been but an attempted disguise to conscious imbecility—not deep policy, but shallow device. But be all this as it might, whether Don Benito's manner was designed or not, the more Captain Delano noted its pervading reserve, the less he felt uneasiness at any particular manifestation of that reserve towards himself.

Neither were his thoughts taken up by the captain alone. Wonted to the quiet orderliness of the sealer's comfortable family of a crew, the noisy confusion of the San Dominick's suffering host repeatedly challenged his eye. Some prominent breaches, not only of discipline but of decency, were observed. These Captain Delano could not but ascribe, in the main, to the absence of those subordinate deck-officers to whom, along with higher duties, is intrusted what may be styled the police department of a populous ship. True, the old oakum-pickers appeared

---

9 seemed as the
10 then in Don Benito

at times to act the part of monitorial constables to their countrymen, the blacks; but though occasionally succeeding in allaying trifling outbreaks now and then between man and man, they could do little or nothing toward establishing general quiet. The San Dominick was in the condition of a transatlantic emigrant ship, among whose multitude of living freight are some individuals, doubtless, as little troublesome as crates and bales; but the friendly remonstrances of such with their ruder companions are of not so much avail as the unfriendly arm of the mate. What the San Dominick wanted was, what the emigrant ship has, stern superior officers. But on these decks not so much as a fourth-mate was to be seen.

The visitor's curiosity was roused to learn the particulars of those mishaps which had brought about such absenteeism, with its consequences; because, though deriving some inkling of the voyage from the wails which at the first moment had greeted him, yet of the details no clear understanding had been had. The best account would, doubtless, be given by the captain. Yet at first the visitor was loth to ask it, unwilling to provoke some distant rebuff. But plucking up courage, he at last accosted Don Benito, renewing the expression of his benevolent interest, adding, that did he (Captain Delano) but know the particulars of the ship's misfortunes, he would, perhaps, be better able in the end to relieve them. Would Don Benito favor him with the whole story.

Don Benito faltered; then, like some somnambulist suddenly interfered with, vacantly stared at his visitor, and ended by looking down on the deck. He maintained this posture so long, that Captain Delano, almost equally disconcerted, and involuntarily almost as rude, turned suddenly from him, walking forward to accost one of the Spanish seamen for the desired information. But he had hardly gone five paces, when, with a sort of eagerness, Don Benito invited him back, regretting his momentary absence of mind, and professing readiness to gratify him.

While most part of the story was being given, the two captains stood on the after part of the main-deck, a privileged spot, no one being near but the servant.

"It is now a hundred and ninety days," began the Spaniard, in his husky whisper, "that this ship, well officered and well manned, with several cabin passengers—some fifty Spaniards in all—sailed from Buenos Ayres bound to Lima, with a general cargo, [hardware,][11] Paraguay tca and the like—and," pointing forward, "that parcel of negroes, now not more than a hundred and fifty, as you see, but then numbering over three hundred souls. Off Cape Horn we had heavy gales. In one moment, by night, three of my best officers, with fifteen sailors, were lost, with the main-yard; the spar snapping under them in the slings, as they sought, with heavers, to beat down the icy sail. To lighten the

---

11 "hardware," was omitted in the *Putnam* version.

hull, the heavier sacks of mata were thrown into the sea, with most of the water-pipes lashed on deck at the time. And this last necessity it was, combined with the prolonged detentions afterwards experienced, which eventually brought about our chief causes of suffering. When——"

Here there was a sudden fainting attack of his cough, brought on, no doubt, by his mental distress. His servant sustained him, and drawing a cordial from his pocket placed it to his lips. He a little revived. But unwilling to leave him unsupported while yet imperfectly restored, the black with one arm still encircled his master, at the same time keeping his eye fixed on his face, as if to watch for the first sign of complete restoration, or relapse, as the event might prove.

The Spaniard proceeded, but brokenly and obscurely, as one in a dream.

—"Oh, my God! rather than pass through what I have, with joy I would have hailed the most terrible gales; but——"

His cough returned and with increased violence; this subsiding, with reddened lips and closed eyes he fell heavily against his supporter.

"His mind wanders. He was thinking of the plague that followed the gales," plaintively sighed the servant; "my poor, poor master!" wringing one hand, and with the other wiping the mouth. "But be patient, Señor," again turning to Captain Delano, "these fits do not last long; master will soon be himself."

Don Benito reviving, went on; but as this portion of the story was very brokenly delivered, the substance only will here be set down.

It appeared that after the ship had been many days tossed in storms off the Cape, the scurvy broke out, carrying off numbers of the whites and blacks. When at last they had worked round into the Pacific, their spars and sails were so damaged, and so inadequately handled by the surviving mariners, most of whom were become invalids, that, unable to lay her northerly course by the wind, which was powerful, the unmanageable ship, for successive days and nights, was blown northwestward, where the breeze suddenly deserted her, in unknown waters, to sultry calms. The absence of the water-pipes now proved as fatal to life as before their presence had menaced it. Induced, or at least aggravated, by the more than scanty allowance of water, a malignant fever followed the scurvy; with the excessive heat of the lengthened calm, making such short work of it as to sweep away, as by billows, whole families of the Africans, and a yet larger number, proportionably, of the Spaniards, including, by a luckless fatality, every [remaining][12] officer on board. Consequently, in the smart west winds eventually following the calm, the already rent sails, having to be simply dropped, not furled, at need, had been gradually reduced to the beggars' rags they were now. To procure substitutes for his lost

---

[12] "remaining" was omitted in the *Putnam* version.

sailors, as well as supplies of water and sails, the captain, at the earliest opportunity, had made for [Valdivia],[13] the southernmost civilized port of Chili and South America; but upon nearing the coast the thick weather had prevented him from so much as sighting that harbor. Since which period, almost without a crew, and almost without canvas and almost without water, and, at intervals, giving its added dead to the sea, the San Dominick had been battle-dored about by contrary winds, inveigled by currents, or grown weedy in calms. Like a man lost in woods, more than once she had doubled upon her own track.

"But throughout these calamities," huskily continued Don Benito, painfully turning in the half embrace of his servant, "I have to thank those negroes you see, who, though to your inexperienced eyes appearing unruly, have, indeed, conducted themselves with less of restlessness than even their owner could have thought possible under such circumstances."

Here he again fell faintly back. Again his mind wandered; but he rallied, and less obscurely proceeded.

"Yes, their owner was quite right in assuring me that no fetters would be needed with his blacks; so that while, as is wont in this transportation, those negroes have always remained upon deck—not thrust below, as in the Guineamen—they have, also, from the beginning, been freely permitted to range within given bounds at their pleasure."

Once more the faintness returned—his mind roved—but, recovering, he resumed:

"But it is Babo here to whom, under God, I owe not only my own preservation, but likewise to him, chiefly, the merit is due, of pacifying his more ignorant brethren, when at intervals tempted to murmurings."

"Ah, master," sighed the black, bowing his face, "don't speak of me; Babo is nothing; what Babo has done was but duty."

"Faithful fellow!" cried Captain Delano. "Don Benito, I envy you such a friend; slave I cannot call him."

As master and man stood before him, the black upholding the white, Captain Delano could not but bethink him of the beauty of that relationship which could present such a spectacle of fidelity on the one hand and confidence on the other. The scene was heightened by the contrast in dress, denoting their relative positions. The Spaniard wore a loose Chili jacket of dark velvet; white small-clothes and stockings, with silver buckles at the knee and instep; a high-crowned sombrero, of fine grass; a slender sword, silver mounted, hung from a knot in his sash—the last being an almost invariable adjunct, more for utility than ornament, of a South American gentleman's dress to this hour. Ex-

---

[13] Melville's notoriously bad handwriting and his subsequent missing of the error during the various prepublication stages of *The Piazza Tales* probably accounts for "Valdivia" appearing as "Baldivia" in both the *Putnam* and *Piazza* versions. The source spells it correctly.

cepting when his occasional nervous contortions brought about disarray, there was a certain precision in his attire curiously at variance
with the unsightly disorder around; especially in the belittered Ghetto,
forward of the mainmast, wholly occupied by the blacks.

The servant wore nothing but wide trowsers, apparently, from
their coarseness and patches, made out of some old topsail; they were
clean, and confined at the waist by a bit of unstranded rope, which,
with his composed, deprecatory air at times, made him look something
like a begging friar of St. Francis.

However unsuitable for the time and place, at least in the blunt-
thinking American's eyes, and however strangely surviving in the midst
of all his afflictions, the toilette of Don Benito might not, in fashion
at least, have gone beyond the style of the day among South Americans
of his class. Though on the present voyage sailing from Buenos Ayres,
he had avowed himself a native and resident of Chili, whose inhabitants
had not so generally adopted the plain coat and once plebeian panta-
loons; but, with a becoming modification, adhered to their provincial
costume, picturesque as any in the world. Still, relatively to the pale
history of the voyage, and his own pale face, there seemed something
so incongruous in the Spaniard's apparel, as almost to suggest the image
of an invalid courtier tottering about London streets in the time of the
plague.

The portion of the narrative which, perhaps, most excited interest,
as well as some surprise, considering the latitudes in question, was the
long calms spoken of, and more particularly the ship's so long drifting
about. Without communicating the opinion, of course, the American
could not but impute at least part of the detentions both to clumsy
seamanship and faulty navigation. Eyeing Don Benito's small, yellow
hands, he easily inferred that the young captain had not got into command at the hawse-hole, but the cabin-window; and if so, why wonder
at incompetence, in youth, sickness, and [gentility united?][14]

But drowning criticism in compassion, after a fresh repetition of
his sympathies, Captain Delano, having heard out his story, not only
engaged, as in the first place, to see Don Benito and his people supplied
in their immediate bodily needs, but, also, now further promised to
assist him in procuring a large permanent supply of water, as well as
some sails and rigging; and, though it would involve no small embarrassment to himself, yet he would spare three of his best seamen for
temporary deck officers; so that without delay the ship might proceed
to Conception, there fully to refit for Lima, her destined port.

Such generosity was not without its effect, even upon the invalid.
His face lighted up; eager and hectic, he met the honest glance of his
visitor. With gratitude he seemed overcome.

---

[14] aristocracy united? Such was his democratic conclusion.

"This excitement is bad for master," whispered the servant, taking his arm, and with soothing words gently drawing him aside.

When Don Benito returned, the American was pained to observe that his hopefulness, like the sudden kindling in his cheek, was but febrile and transient.

Ere long, with a joyless mien, looking up towards the poop, the host invited his guest to accompany him there, for the benefit of what little breath of wind might be stirring.

As, during the telling of the story, Captain Delano had once or twice started at the occasional cymballing of the hatchet-polishers, wondering why such an interruption should be allowed, especially in that part of the ship, and in the ears of an invalid; and moreover, as the hatchets had anything but an attractive look, and the handlers of them still less so, it was, therefore, to tell the truth, not without some lurking reluctance, or even shrinking, it may be, that Captain Delano, with apparent complaisance, acquiesced in his host's invitation. The more so, since, with an untimely caprice of punctilio, rendered distressing by his cadaverous aspect, Don Benito, with Castilian bows, solemnly insisted upon his guest's preceding him up the ladder leading to the elevation; where, one on each side of the last step, sat for armorial supporters and sentries two of the ominous file. Gingerly enough stepped good Captain Delano between them, and in the instant of leaving them behind, like one running the gauntlet, he felt an apprehensive twitch in the calves of his legs.

But when, facing about, he saw the whole file, like so many organ-grinders, still stupidly intent on their work, unmindful of everything beside, he could not but smile at his late [fidgety][15] panic.

Presently, while standing with [his host],[16] looking forward upon the decks below, he was struck by one of those instances of insubordination previously alluded to. Three black boys, with two Spanish boys, were sitting together on the [hatches],[17] scraping a rude wooden platter, in which some scanty mess had recently been cooked. Suddenly, one of the black boys, enraged at a word dropped by one of his white companions, seized a knife, and, though called to forbear by one of the oakum-pickers, struck the lad over the head, inflicting a gash from which blood flowed.

In amazement, Captain Delano inquired what this meant. To which the pale [Don][18] Benito dully muttered, that it was merely the sport of the lad.

"Pretty serious sport, truly," rejoined Captain Delano. "Had such

---

[15] fidgeting
[16] Don Benito
[17] hatchets
[18] "Don" was omitted in the *Putnam* version.

a thing happened on board the Bachelor's Delight, instant punishment would have followed."

At these words the Spaniard turned upon the American one of his sudden, staring, half-lunatic looks; then, relapsing into his torpor, answered, "Doubtless, doubtless, Señor."

Is it, thought Captain Delano, that this [hapless][19] man is one of those paper captains I've known, who by policy wink at what by power they cannot put down? I know no sadder sight than a commander who has little of command but the name.

"I should think, Don Benito," he now said, glancing towards the oakum-picker who had sought to interfere with the boys, "that you would find it advantageous to keep all your blacks employed, especially the younger ones, no matter at what useless task, and no matter what happens to the ship. Why, even with my little band, I find such a course indispensable. I once kept a crew on my quarter-deck thrumming mats for my cabin, when, for three days, I had given up my ship—mats, men, and all—for a speedy loss, owing to the violence of a gale, in which we could do nothing but helplessly drive before it."

"Doubtless, doubtless," muttered Don Benito.

"But," continued Captain Delano, again glancing upon the oakum-pickers and then at the hatchet-polishers, near by, "I see you keep some, at least, of your host employed."

"Yes," was again the vacant response.

"Those old men there, shaking their pows from their pulpits," continued Captain Delano, pointing to the oakum-pickers, "seem to act the part of old dominies to the rest, little heeded as their admonitions are at times. Is this voluntary on their part, Don Benito, or have you appointed them shepherds to your flock of black sheep?"

"What posts they fill, I appointed them," rejoined the Spaniard, in an acrid tone, as if resenting some supposed satiric reflection.

"And these others, these Ashantee conjurors here," continued Captain Delano, rather uneasily eyeing the brandished steel of the hatchet-polishers, where, in spots, it had been brought to a shine, "this seems a curious business they are at, Don Benito?"

"In the gales we met," answered the Spaniard, "what of our general cargo was not thrown overboard was much damaged by the brine. Since coming into calm weather, I have had several cases of knives and hatchets daily brought up for overhauling and cleaning."

"A prudent idea, Don Benito. You are part owner of ship and cargo, I presume; but [none][20] of the slaves, perhaps?"

"I am owner of all you see," impatiently returned Don Benito, "except the main company of blacks, who belonged to my late friend, Alexandro Aranda."

---

19 helpless
20 not

As he mentioned this name, his air was heart-broken; his knees shook; his servant supported him.

Thinking he divined the cause of such unusual emotion, to confirm his surmise, Captain Delano, after a pause, said: "And may I ask, Don Benito, whether—since awhile ago you spoke of some cabin passengers—the friend, whose loss so afflicts you, at the outset of the voyage accompanied his blacks?"

"Yes."

"But died of the fever?"

"Died of the fever. Oh, could I but——"

Again quivering, the Spaniard paused.

"Pardon me," said Captain Delano, lowly, "but I think that, by a sympathetic experience, I conjecture, Don Benito, what it is that gives the keener edge to your grief. It was once my hard fortune to lose, at sea, a dear friend, my own brother, then supercargo. Assured of the welfare of his spirit, its departure I could have borne like a man; but that honest eye, that honest hand—both of which had so often met mine —and that warm heart; all, all—like scraps to the dogs—to throw all to the sharks! It was then I vowed never to have for fellow-voyager a man I loved, unless, unbeknown to him, I had provided every requisite, in case of a fatality, for embalming his mortal part for interment on shore. Were your friend's remains now on board this ship, Don Benito, not thus strangely would the mention of his name affect you."

"On board this ship?" echoed the Spaniard. Then, with horrified gestures, as directed against some spectre, he unconsciously fell into the ready arms of his attendant, who, with a silent appeal toward Captain Delano, seemed beseeching him not again to broach a theme so unspeakably distressing to his master.

This poor fellow now, thought the pained American, is the victim of that sad superstition which associates goblins with the deserted body of man, as ghosts with an abandoned house. How unlike are we made! What to me, in like case, would have been a solemn satisfaction, the bare suggestion, even, terrifies the Spaniard into this trance. Poor Alexandro Aranda! what would you say could you here see your friend —who, on former voyages, when you, for months, were left behind, has, I dare say, often longed, and longed, for one peep at you—now transported with terror at the least thought of having you anyway nigh him.

At this moment, with a dreary grave-yard toll, betokening a flaw, the ship's forecastle bell, smote by one of the grizzled oakum-pickers, proclaimed ten o'clock, through the leaden calm; when Captain Delano's attention was caught by the moving figure of a gigantic black, emerging from the general crowd below, and slowly advancing towards the elevated poop. An iron collar was about his neck, from which depended a chain, thrice wound round his body; the terminating links padlocked together at a broad band of iron, his girdle.

"How like a mute Atufal moves," murmured the servant.

The black mounted the steps of the poop, and, like a brave prisoner, brought up to receive sentence, stood in unquailing muteness before Don Benito, now recovered from his attack.

At the first glimpse of his approach, Don Benito had started, a resentful shadow swept over his face; and, as with the sudden memory of bootless rage, his white lips glued together.

This is some mulish mutineer, thought Captain Delano, surveying, not without a mixture of admiration, the colossal form of the negro.

"See, he waits your question, master," said the servant.

Thus reminded, Don Benito, nervously averting his glance, as if shunning, by anticipation, some rebellious response, in a disconcerted voice, thus spoke:—

"Atufal, will you ask my pardon, now?"

The black was silent.

"Again, master," murmured the servant, with bitter upbraiding eyeing his countryman, "Again, master; he will bend to master yet."

"Answer," said Don Benito, still averting his glance, "say but the one word, *pardon,* and your chains shall be off."

Upon this, the black, slowly raising both arms, let them lifelessly fall, his links clanking, his head bowed; as much as to say, "no, I am content."

"Go," said Don Benito, with inkept and unknown emotion.

Deliberately as he had come, the black obeyed.

"Excuse me, Don Benito," said Captain Delano, "but this scene surprises me; what means it, pray?"

"It means that that negro alone, of all the band, has given me peculiar cause of offense. I have put him in chains; I——"

Here he paused; his hand to his head, as if there were a swimming there, or a sudden bewilderment of memory had come over him; but meeting his servant's kindly glance seemed reassured, and proceeded:——

"I could not scourge such a form. But I told him he must ask my pardon. As yet he has not. At my command, every two hours he stands before me."

"And how long has this been?"

"Some sixty days."

"And obedient in all else? And respectful?"

"Yes."

"Upon my conscience, then," exclaimed Captain Delano, impulsively, "he has a royal spirit in him, this fellow."

"He may have some right to it," bitterly returned Don Benito, "he says he was king in his own land."

"Yes," said the servant, entering a word, "those slits in Atufal's ears once held wedges of gold; but poor Babo here, in his own land, was only a poor slave; a black man's slave was Babo, who now is the white's."

Somewhat annoyed by these conversational familiarities, Captain Delano turned curiously upon the attendant, then glanced inquiringly at his master; but, as if long wonted to these little informalities, neither master nor man seemed to understand him.

"What, pray, was Atufal's offense, Don Benito?" asked Captain Delano; "if it was not something very serious, take a fool's advice, and, in view of his general docility, as well as in some natural respect for his spirit, remit him his penalty."

"No, no, master never will do that," here murmured the servant to himself, "proud Atufal must first ask master's pardon. The slave there carries the padlock, but master here carries the key."

His attention thus directed, Captain Delano now noticed for the first [time][21] that, suspended by a slender silken cord, from Don Benito's neck, hung a key. At once, from the servant's muttered syllables, divining the key's purpose, he smiled and said:— "So, Don Benito— padlock and key—significant symbols, truly."

Biting his lip, Don Benito faltered.

Though the remark of Captain Delano, a man of such native simplicity as to be incapable of satire or irony, had been dropped in playful allusion to the Spaniard's singularly evidenced lordship over the black; yet the hypochondriac [seemed some way][22] to have taken it as a malicious reflection upon his confessed inability thus far to break down, at least, on a verbal summons, the entrenched will of the slave. Deploring this supposed misconception, yet despairing of correcting it, Captain Delano shifted the subject; but finding his companion more than ever withdrawn, as if still [sourly][23] digesting the lees of the presumed affront above-mentioned, by-and-by Captain Delano likewise became less talkative, oppressed, against his own will, by what seemed the secret vindictiveness of the morbidly sensitive Spaniard. But the good sailor, himself of a quite contrary disposition, refrained, on his part, alike from the appearance as from the feeling of resentment, and if silent, was only so from contagion.

Presently the Spaniard, assisted by his servant somewhat discourteously crossed over from [his guest];[24] a procedure which, sensibly enough, might have been allowed to pass for idle caprice of ill-humor, had not master and man, lingering round the corner of the elevated skylight, began whispering together in low voices. This was unpleasing. And more: the moody air of the Spaniard, which at times had not been without a sort of valetudinarian stateliness, now seemed anything but dignified; while the menial familiarity of the servant lost its original charm of simple-hearted attachment.

---

21 "time" from the *Putnam* version was most probably inadvertently omitted in the *Piazza* version and should be replaced.

22 seemed in some way

23 slowly

24 Captain Delano

In his embarrassment, the visitor turned his face to the other side of the ship. By so doing, his glance accidentally fell on a young Spanish sailor, a coil of rope in his hand, just stepped from the deck to the first round of the mizzen-rigging. Perhaps the man would not have been particularly noticed, were it not that, during his ascent to one of the yards, he, with a sort of covert intentness, kept his eye fixed on Captain Delano, from whom, presently, it passed, as if by a natural sequence, to the two whisperers.

His own attention thus redirected to that quarter, Captain Delano gave a slight start. From something in Don Benito's manner just then, it seemed as if the visitor had, at least partly, been the subject of the withdrawn consultation going on—a conjecture as little agreeable to the guest as it was little flattering to the host.

The singular alternations of courtesy and ill-breeding in the Spanish captain were unaccountable, except on one of two suppositions—innocent lunacy, or wicked imposture.

But the first idea, though it might naturally have occurred to an indifferent observer, and, in some respect, had not hitherto been wholly a stranger to Captain Delano's mind, yet, now that, in an incipient way, he began to regard the stranger's conduct something in the light of an intentional affront, of course the idea of lunacy was virtually vacated. But if not a lunatic, what then? Under the circumstances, would a gentleman, nay, any honest boor, act the part now acted by his host? The man was an imposter. Some low-born adventurer, masquerading as an oceanic grandee; yet so ignorant of the first requisites of mere gentlemanhood as to be betrayed into the present remarkable indecorum. That strange ceremoniousness, too, at other times evinced, seemed not uncharacteristic of one playing a part above his real level. Benito Cereno—Don Benito Cereno—a sounding name. One, too, at that period, not unknown, in the surname, to supercargoes and sea captains trading along the Spanish Main, as belonging to one of the most enterprising and extensive mercantile families in all those provinces; several members of it having titles; a sort of Castilian Rothschild, with a noble brother, or cousin, in every great trading town of South America. The alleged Don Benito was in early manhood, about twenty-nine or thirty. To assume a sort of roving cadetship in the maritime affairs of such a house, what more likely scheme for a young knave of talent and spirit? But the Spaniard was a pale invalid. Never mind. For even to the degree of simulating mortal disease, the craft of some tricksters had been known to attain. To think that, under the aspect of infantile weakness, the most savage energies might be couched—those velvets of the Spaniard but the [silky]25 paw to his fangs.

From no train of thought did these fancies come; not from within, but from without; suddenly, too, and in one throng, like hoar frost;

---

25 velvet

yet as soon to vanish as the mild sun of Captain Delano's good-nature regained its meridian.

Glancing over once more towards [his host][26]—whose side-face, revealed above the skylight, was now turned towards him—[he][27] was struck by the profile, whose clearness of cut was refined by the thinness, incident to ill-health, as well as ennobled about the chin by the beard. Away with suspicion. He was a true off-shoot of a true hidalgo Cereno.

Relieved by these and other better thoughts, the visitor, lightly humming a tune, now began indifferently pacing the poop, so as not to betray to Don Benito that he had at all mistrusted incivility, much less duplicity; for such mistrust would yet be proved illusory, and by the event; though, for the present, the circumstance which had provoked that distrust remained unexplained. But when that little mystery should have been cleared up, Captain Delano thought he might extremely regret it, did he allow Don Benito to become aware that he had indulged in ungenerous surmises. In short, to the Spaniard's black-letter text, it was best, for awhile, to leave open margin.

Presently, his pale face twitching and overcast, the Spaniard, still supported by his attendant, moved over towards his guest, when, with even more than his usual embarrassment, and a strange sort of intriguing intonation in his husky whisper, the following conversation began:—

"Señor, may I ask how long you have lain at this isle?"

"Oh, but a day or two, Don Benito."

"And from what port are you last?"

"Canton."

"And there, Señor, you exchanged your sealskins for teas and silks, I think you said?"

"Yes. Silks, mostly."

"And the balance you took in specie, perhaps?"

Captain Delano, fidgeting a little, answered—

"Yes; some silver; not a very great deal, though."

"Ah—well. May I ask how many men [have you],[28] Señor?"

Captain Delano slightly started, but answered—

"About five-and-twenty, all told."

"And at present, Señor, all on board, I suppose?"

"All on board, Don Benito," replied the Captain, now with satisfaction.

"And will be to-night, Señor?"

At this last question, following so many pertinacious ones, for the soul of him Captain Delano could not but look very earnestly at the questioner, who, instead of meeting the glance, with every token of

---

[26] Don Benito
[27] Captain Delano
[28] have you on board

craven discomposure dropped his eyes to the deck; presenting an un-
worthy contrast to his servant, who, just then, was kneeling at his feet,
adjusting a loose shoe-buckle; his disengaged face meantime, with
humble curiosity, turned openly up into his master's downcast one.

The Spaniard, still with a guilty shuffle, repeated his question:

"And—and will be to-night, Señor?"

"Yes, for aught I know," returned Captain Delano—"but nay,"
rallying himself into fearless truth, "some of them talked of going off
on another fishing party about midnight."

"Your ships generally go—go more or less armed, I believe, Señor?"

"Oh, a six-pounder or two, in case of emergency," was the in-
trepidly indifferent reply, "with a small stock of muskets, sealing-spears,
and cutlasses, you know."

As he thus responded, Captain Delano again glanced at Don
Benito, but the latter's eyes were averted; while abruptly and awkwardly shifting the subject, he made some peevish allusion to the calm,
and then, without apology, once more, with his attendant, withdrew
to the opposite bulwarks, where the whispering was resumed.

At this moment, and ere Captain Delano could cast a cool thought
upon what had just passed, the young Spanish sailor, before mentioned,
was seen descending from the rigging. In act of stooping over to spring
inboard to the deck, his voluminous, unconfined frock, or shirt, of
coarse woolen, much spotted with tar, opened out far down the chest,
revealing a soiled under garment of what seemed the finest linen,
edged, about the neck, with a narrow blue ribbon, sadly faded and
worn. At this moment the young sailor's eye was again fixed on the
whisperers, and Captain Delano thought he observed a lurking significance in it, as if silent signs, of some Freemason sort, had that instant
been interchanged.

This once more impelled his own glance in the direction of Don
Benito, and, as before, he could not but infer that himself formed the
subject of the conference. He paused. The sound of the hatchet-polish-
ing fell on his ears. He cast another swift side-look at the two. They had
the air of conspirators. In connection with the late questionings, and
the incident of the young sailor, these things now begat such return of
involuntary suspicion, that the singular guilelessness of the American
could not endure it. Plucking up a gay and humorous expression, he
crossed over to the two rapidly, saying:—"Ha, Don Benito, your black
here seems high in your trust; a sort of privy-counselor, in fact."

Upon this, the servant looked up with a good-natured grin, but
the master started as from a venomous bite. It was a moment or two
before the Spaniard sufficiently recovered himself to reply; which he
did, at last, with cold constraint:—"Yes, Señor, I have trust in Babo."

Here Babo, changing his previous grin of mere animal humor
into an intelligent smile, not ungratefully eyed his master.

Finding that the Spaniard now stood silent and reserved, as if involuntarily, or purposely giving hint that his guest's proximity was inconvenient just then, Captain Delano, unwilling to appear uncivil even to incivility itself, made some trivial remark and moved off; again and again turning over in his mind the mysterious demeanor of Don Benito Cereno.

He had descended from the poop, and, wrapped in thought, was passing near a dark hatchway, leading down into the steerage, when, perceiving motion there, he looked to see what moved. The same instant there was a sparkle in the shadowy hatchway, and he saw one of the Spanish sailors, prowling there, hurriedly placing his hand in the bosom of his frock, as if hiding something. Before the man could have been certain who it was that was passing, he slunk below out of sight. But enough was seen of him to make it sure that he was the same young sailor before noticed in the rigging.

What was that which so sparkled? thought Captain Delano. It was no lamp—no match—no live coal. Could it have been a jewel? But how come sailors with jewels?—or with silk-trimmed under-shirts either? Has he been robbing the trunks of the dead cabin-passengers? But if so, he would hardly wear one of the stolen articles on board ship here. Ah, ah —if, now, that was, indeed, a secret sign I saw passing between this suspicious fellow and his captain awhile since; if I could only be certain that, in my uneasiness, my senses did not deceive me, then——

Here, passing from one suspicious thing to another, his mind [revolved the strange questions]29 put to him concerning his ship.

By a curious coincidence, as each point was recalled, the black wizards of Ashantee would strike up with their hatchets, as in ominous comment on the white stranger's thoughts. Pressed by such enigmas and portents, it would have been almost against nature, had not, even into the least distrustful heart, some ugly misgivings obtruded.

Observing the ship, now helplessly fallen into a current, with enchanted sails, drifting with increased rapidity seaward; and noting that, from a lately intercepted projection of the land, the sealer was hidden, the stout mariner began to quake at thoughts which he barely durst confess to himself. Above all, he began to feel a ghostly dread of Don Benito. And yet, when he roused himself, dilated his chest, felt himself strong on his legs, and coolly considered it—what did all these phantoms amount to?

Had the Spaniard any sinister scheme, it must have reference not so much to him (Captain Delano) as to his ship (the Bachelor's Delight). Hence the present drifting away of the one ship from the other, instead of favoring any such possible scheme, was, for the time, at least, opposed to it. Clearly any suspicion, combining such contradictions, must need be delusive. Beside, was it not absurd to think of a vessel in distress— a vessel by sickness almost dismanned of her crew—a vessel whose in-

---

29 revolved the point of the strange questions

mates were parched for water—was it not a thousand times absurd that such a craft should, at present, be of a piratical character; or her commander, either for himself or those under him, cherish any desire but for speedy relief and refreshment? But then, might not general distress, and thirst in particular, be affected? And might not that same undiminished Spanish crew, alleged to have perished off to a remnant, be at that very moment lurking in the hold? On heart-broken pretense of entreating a cup of cold water, fiends in human form had got into lonely dwellings, nor retired until a dark deed had been done. And among the Malay pirates, it was no unusual thing to lure ships after them into their treacherous harbors, or entice boarders from a declared enemy at sea, by the spectacle of thinly manned or vacant decks, beneath which prowled a hundred spears with yellow arms ready to upthrust them through the mats. Not that Captain Delano had entirely credited such things. He had heard of them—and now, as stories, they recurred. The present destination of the ship was the anchorage. There she would be near his own vessel. Upon gaining that vicinity, might not the San Dominick, like a slumbering volcano, suddenly let loose energies now hid?

He recalled the Spaniard's manner while telling his story. There was a gloomy hesitancy and subterfuge about it. It was just the manner of one making up his tale for evil purposes, as he goes. But if that story was not true, what was the truth? That the ship had unlawfully come into the Spaniard's possession? But in many of its details, especially in reference to the more calamitous parts, such as the fatalities among the seamen, the consequent prolonged beating about, the past sufferings from obstinate calms, and still continued suffering from thirst; in all these points, as well as others, Don Benito's story had corroborated not only the wailing ejaculations of the indiscriminate multitude, white and black, but likewise—what seemed impossible to be counterfeit—by the very expression and play of every human feature, which Captain Delano saw. If Don Benito's story was, throughout, an invention, then every soul on board, down to the youngest negress, was his carefully drilled recruit in the plot: an incredible inference. And yet, if there was ground for mistrusting [his][30] veracity, that inference was a legitimate one.

[But those questions of the Spaniard. There, indeed, one might pause. Did they not seem put with much the same object with which the burglar or assassin, by day-time, reconnoitres the walls of a house? But, with ill purposes, to solicit such information openly of the chief person endangered, and so, in effect, setting him on his guard; how unlikely a procedure was that? Absurd, then, to suppose that those questions had been prompted by evil designs. Thus, the same conduct,

---

[30] the Spanish captain's

which, in this instance, had raised the alarm, served to dispel it. In short, scarce any suspicion or uneasiness, however apparently reasonable at the time, which was not now, with equal apparent reason, dismissed.][31]

At last he began to laugh at [his former][32] forebodings; and laugh at the strange ship for, in its aspect, someway siding with them, as it were; and laugh, too, at the odd-looking blacks, particularly those old scissors-grinders, the Ashantees; and those bed-ridden old knitting women, the oakum-pickers; and [almost at the dark Spaniard himself],[33] the central hobgoblin of all.

For the rest, whatever in a serious way seemed enigmatical, was now good-naturedly explained away by the thought that, for the most part, the poor invalid scarcely knew what he was about; either sulking in black vapors, or putting [idle][34] questions without sense or object. Evidently, for the present, the man was not fit to be intrusted with the ship. On some benevolent plea withdrawing the command from him, Captain Delano would yet have to send her to Conception, in charge of his second mate, a worthy person and good navigator—a plan [not more convenient][35] for the San Dominick than for Don Benito; for, relieved from all anxiety, keeping wholly to his cabin, the sick man, under the good nursing of his servant, would, probably, by the end of the passage, be in a measure restored to health, and with that he should also be restored to authority.

Such were the American's thoughts. They were tranquilizing. There was a difference between the idea of Don Benito's darkly preordaining Captain Delano's fate, and Captain Delano's lightly arranging Don Benito's. Nevertheless, it was not without something of relief that the good seaman presently perceived his whale-boat in the distance. Its absence had been prolonged by unexpected detention at the sealer's side, as well as its returning trip lengthened by the continual recession of the goal.

The advancing speck was observed by the blacks. Their shouts attracted the attention of Don Benito, who, with a return of courtesy, approaching Captain Delano, expressed satisfaction at the coming of some supplies, slight and temporary as they must necessarily prove.

Captain Delano responded; but while doing so, his attention was drawn to something passing on the deck below: among the crowd climbing the landward bulwarks, anxiously watching the coming boat, two blacks, to all appearances accidentally incommoded by one of the sailors, [violently pushed him aside],[36] which the sailor someway re-

---

[31] In short, scarce an uneasiness entered the honest sailor's mind but, by a subsequent spontaneous act of good sense, it was ejected.

[32] these

[33] in a human way, he almost began to laugh at the dark Spaniard himself

[34] random

[35] which would prove no wiser

[36] flew out against him with horrible curses

senting, [they dashed him to the deck],[37] despite the earnest cries of the oakum-pickers.

"Don Benito," said Captain Delano quickly, "do you see what is going on there? Look!"

But, seized by his cough, the Spaniard staggered, with both hands to his face, on the point of falling. Captain Delano would have supported him, but the servant was more alert, who, with one hand sustaining his master, with the other applied the cordial. Don Benito restored, the black withdrew his support, slipping aside a little, but dutifully remaining within call of a whisper. Such discretion was here evinced as quite wiped away, in the visitor's eyes, any blemish of impropriety which might have attached to the attendant, from the indecorous conferences before mentioned; showing, too, that if the servant were to blame, it might be more the master's fault than his own, since, when left to himself, he could conduct thus well.

His [glance called][38] away from the spectacle of disorder to the more pleasing one before him, Captain Delano could not avoid again congratulating [his host][39] upon possessing such a servant, who, though perhaps a little too forward now and then, must upon the whole be invaluable to one in the invalid's situation.

"Tell me, Don Benito," he added, with a smile—"I should like to have your man here, myself—what will you take for him? Would fifty doubloons be any object?"

"Master wouldn't part with Babo for a thousand doubloons," murmured the black, overhearing the offer, and taking it in earnest, and, with the strange vanity of a faithful slave, appreciated by his master, scorning to hear so paltry a valuation put upon him by a stranger. But Don Benito, apparently hardly yet completely restored, and again interrupted by his cough, made but some broken reply.

Soon his physical distress became so great, affecting his mind, too, apparently, that, as if to screen the sad spectacle, the servant gently conducted his master below.

Left to himself, the American, to while away the time till his boat should arrive, would have pleasantly accosted some one of the few Spanish seamen he saw; but recalling something that Don Benito had said touching their ill conduct, he refrained; as a shipmaster indisposed to countenance cowardice or unfaithfulness in seamen.

While, with these thoughts, standing with eye directed forward towards that handful of sailors, suddenly he thought that [one or two][40] of them returned the glance and with a sort of meaning. He rubbed his eyes, and looked again; but again seemed to see the same thing.

---

37 the two blacks dashed him to the deck and jumped upon him
38 glance thus called
39 Don Benito
40 some

Under a new form, but more obscure than any previous one, the old suspicions recurred, but, in the absence of Don Benito, with less of panic than before. Despite the bad account given of the sailors, Captain Delano resolved forthwith to accost one of them. Descending the poop, he made his way through the blacks, his movement drawing a queer cry from the oakum-pickers, prompted by whom, the negroes, twitching each other aside, divided before him; but, as if curious to see what was the object of this deliberate visit to their Ghetto, closing in behind, in tolerable order, followed the white stranger up. His progress thus proclaimed as by mounted kings-at-arms, and escorted as by a Caffre guard of honor, Captain Delano, assuming a good-humored, off-handed air, continued to advance; now and then saying a blithe word to the negroes, and his eye curiously surveying the white faces, here and there sparsely mixed in with the blacks, like stray white pawns venturously involved in the ranks of the chess-men opposed.

While thinking which of them to select for his purpose, he chanced to observe a sailor seated on the deck engaged in tarring the strap of a large block, [a circle][41] of blacks squatted round him inquisitively eyeing the process.

The mean employment of the man was in contrast with something superior in his figure. His hand, black with continually thrusting it into the tar-pot held for him by a negro, seemed not naturally allied to his face, a face which would have been a very fine one but for its haggardness. Whether this haggardness had aught to do with criminality, could not be determined; since, as intense heat and cold, though unlike, produce like sensations, so innocence and guilt, when, through casual association with mental pain, stamping any visible impress, use one seal—a hacked one.

Not again that this reflection occurred to Captain Delano at the time, charitable man as he was. Rather another idea. Because observing so singular a haggardness [combined][42] with a dark eye, averted as in trouble and shame, and then [again recalling Don Benito's confessed ill opinion of his crew, insensibly he was operated upon by certain general notions which, while disconnecting pain and abashment from virtue, invariably link them with vice.][43]

If, indeed, there be any wickedness on board this ship, thought Captain Delano, be sure that man there has fouled his hand in it, even as now he fouls it in the pitch. I don't like to accost him. I will speak to this other, this old Jack here on the windlass.

He advanced to an old Barcelona tar, in ragged red breeches and

41 with a circle

42 to be combined

43 ,however illogically, uniting in his mind his own private suspicions of the crew with the confessed ill-opinion on the part of their Captain, he was insensibly operated upon by certain general notions, which, while disconnecting pain and abashment from virtue, as invariably link them with vice.

dirty night-cap, cheeks trenched and bronzed, whiskers dense as thorn hedges. Seated between two sleepy-looking Africans, this mariner, like his younger shipmate, was employed upon some rigging—splicing a cable—the sleepy-looking blacks performing the inferior function of holding the outer parts of the ropes for him.

Upon Captain Delano's approach, the man at once hung his head below its previous level; the one necessary for business. It appeared as if he desired to be thought absorbed, with more than common fidelity, in his task. Being addressed, he glanced up, but with what seemed a furtive, diffident air, which sat strangely enough on his weather-beaten visage, much as if a grizzly bear, instead of growling and biting, should simper and cast sheep's eyes. He was asked several questions concerning the voyage—questions purposely referring to several particulars in Don Benito's narrative, not previously corroborated by those impulsive cries greeting the visitor on first coming on board. The questions were briefly answered, confirming all that remained to be confirmed of the story. The negroes about the windlass joined in with the old sailor; but, as they became talkative, he by degrees became mute, and at length quite glum, seemed morosely unwilling to answer more questions, and yet, all the while, this ursine air was somehow mixed with his sheepish one.

Despairing of getting into unembarrassed talk with such a centaur, Captain Delano, after glancing round for a more promising countenance, but seeing none, spoke pleasantly to the blacks to make way for him; and so, amid various grins and grimaces, returned to the poop, feeling a little strange at first, he could hardly tell why, but upon the whole with regained confidence in Benito Cereno.

How plainly, thought he, did that old whiskerando yonder betray a consciousness of ill desert. No doubt, when he saw me coming, he dreaded lest I, apprised by his Captain of the crew's general misbehavior, came with sharp words for him, and so down with his head. And yet—and yet, now that I think of it, that very old fellow, if I err not, was one of those who seemed so earnestly eyeing me here awhile since. Ah, these currents spin one's head round almost as much as they do the ship. Ha, there now's a pleasant sort of sunny sight; quite sociable, too.

His attention had been drawn to a slumbering negress, partly disclosed through the lace-work of some rigging, lying, with youthful limbs carelessly disposed, under the lee of the bulwarks, like a doe in the shade of a woodland rock. Sprawling at her lapped breasts, was her wide-awake fawn, stark naked, its black little body half lifted from the deck, crosswise with its dam's; its hands, like two paws, clambering upon her; its mouth and nose ineffectually rooting to get at the mark; and meantime giving a vexatious half-grunt, blending with the composed snore of the negress.

The uncommon vigor of the child at length roused the mother.

She started up, at [a]⁴⁴ distance facing Captain Delano. But as if not at all concerned at the attitude in which she had been caught, delightedly she caught the child up, with maternal transports, covering it with kisses.

There's naked nature, now; pure tenderness and love, thought Captain Delano, well pleased.

This incident prompted him to remark the other negresses more particularly than before. He was gratified with their manners: like most uncivilized women, they seemed at once tender of heart and tough of constitution; equally ready to die for their infants or fight for them. Unsophisticated as leopardesses; loving as doves. Ah! thought Captain Delano, these, perhaps, are some of the very women whom [Ledyard]⁴⁵ saw in Africa, and gave such a noble account of.

These natural sights somehow insensibly deepened his confidence and ease. At last he looked to see how his boat was getting on; but it was still pretty remote. He turned to see if Don Benito had returned; but he had not.

To change the scene, as well as to please himself with a leisurely observation of the coming boat, stepping over into the mizzen-chains, he clambered his way into the starboard quarter-gallery—one of those abandoned Venetian-looking water-balconies previously mentioned— retreats cut off from the deck. As his foot pressed the half-damp, half-dry sea-mosses matting the place, and a chance phantom cats-paw—an islet of breeze, unheralded, unfollowed—as this ghostly cats-paw came fanning his cheek; as his glance fell upon the row of small, round dead-lights—all closed like coppered eyes of the coffined—and the state-cabin door, once connecting with the gallery, even as the dead-lights had once looked out upon it, but now calked fast like a sarcophagus lid; [and]⁴⁶ to a purple-black tarred-over, panel, threshold, and post; and he bethought him of the time when that state-cabin and this state-balcony had heard the voices of the Spanish king's officers, and the forms of the Lima viceroy's daughters had perhaps leaned where he stood—as these and other images flitted through his mind, as the cats-paw through the calm, gradually he felt rising a dreamy inquietude, like that of one who alone on the prairie feels unrest from the repose of the noon.

---

⁴⁴ "a" was omitted in the *Putnam* version.

⁴⁵ Mungo Park (In the issue of *Putnam's* in which the third installment of *Benito Cereno* was printed, there also appeared an anonymous essay entitled "About Niggers." By an extraordinary coincidence, the author of this essay quoted the exact passage to which Melville here alludes. What Melville had forgotten was that Park cites Ledyard as the source for the passage—"as Mr. Ledyard has eloquently said before me"—and so in the interests of scholarly fairness he changed the names when he revised the story the following month [January 1856] for *The Piazza Tales* edition.)

⁴⁶ "and" was omitted in the *Putnam* version.

He leaned against the curved balustrade, again looking off toward his boat; but found his eye falling upon the [ribbon][47] grass, trailing along the ship's water-line, straight as a border of green box; and parterres of sea-weed, broad ovals and crescents, floating nigh and far, with what seemed long formal alleys between, crossing the terraces of swells, and sweeping round as if leading to the grottoes below. And overhanging all was the balustrade by his arm, which, partly stained with pitch and partly embossed with moss, seemed the charred ruin of some summer-house in a grand garden long running to waste.

Trying to break one charm, he was but becharmed anew. Though upon the wide sea, he seemed in some far inland country; prisoner in some deserted château, left to stare at empty grounds, and peer out at vague roads, where never wagon or wayfarer passed.

But these enchantments were a little disenchanted as his eye fell on the corroded main-chains. Of an ancient style, massy and rusty in link, shackle and bolt, they seemed even more fit for the ship's present business than the one for [which she][48] had been built.

Presently he thought something moved nigh the chains. He rubbed his eyes, and looked hard. Groves of rigging were about the chains; and there, peering from behind a great stay, like an Indian from behind a hemlock, a Spanish sailor, a marlingspike in his hand, was seen, who made what seemed an imperfect gesture towards the balcony, but immediately, as if alarmed by some advancing step along the deck within, vanished into the recesses of the hempen forest, like a poacher.

What meant this? Something the man had sought to communicate, unbeknown to any one, even to his captain. Did the secret involve aught unfavorable to his captain? Were those previous misgivings of Captain Delano's about to be verified? Or, in his haunted mood at the moment, had some random, unintentional motion of the man, while busy with the stay, as if repairing it, been mistaken for a significant beckoning?

Not unbewildered, again he gazed off for his boat. But it was temporarily hidden by a rocky spur of the isle. As with some eagerness he bent forward, watching for the first shooting view of its beak, the balustrade gave way before him like charcoal. Had he not clutched an outreaching rope he would have fallen into the sea. The crash, though feeble, and the fall, though hollow, of the rotten fragments, must have been overheard. He glanced up. With sober curiosity peering down upon him was one of the old oakum-pickers, slipped from his perch to an outside boom; while below the old negro, and, invisible to him, reconnoitering from a port-hole like a fox from the mouth of its den, crouched the Spanish sailor again. From something suddenly suggested by the man's air, the mad idea now darted into Captain Delano's mind,

---

[47] ribboned
[48] which probably she

that Don Benito's plea of indisposition, in withdrawing below, was but a pretense: that he was engaged there maturing [his][49] plot, of which the sailor, by some means gaining an inkling, had a mind to warn the stranger against; incited, it may be, by gratitude for a kind word on first boarding the ship. Was it from foreseeing some possible interference like this, that Don Benito had, beforehand, given such a bad character of his sailors, while praising the negroes; though, indeed, the former seemed as docile as the latter the contrary? The whites, too, by nature, were the shrewder race. A man with some evil design, would he not be likely to speak well of that stupidity which was blind to his depravity, and malign that intelligence from which it might not be hidden? Not unlikely, perhaps. But if the whites had dark secrets concerning Don Benito, could then Don Benito be any way in complicity with the blacks? But they were too stupid. Besides, who ever heard of a white so far a renegade as to apostatize from his very species almost, by leaguing in against it with negroes? These difficulties recalled former ones. Lost in their mazes, Captain Delano, who had now regained the deck, was uneasily advancing along it, when he observed a new face; an aged sailor seated cross-legged near the main hatchway. His skin was shrunk up with wrinkles like a pelican's empty pouch; his hair frosted; his countenance grave and composed. His hands were full of ropes, which he was working into a large knot. Some blacks were about him obligingly dipping the strands for him, here and there, as the exigencies of the operation demanded.

Captain Delano crossed over to him, and stood in silence surveying the knot; his mind, by a not uncongenial transition, passing from its own entanglements to those of the hemp. For intricacy, such a knot he had never seen in an American ship, nor indeed any other. The old man looked liked an Egyptian priest, making Gordian knots for the temple of Ammon. The knot seemed a combination of double-bowline-knot, treble-crown-knot, back-handed-well-knot, knot-in-and-out-knot, and jamming-knot.

At last, puzzled to comprehend the meaning of such a knot, Captain Delano addressed the knotter:—

"What are you knotting there, my man?"

"The knot," was the brief reply, without looking up.

"So it seems; but what is it for?"

"For some one else to undo," muttered back the old man, plying his fingers harder than ever, the knot being now nearly completed.

While Captain Delano stood watching him, suddenly the old man threw the knot towards him, saying in broken English—the first heard in the ship—something to this effect: "Undo it, cut it, quick." It was said lowly, but with such condensation of rapidity, that the long, slow

---

[49] some

words in Spanish, which had preceded and followed, almost operated as covers to the brief English between.

For a moment, knot in hand, and knot in head, Captain Delano stood mute; while, without further heeding him, the old man was now intent upon other ropes. Presently there was a slight stir behind Captain Delano. Turning, he saw the chained negro, Atufal, standing quietly there. The next moment the old sailor rose, muttering, and, followed by his subordinate negroes, removed to the forward part of the ship, where in the crowd he disappeared.

An elderly negro, in a clout like an infant's, and with a pepper and salt head, and a kind of attorney air, now approached Captain Delano. In tolerable Spanish, and with a good-natured, knowing wink, he informed him that the old knotter was simple-witted, but harmless; often playing his [odd][50] tricks. The negro concluded by begging the knot, for of course the stranger would not care to be troubled with it. Unconsciously, it was handed to him. With a sort of congé, the negro received it, and, turning his back, ferreted into it like a detective custom-house office after smuggled laces. Soon, with some African word, equivalent to pshaw, he tossed the knot overboard.

All this is very queer now, thought Captain Delano, with a qualmish sort of emotion; but, as one feeling incipient sea-sickness, he strove, by ignoring the symptoms, to get rid of the malady. Once more he looked off for his boat. To his delight, it was now again in view, leaving the rocky spur astern.

The sensation here experienced, after at first relieving his uneasiness, with unforeseen [efficacy][51] soon began to remove it. The less distant sight of that well-known boat—showing it, not as before, half blended with the haze, but with outline defined, so that its individuality, like a man's, was manifest; that boat, Rover by name, which, though now in strange seas, had often pressed the beach of Captain Delano's home, and, brought to its threshold for repairs, had familiarly lain there, as a Newfoundland dog; the sight of that household boat evoked a thousand trustful associations, which, contrasted with previous suspicions, filled him not only with lightsome confidence, but somehow with half humorous self-reproaches at his former lack of it.

"What, I, Amasa Delano—Jack of the Beach, as they called me when a lad—I, Amasa; the same that, duck-satchel in hand, used to paddle along the water-side to the schoolhouse made from the old hulk—I, little Jack of the Beach, that used to go berrying with cousin Nat and the rest; I to be murdered here at the ends of the earth, on board a haunted pirate-ship by a horrible Spaniard? Too nonsensical to think of! Who would murder Amasa Delano? His conscience is clean. There is some one above. Fie, fie, Jack of the Beach! you are a child

---

[50] old
[51] efficiency,

indeed; a child of the second childhood, old boy; you are beginning to dote and drule, I'm afraid."

Light of heart and foot, he stepped aft, and there was met by Don Benito's servant, who, with a pleasing expression, responsive to his own present feelings, informed him that his master had recovered from the effects of his coughing fit, and had just ordered him to go present his compliments to his good guest, Don Amasa, and say that he (Don Benito) would soon have the happiness to rejoin him.

There now, do you mark that? again thought Captain Delano, walking the poop. What a donkey I was. This kind gentleman who here sends me his kind compliments, he, but ten minutes ago, dark-lantern in [hand],[52] was dodging round some old grind-stone in the hold, sharpening a hatchet for me, I thought. Well, well; these long calms have a morbid effect on the mind, I've often heard, though I never believed it before. Ha! glancing towards the boat; there's Rover; good dog; a white bone in her mouth. A pretty big bone though, seems to me.—What? Yes, she has fallen afoul of the bubbling tide-rip there. It sets her the other way, too, for the time. Patience.

It was now about noon, though, from the grayness of everything, it seemed to be getting towards dusk.

The calm was confirmed. In the far distance, away from the influence of land, the leaden ocean seemed laid out and leaded up, its course finished, soul gone, defunct. But the current from landward, where the ship was, increased; silently sweeping her further and further towards the tranced waters beyond.

Still, from his knowledge of those latitudes, cherishing hopes of a breeze, and a fair and fresh one, at any moment, Captain Delano, despite present prospects, buoyantly counted upon bringing the San Dominick safely to anchor ere night. The distance swept over was nothing; since, with a good wind, ten minutes' sailing would retrace more than sixty minutes, drifting. Meantime, one moment turning to mark "Rover" fighting the tide-rip, and the next to see Don Benito approaching, he continued walking the poop.

Gradually he felt a vexation arising from the delay of his boat; this soon merged into uneasiness; and at last—his eye falling continually, as from a stage-box into the pit, upon the strange crowd before and below him, and, by-and-by, recognizing there the face— now composed to indifference—of the Spanish sailor who had seemed to beckon from the main-chains—something of his old trepidations returned.

Ah, thought he—gravely enough—this is like the ague: because it went off, it follows not that it won't come back.

Though ashamed of the relapse, he could not altogether subdue

---

[52] "hand" from the *Putnam* version, not "had" from *Piazza* is obviously correct.

it; and so, exerting his good-nature to the utmost, insensibly he came to a compromise.

Yes, this is a strange craft; a strange history, too, and strange folks on board. But—nothing more.

By way of keeping his mind out of mischief till the boat should arrive, he tried to occupy it with turning over and over, in a purely speculative sort of way, some lesser peculiarities of the captain and crew. Among others, four curious points recurred:

First, the affair of the Spanish lad assailed with a knife by the slave boy; an act winked at by Don Benito. Second, the tyranny in Don Benito's treatment of Atufal, the black; as if a child should lead a bull of the Nile by the ring in his nose. Third, the trampling of the sailor by the two negroes; a piece of insolence passed over without so much as a reprimand. Fourth, the cringing submission to their master, of all the ship's underlings, mostly blacks; as if by the least inadvertence they feared to draw down his despotic displeasure.

Coupling these points, they seemed somewhat contradictory. But what then, thought Captain Delano, glancing towards his now nearing boat—what then? Why, Don Benito is a very capricious commander. But he is not the first of the sort I have seen; though it's true he rather exceeds any other. But as a nation—continued he in his reveries—these Spaniards are all an odd set; the very word Spaniard has a curious, conspirator, Guy-Fawkish twang to it. And yet, I dare say, Spaniards in the main are as good folks as any in Duxbury, Massachusetts. Ah good! At last "Rover" has come.

As, with its welcome freight, the boat touched the side, the oakum-pickers, with venerable gestures, sought to restrain the blacks, who, at the sight of three gurried water-casks in its bottom, and a pile of wilted pumpkins in its bow, hung over the bulwarks in disorderly raptures.

Don Benito, with his servant, now appeared; his coming, perhaps, hastened by hearing the noise. Of him Captain Delano sought permission to serve out the water, so that all might share alike, and none injure themselves by unfair excess. But sensible, and, on Don Benito's account, kind as this offer was, it was received with what seemed impatience; as if aware that he lacked energy as a commander, Don Benito, with the true jealousy of weakness, resented as an affront any interference. So, at least, Captain Delano inferred.

In another moment the casks were being hoisted in, when some of the eager negroes accidentally jostled Captain Delano, where he stood by the gangway; so that, unmindful of Don Benito, yielding to the impulse of the moment, with good-natured authority he bade the blacks stand back; to enforce his words making use of a half-mirthful, half-menacing gesture. Instantly the blacks paused, just where they were, each negro and negress suspended in his or her posture, exactly as the word had found them—for a few seconds continuing so—while, as between the responsive posts of a telegraph, an unknown syllable ran from man to man among the perched oakum-pickers. While the [visitor's][53] attention was fixed by this scene, suddenly the hatchet-polishers half rose, and a rapid cry came from Don Benito.

Thinking that at the signal of the Spaniard he was about to be massacred, Captain Delano would have sprung for his boat, but paused, as the oakum-pickers, dropping down into the crowd with earnest exclamations, forced every white and every negro back, at the same moment, with gestures friendly and familiar, almost jocose, bidding him, in substance, not be a fool. Simultaneously the hatchet-polishers resumed their seats, quietly as so many tailors, and at once, as if nothing had happened, the work of hoisting in the casks was resumed, whites and blacks singing at the tackle.

Captain Delano glanced towards Don Benito. As he saw his meagre form in the act of recovering itself from reclining in the servant's arms, into which the agitated invalid had fallen, he could not but marvel at the panic by which himself had been surprised, on the darting supposition that such a commander, who, upon a legitimate occasion, so trivial, too, as it now appeared, could lose all self-command, was, with energetic iniquity, going to bring about his murder.

The casks being on deck, Captain Delano was handed a number of jars and cups by one of the steward's aids, who, in the name of [his captain],[54] entreated him to do as he had proposed—dole out the water. He complied, with republican impartiality as to this republican element, which always seeks one level, serving the oldest white no better than the youngest black; excepting, indeed, poor Don Benito, whose condition, if not rank, demanded an extra allowance. To him, in the first place, Captain Delano presented a fair pitcher of the fluid; but, thirsting as he was for [it, the Spaniard][55] quaffed not a drop until after several grave bows and salutes. A reciprocation of courtesies which the sight-loving Africans hailed with clapping of hands.

Two of the less wilted pumpkins being reserved for the cabin table, the residue were minced up on the spot for the general regalement. But the soft bread, sugar, and bottled cider, Captain Delano would have given the [whites][56] alone, and in chief Don Benito; but the latter objected; which [disinterestedness not][57] a little pleased the American; and so mouthfuls all around were given alike to whites and blacks; excepting one bottle of cider, which Babo insisted upon setting aside for his master.

Here it may be observed that as, on the first visit of the boat, the

---

[53] Captain Delano's
[54] Don Benito
[55] fresh water, Don Benito
[56] Spaniards
[57] disinterestedness, on his part, not

American had not permitted his men to board the ship, neither did he now; being unwilling to add to the confusion of the decks.

Not uninfluenced by the peculiar good-humor at present prevailing, and for the time oblivious of any but benevolent thoughts, Captain Delano, who, from recent indications, counted upon a breeze within an hour or two at furthest, dispatched the boat back to the sealer, with orders for all the hands that could be spared immediately to set about rafting casks to the watering-place and filling them. Likewise he bade word be carried to his chief officer, that if, against present expectation, the ship was not brought to anchor by sunset, he need be under no concern; for as there was to be a full moon that night, he (Captain Delano) would remain on board ready to play the pilot, [come the wind][58] soon or late.

As the two captains stood together, observing the departing boat—the servant, as it happened, having just spied a spot on his master's velvet sleeve, and silently engaged rubbing it out—the American expressed his regrets that the San Dominick had no boats; none, at least, but the unseaworthy old hulk of the long-boat, which, warped as a camel's skeleton in the desert, and almost as bleached, lay pot-wise inverted amidships, one side a little tipped, furnishing a subterranean sort of den for family groups of the blacks, mostly women and small children; who, squatting on old mats below, or perched above in the dark dome, on the elevated seats, were descried, some distance within, like a social circle of bats, sheltering in some friendly cave; at intervals, ebon flights of naked boys and girls, three or four years old, darting in and out of the den's mouth.

"Had you three or four boats now, Don Benito," said Captain Delano, "I think that, by tugging at the oars, your negroes here might help along matters some. Did you sail from port without boats, Don Benito?"

"They were stove in the gales, Señor."

"That was bad. Many men, too, you lost then. Boats and men. Those must have been hard gales, Don Benito."

"Past all speech," cringed the Spaniard.

"Tell me, Don Benito," continued his companion with increased interest, "tell me, were these gales immediately off the pitch of Cape Horn?"

"Cape Horn?—who spoke of Cape Horn?"

"Yourself did, when giving me an account of your voyage," answered Captain Delano, with almost equal astonishment at this eating of his own words, even as he ever seemed eating his own heart, on the part of the Spaniard. "You yourself, Don Benito, spoke of Cape Horn," he emphatically repeated.

The Spaniard turned, in a sort of stooping posture, pausing an

---

[58] should the wind come

instant, as one about to make a plunging exchange of elements, as from air to water.

At this moment a messenger-boy, a white, hurried by, in the regular performance of his function carrying the last expired half hour forward to the forecastle, from the cabin time-piece, to have it struck at the ship's large bell.

"Master," said the servant, discontinuing his work on the coat sleeve, and addressing the rapt Spaniard with a sort of timid apprehensiveness, as one charged with a duty, the discharge of which, it was foreseen, would prove irksome to the very person who had imposed it, and for whose benefit it was intended, "master told me never mind where he was, or how engaged, always to remind him, to a minute, when shaving-time comes. Miguel has gone to strike the half-hour afternoon. It is *now* master. Will master go into the cuddy?"

"Ah—yes," answered the Spaniard, [starting],[59] as from dreams into realities; then turning upon Captain Delano, he said that ere long he would resume the conversation.

"Then if master means to talk more to Don Amasa," said the servant, "why not let Don Amasa sit by master in the cuddy, and master can talk, and Don Amasa can listen, while Babo here lathers and strops."

"Yes," said Captain Delano, not unpleased with this sociable plan, "yes, Don Benito, unless you had rather not, I will go with you."

"Be it so, Señor."

As the three passed aft, the American could not but think it another strange instance of his host's capriciousness, this being shaved with such uncommon punctuality in the middle of the day. But he deemed it more than likely that the servant's anxious fidelity had something to do with the matter; inasmuch as the timely interruption served to rally his master from the mood which had evidently been coming upon him.

The place called the cuddy was a light deck-cabin formed by the poop, a sort of attic to the large cabin below. Part of it had formerly been the quarters of the officers; but since their death all the partitionings had been thrown down, and the whole interior converted into one spacious and airy marine hall; for absence of fine furniture and picturesque disarray of odd appurtenances, somewhat answering to the wide, cluttered hall of some eccentric bachelor-squire in the country, who hangs his shooting-jacket and tobacco-pouch on deer antlers, and keeps his fishing-rod, tongs, and walking-stick in the same corner.

The similitude was heightened, if not originally suggested, by glimpses of the surrounding sea; since, in one aspect, the country and the ocean seem cousins-german.

The floor of the cuddy was matted. Overhead, four or five old

---

[59] starting somewhat

muskets were stuck into horizontal holes along the beams. On one side was a claw-footed old table lashed to the deck; a thumbed missal on it, and over it a small, meagre crucifix attached to the bulk-head. Under the table lay a dented cutlass or two, with a hacked harpoon, among some melancholy old rigging, like a heap of poor friars' girdles. There were also two long, sharp-ribbed settees of Malacca cane, black with age, and uncomfortable to look at as inquisitors' racks, with a large, misshapen arm-chair, which, furnished with a rude barber's [crotch][60] at the back, working with a screw, seemed some [grotesque engine][61] of torment. A flag locker was in one corner, open, exposing various colored bunting, some rolled up, others half unrolled, still others tumbled. Opposite was a cumbrous washstand, of black mahogany, all of one block, with a pedestal, like a font, and over it a railed shelf, containing combs, brushes, and other implements of the toilet. A torn hammock of stained grass swung near; the sheets tossed, and the pillow wrinkled up like a brow, as if whoever slept here slept but illy, with alternate visitations of sad thoughts and bad dreams.

The further extremity of the cuddy, overhanging the ship's stern, was pierced with three openings, windows or port-holes, according as men or cannon might peer, socially or unsocially, out of them. At present neither men nor cannon were seen, though huge ring-bolts and other rusty iron fixtures of the wood-work hinted of twenty-four-pounders.

Glancing towards the hammock as he entered, Captain Delano said, "You sleep here, Don Benito?"

"Yes, Señor, since we got into mild weather."

"This seems a sort of dormitory, sitting-room, sail-loft, chapel, armory, and private closet all together, Don Benito," added Captain Delano, looking round.

"Yes, Señor; events have not been favorable to much order in my arrangements."

Here the servant, napkin on arm, made a motion as if waiting his master's good pleasure. Don Benito signified his readiness, when, seating him in the Malacca arm-chair, and for the guest's convenience drawing [opposite one][62] of the settees, the servant commenced operations by throwing back his master's collar and loosening his cravat.

There is something in the negro which, in a peculiar way, fits him for avocations about one's person. Most negroes are natural valets and hair-dressers; taking to the comb and brush congenially as to the castanets, and flourishing them apparently with almost equal satisfaction. There is, too, a smooth tact about them in this employment, with a marvelous, noiseless, gliding briskness, not ungraceful in its way,

---

60 crutch
61 grotesque, middle-age engine
62 opposite it one

singularly pleasing to behold, and still more so to be the manipulated subject of. And above all is the great gift of good-humor. Not the mere grin or laugh is here meant. Those were unsuitable. But a certain easy cheerfulness, harmonious in every glance and gesture; as though God had set the whole negro to some pleasant tune.

When [to this][63] is added the docility arising from the unaspiring contentment of a limited mind, and that susceptibility of blind attachment sometimes inhering in indisputable inferiors, one readily perceives why those hypochondriacs, Johnson and Byron—it may be, something like the hypochondriac Benito Cereno—took to their hearts, almost to the exclusion of the entire white race, their serving men, the negroes, Barber and Fletcher. But if there be that in the negro which exempts him from the inflicted sourness of the morbid or cynical mind, how, in his most prepossessing aspects, must he appear to a benevolent one? When at ease with respect to exterior things, Captain Delano's nature was not only benign, but familiarly and humorously so. At home, he had often taken rare satisfaction in sitting in his door, watching some free man of color at his work or play. If on a voyage he chanced to have a black sailor, invariably he was on chatty and half-gamesome terms with him. In fact, like most men of a good, blithe heart, Captain Delano took to negroes, not philanthropically, but genially, just as other men to Newfoundland dogs.

Hitherto, the circumstances in which he found the San Dominick had repressed the tendency. But in the cuddy, relieved from his former uneasiness, and, for various reasons, more sociably inclined than at any previous period of the day, and seeing the colored servant, napkin on arm, so debonair about his master, in a business so familiar as that of shaving, too, all his old weakness for negroes returned.

Among other things, he was amused with an odd instance of the African love of bright colors and fine shows, in the black's informally taking from the flag-locker a great piece of bunting of all hues, and lavishly tucking it under his master's chin for an apron.

The mode of shaving among the Spaniards is a little different from what it is with other nations. They have a basin, specifically called a barber's basin, which on one side is scooped out, so as accurately to receive the chin, against which it is closely held in lathering; which is done, not with a brush, but with soap dipped in the water of the basin and rubbed on the face.

In the present instance salt-water was used for lack of better; and the parts lathered were only the upper lip, and low down under the throat, all the rest being cultivated beard.

The preliminaries being somewhat novel to Captain Delano, he sat curiously eyeing them, so that no conversation took place, nor, for the present, did Don Benito appear disposed to renew any.

---

[63] to all this

Setting down his basin, the negro searched among the razors, as for the sharpest, and having found it, gave it an additional edge by expertly strapping it on the firm, smooth, oily skin of his open palm; he then made a gesture as if to begin, but midway stood suspended for an instant, one hand elevating the razor, the other professionally dabbling among the bubbling suds on the Spaniard's lank neck. Not unaffected by the close sight of the gleaming steel, Don Benito nervously shuddered; his usual ghastliness was heightened by the lather, which lather, again, was intensified in its hue by the contrasting sootiness of the negro's body. Altogether the scene was somewhat peculiar, at least to Captain Delano, nor, as he saw the two thus postured, could he resist the vagary, that in the black he saw a headsman, and in the white a man at the block. But this was one of those antic conceits, appearing and vanishing in a breath, from which, perhaps, the best regulated mind is not [always][64] free.

Meantime the agitation of the Spaniard had a little loosened the bunting from around him, so that one broad fold swept curtain-like over the chair-arm to the floor, revealing, amid a profusion of armorial bars and ground-colors—black, blue, and yellow—a closed castle in a blood-red field diagonal with a lion rampant in a white.

"The castle and the lion," exclaimed Captain Delano—"why, Don Benito, this is the flag of Spain you use here. It's well it's only I, and not the King, that sees this," he added, with a smile, "but"—turning towards the black—"it's all one, I suppose, so the colors be gay;" which playful remark did not fail somewhat to tickle the negro.

"Now, master," he said, readjusting the flag, and pressing the head gently further back into the crotch of the chair; "now, master," and the steel glanced nigh the throat.

Again Don Benito faintly shuddered.

"You must not shake so, master. See, Don Amasa, master always shakes when I shave him. And yet master knows I never yet have drawn blood, though it's true, if master will shake so, I may some of these times. Now master," he continued. "And now, Don Amasa, please go on with your talk about the gale, and all that; master can hear, and, between times, master can answer."

"Ah yes, these gales," said Captain Delano; "but the more I think of your voyage, Don Benito, the more I wonder, not at the gales, terrible as they must have been, but at the disastrous interval following them. For here, by your account, have you been these two months and more getting from Cape Horn to St. Maria, a distance which I myself, with a good wind, have sailed in a few days. True, you had calms, and long ones, but to be becalmed for two months, that is, at least, unusual. Why, Don Benito, had almost any other gentleman told me such a story, I should have been half disposed to a little incredulity."

---

[64] "always" was omitted in the *Putnam* version.

Here an involuntary expression came over the Spaniard, similar to that just before on the deck, and whether it was the start he gave, or a sudden gawky roll of the hull in the calm, or a momentary unsteadiness of the servant's hand, however it was, just then the razor drew blood, spots of which stained the creamy lather under the throat: immediately the black barber drew back his steel, and, remaining in his professional attitude, back to Captain Delano, and face to Don Benito, held up the trickling razor, saying, with a sort of half humorous sorrow, "See, master—you shook so—here's Babo's first blood."

No sword drawn before James the First of England, no assassination in that timid King's presence, could have produced a more terrified aspect than was now presented by Don Benito.

Poor fellow, thought Captain Delano, so nervous he can't even bear the sight of barber's blood; and this unstrung, sick man, is it credible that I should have imagined he meant to spill all my blood, who can't endure the sight of one little drop of his own? Surely, Amasa Delano, you have been beside yourself this day. Tell it not when you get home, sappy Amasa. Well, well, he looks like a murderer, doesn't he? More like as if himself were to be done for. Well, well, this day's experience shall be a good lesson.

Meantime, while these things were running through the honest seaman's mind, the servant had taken the napkin from his arm, and to Don Benito had said—"But answer Don Amasa, please, master, while I wipe this ugly stuff off the razor, and strop it again."

As he said the words, his face was turned half round, so as to be alike visible to the Spaniard and the American, and seemed, by its expression, to hint, that he was desirous, by getting his master to go on with the conversation, considerately to withdraw his attention from the recent annoying accident. As if glad to snatch the offered relief. Don Benito resumed, rehearsing to Captain Delano, that not only were the calms of unusual duration, but the ship had fallen in with obstinate currents; and other things he added, some of which were but repetitions of former statements, to explain how it came to pass that the passage from Cape Horn to St. Maria had been so exceedingly long; now and then mingling with his words, incidental praises, less qualified than before, to the blacks, for their general good conduct. These particulars were not given consecutively, the servant [, at convenient times,][65] using his razor, and so, between the intervals of shaving, the story and panegyric went on with more than usual huskiness.

To Captain Delano's imagination, now again not wholly at rest, there was something so hollow in the Spaniard's manner, with apparently some reciprocal hollowness in the servant's dusky comment of silence, that the idea flashed across him, that possibly master and man, for some unknown purpose, were acting out, both in word and deed,

---

[65] now and then

nay, to the very tremor of Don Benito's limbs, some juggling play before him. Neither did the suspicion of collusion lack apparent support, from the fact of those whispered conferences before mentioned. But then, what could be the object of enacting this play of the barber before him? At last, regarding the notion as a whimsy, insensibly suggested, perhaps, by the theatrical aspect of Don Benito in his harlequin ensign, Captain Delano speedily banished it.

The shaving over, the servant bestirred himself with a small bottle of scented waters, pouring a few drops on the head, and then diligently rubbing; the vehemence of the exercise causing the muscles of his face to twitch rather strangely.

His next operation was with comb, scissors, and brush; going round and round, smoothing a curl here, clipping an unruly whisker-hair there, giving a graceful sweep to the temple-lock, with other impromptu touches evincing the hand of a master; while, like any resigned gentleman in barber's hands, Don Benito bore all, much less uneasily, at least, than he had done the razoring; indeed, he sat so pale and rigid now, that the negro seemed a Nubian sculptor finishing off a white statue-head.

All being over at last, the standard of Spain removed, tumbled up, and tossed back into the flag-locker, the negro's warm breath blowing away any stray hair which might have lodged down his master's neck; collar and cravat readjusted; a speck of lint whisked off the velvet lapel; all this being done; backing off a little space, and pausing with an expression of subdued self-complacency, the servant for a moment surveyed his master, as, in toilet at least, the creature of his own tasteful hands.

Captain Delano playfully complimented him upon his achievement; at the same time congratulating Don Benito.

But neither sweet waters, nor shampooing, nor fidelity, nor sociality, delighted the Spaniard. Seeing him relapsing into forbidding gloom, and still remaining seated, Captain Delano, thinking that his presence was undesired just then, withdrew, on pretense of seeing whether, as he had prophesied, any signs of a breeze were visible.

Walking forward to the main-mast, he stood awhile thinking over the scene, and not without some undefined misgivings, when he heard a noise near the cuddy, and turning, saw the negro, his hand to his cheek. Advancing, Captain Delano perceived that the cheek was bleeding. He was about to ask the cause, when the negro's wailing soliloquy enlightened him.

"Ah, when will master get better from his sickness; only the sour heart that sour sickness breeds made him serve Babo so; cutting Babo with the razor, because, only by accident, Babo had given master one little scratch; and for the first time in so many a day, too. Ah, ah, ah," holding his hand to his face.

Is it possible, thought Captain Delano; was it to wreak in private his Spanish spite against this poor friend of his, that Don Benito, by his sullen manner, impelled me to withdraw? Ah, this slavery breeds ugly passions in man.—Poor fellow!

He was about to speak in sympathy to the negro, but with a timid reluctance he now re-entered the cuddy.

Presently master and man came forth; Don Benito leaning on his servant as if nothing had happened.

But a sort of love-quarrel, after all, thought Captain Delano.

He accosted Don Benito, and they slowly walked together. They had gone but a few paces, when the steward—a tall, rajah-looking mulatto, orientally set off with a pagoda turban formed by three or four Madras handkerchiefs wound about his head, tier on tier—approaching with a saalam, announced lunch in the cabin.

On their way thither, the two captains were preceded by the mulatto, who, turning round as he advanced, with continual smiles and bows, ushered them [on],[66] a display of elegance which quite completed the insignificance of the small bare-headed Babo, who, as if not unconscious of inferiority, eyed askance the graceful steward. But in part, Captain Delano imputed his jealous watchfulness to that peculiar feeling which the full-blooded African entertains for the adulterated one. As for the steward, his manner, if not bespeaking much dignity of self-respect, yet evidenced his extreme desire to please; which is doubly meritorious, as at once Christian and Chesterfieldian.

Captain Delano observed with interest that while the complexion of the mulatto was hybrid, his physiognomy was European—classically so.

"Don Benito," whispered he, "I am glad to see this usher-of-the-golden-rod of yours; the sight refutes an ugly remark once made to me by a Barbadoes planter; that when a mulatto has a regular European face, look out for him; he is a devil. But see, your steward here has features more regular than King George's of England; and yet there he nods, and bows, and smiles; a king, indeed—the king of kind hearts and polite fellows. What a pleasant voice he has, too?"

"He has, Señor."

"But tell me, has he not, so far as you have known him, always proved a good, worthy fellow?" said Captain Delano, pausing, while with a final genuflexion the steward disappeared into the cabin; "come, for the reason just mentioned, I am curious to know."

"Francesco is a good man," [a sort of][67] sluggishly responded Don Benito, like a phlegmatic appreciator, who would neither find fault nor flatter.

---

66 in

67 Unfortunately, there seems to be no reasonable way to correct this misconstruction, which appears in both the *Putnam* and *Piazza* versions; Weaver (1928) and Chase (1950) substitute, respectively, "rather" and "somewhat" for "a sort of," but without any apparent justification.

"Ah, I thought so. For it were strange, indeed, and not very creditable to us white-skins, if a little of our blood mixed with the African's, should, far from improving the latter's quality, have the sad effect of pouring vitriolic acid into black broth; improving the hue, perhaps, but not the wholesomeness."

"Doubtless, doubtless, Señor, but"—glancing at Babo—"not to speak of negroes, your planter's remark I have heard applied to the Spanish and Indian intermixtures in our provinces. But I know nothing about the matter," he listlessly added.

And here they entered the cabin.

The lunch was a frugal one. Some of Captain Delano's fresh fish and pumpkins, biscuit and salt beef, the reserved bottle of cider, and the San Dominick's last bottle of Canary.

As they entered, Francesco, with two or three colored aids, was hovering over the table giving the last adjustments. Upon perceiving their master they withdrew, Francesco making a smiling congé, and the Spaniard, without condescending to notice it, fastidiously remarking to his companion that he relished not superfluous attendance.

Without companions, host and guest sat down, like a childless married couple, at opposite ends of the table, Don Benito waving Captain Delano to his place, and, weak as he was, insisting upon that gentleman being seated before himself.

The negro placed a rug under Don Benito's feet, and a cushion behind his back, and then stood behind, not his master's chair, but Captain Delano's. At first, this a little surprised the latter. But it was soon evident that, in taking his position, the black was still true to his master; since by facing him he could the more readily anticipate his slightest want.

"This is an uncommonly intelligent fellow of yours, Don Benito," whispered Captain Delano across the table.

"You say true, Señor."

During the repast, the guest again reverted to parts of Don Benito's story, begging further particulars here and there. He inquired how it was that the scurvy and fever should have committed such wholesale havoc upon the whites, while destroying less than half of the blacks. As if this question reproduced the whole scene of plague before the Spaniard's eyes, miserably reminding him of his solitude in a cabin where before he had had so many friends and officers round him, his hands shook, his face became hueless, broken words escaped; but directly the sane memory of the past seemed replaced by insane terrors of the present. With starting eyes he stared before him at vacancy. For nothing was to be seen but the hand of his servant pushing the Canary over towards him. At length a few sips served partially to restore him. He made random reference to the different constitution of races, enabling one to offer more resistance to certain maladies than another. The thought was new to his companion.

Presently Captain Delano, intending to say something to his host concerning the pecuniary part of the business he had undertaken for him, especially—since he was strictly accountable to his owners—with reference to the new suit of sails, and other things of that sort; and naturally preferring to conduct such affairs in private, was desirous that the servant should withdraw; imagining that Don Benito for a few minutes could dispense with his attendance. He, however, waited awhile; thinking that, as the conversation proceeded, Don Benito, without being prompted, would perceive the propriety of the step.

But it was otherwise. At last catching his host's eye, Captain Delano, with a slight backward gesture of his thumb, whispered, "Don Benito, pardon me, but there is an interference with the full expression of what I have to say to you."

Upon this the Spaniard changed countenance; which was imputed to his resenting the hint, as in some way a reflection upon his servant. After a moment's pause, he assured his guest that the black's remaining with them could be of no disservice; because since losing his officers he had made Babo (whose original office, it now appeared, had been captain of the slaves) not only his constant attendant and companion, but in all things his confidant.

After this, nothing more could be said; though, indeed, Captain Delano could hardly avoid some little tinge of irritation upon being left ungratified in so inconsiderable a wish, by one, too, for whom he intended such solid services. But it is only his querulousness, thought he; and so filling his glass he proceeded to business.

The price of the sails and other matters was fixed upon. But while this was being done, the American observed that, though his original offer of assistance had been hailed with hectic animation, yet now when it was reduced to a business transaction, indifference and apathy were betrayed. Don Benito, in fact, appeared to submit to hearing the details more out of regard to common propriety, than from any impression that weighty benefit to himself and his voyage was involved.

Soon, [his][68] manner became still more reserved. The effort was vain to seek to draw him into social talk. Gnawed by his splenetic mood, he sat twitching his beard, while to little purpose the hand of his servant, mute as that on the wall, slowly pushed over the Canary.

Lunch being over, they sat down on the cushioned transom; the servant placing a pillow behind his master. The long continuance of the calm had now affected the atmosphere. Don Benito sighed heavily, as if for breath.

"Why not adjourn to the cuddy," said Captain Delano; "there is more air there." But the host sat silent and motionless.

Meantime his servant knelt before him, with a large fan of feathers. And Francesco coming in on tiptoes, handed the negro a

---

[68] this

little cup of aromatic waters, with which at intervals he chafed his master's brow; smoothing the hair along the temples as a nurse does a child's. He spoke no word. He only rested his eye on his master's, as if, amid all Don Benito's distress, a little to refresh his spirit by the silent sight of fidelity.

Presently the ship's bell sounded two o'clock; and through the cabin windows a slight rippling of the sea was discerned; and from the desired direction.

"There," exclaimed Captain Delano, "I told you so, Don Benito, look!"

He had risen to his feet, speaking in a very animated tone, with a view the more to rouse his companion. But though the crimson curtain of the stern-window near him that moment fluttered against his pale cheek, Don Benito seemed to have even less welcome for the breeze than the calm.

Poor fellow, thought Captain Delano, bitter experience has taught him that one ripple does not make a wind, any more than one swallow a summer. But he is mistaken for once. I will get his ship in for him, and prove it.

Briefly alluding to his weak condition, he urged his host to remain quietly where he was, since he (Captain Delano) would with pleasure take upon himself the responsibility of making the best use of the wind.

Upon gaining the deck, Captain Delano started at the unexpected figure of Atufal, monumentally fixed at the threshold, like one of those sculptured porters of black marble guarding the porches of Egyptian tombs.

But this time the start was, perhaps, purely physical. Atufal's presence, singularly attesting docility even in sullenness, was contrasted with that of the hatchet-polishers, who in patience evinced their industry; while both spectacles showed, that lax as Don Benito's general authority might be, still, whenever he chose to exert it, no man so savage or colossal but must, more or less, bow.

Snatching a trumpet which hung from the bulwarks, with a free step Captain Delano advanced to the forward edge of the poop, issuing his orders in his best Spanish. The few sailors and many negroes, all equally pleased, obediently set about heading the ship towards the harbor.

While giving some directions about setting a lower stu'n'-sail, suddenly Captain Delano heard a voice faithfully repeating his orders. Turning, he saw Babo, now for the time acting, under the pilot, his original part of captain of the slaves. This assistance proved valuable. Tattered sails and warped yards were soon brought into some trim. And no brace or halyard was pulled but to the blithe songs of the inspirited negroes.

Good fellows, thought Captain Delano, a little training would make fine sailors of them. Why see, the very women pull and sing too.

These must be some of those Ashantee negresses that make such capital soldiers, I've heard. But who's at the helm? I must have a good hand there.

He went to see.

The San Dominick steered with a cumbrous tiller, with large horizontal pullies attached. At each pulley-end stood a subordinate black, and between them, at the tiller-head, the responsible post, a Spanish seaman, whose countenance evinced his due share in the general hopefulness and confidence at the coming of the breeze.

He proved the same man who had behaved with so shame-faced an air on the windlass.

"Ah,—it is you, my man," exclaimed Captain Delano—"well, no more sheep's-eyes now;—look straight forward and keep the ship so. Good hand, I trust? And want to get into the harbor, don't you?"

[The man assented]⁶⁹ with an inward chuckle, grasping the tiller-head firmly. Upon this, unperceived by the American, the two blacks eyed the sailor [intently].⁷⁰

Finding all right at the helm, the pilot went forward to the forecastle, to see how matters stood there.

The ship now had way enough to breast the current. With the approach of evening, the breeze would be sure to freshen.

Having done all that was needed for the present, Captain Delano, giving his last orders to the sailors, turned aft to report affairs to Don Benito in the cabin; perhaps additionally incited to rejoin him by the hope of snatching a moment's private chat while [the]⁷¹ servant was engaged upon deck.

From opposite sides, there were, beneath the poop, two approaches to the cabin; one further forward than the other, and consequently communicating with a longer passage. Marking the servant still above, Captain Delano, taking the nighest entrance—the one last named, and at whose porch Atufal still stood—hurried on his way, till, arrived at the cabin threshold, he paused an instant, a little to recover from his eagerness. Then, with the words of his intended business upon his lips, he entered. As he advanced toward the [seated Spaniard],⁷² he heard another footstep, keeping time with his. From the opposite door, a salver in hand, the servant was likewise advancing.

"Confound the faithful fellow," thought Captain Delano; "what a vexatious coincidence."

Possibly, the vexation might have been something different, were it not for the [brisk]⁷³ confidence inspired by the breeze. But even as

---

⁶⁹ "Sí, Señor," assented the man
⁷⁰ askance
⁷¹ his
⁷² Spaniard, on the transom
⁷³ buoyant

it was, he felt a slight twinge, from a sudden [indefinite][74] association in his mind of Babo with Atufal.

"Don Benito," said he, "I give you joy; the breeze will hold, and will increase. By the way, your tall man and time-piece, Atufal, stands without. By your order, of course?"

Don Benito recoiled, as if at some bland satirical touch, delivered with such adroit garnish of apparent good breeding as to present no handle for retort.

He is like one flayed alive, thought Captain Delano; where may one touch him without causing a shrink?

The servant moved before his master, adjusting a cushion; recalled to civility, the Spaniard stiffly replied: "You are right. The slave appears where you saw him, according to my command; which is, that if at the given hour I am below, he must take his stand and abide my coming."

"Ah now, pardon me, but that is treating the poor fellow like an ex-king [indeed].[75] Ah, Don Benito," smiling, "for all the license you permit in some things, I fear lest, at bottom, you are a bitter hard master."

Again Don Benito shrank; and this time, as the good sailor thought, from a genuine twinge of his conscience.

[Again conversation][76] became constrained. In vain Captain Delano called attention to the now perceptible motion of the keel gently cleaving the sea; with lack-lustre eye, Don Benito returned words few and reserved.

By-and-by, the wind having steadily risen, and still blowing right into the harbor, bore the San Dominick swiftly on. Rounding a point of land, the sealer at distance came into open view.

Meantime Captain Delano had again repaired to the deck, remaining there sometime. Having at last altered the ship's course, so as to give the reef a wide berth, he returned for a few moments below.

I will cheer up my poor friend, this time, thought he.

"Better and better, Don Benito," he cried as he blithely reentered: "there will soon be an end to your cares, at least for awhile. For when, after a long, sad voyage, you know, the anchor drops into the haven, all its vast weight seems lifted from the captain's heart. We are getting on famously, Don Benito. My ship is in sight. Look through this side-light here; there she is; all a-taunt-o! The Bachelor's Delight, my good friend. Ah, how this wind braces one up. Come, you must take a cup of coffee with me this evening. My old steward will give you as fine a cup as ever any sultan tasted. What say you, Don Benito, will you?"

---

[74] involuntary
[75] denied
[76] Conversation now

At first, the Spaniard glanced feverishly up, casting a longing look towards the sealer, while with mute concern his servant gazed into his face. Suddenly the old ague of coldness returned, and dropping back to his cushions he was silent.

"You do not answer. Come, all day you have been my host; would you have hospitality all on one side?"

"I cannot go," was the response.

"What? it will not fatigue you. The ships will lie together as near as they can, without swinging foul. It will be little more than stepping from deck to deck; which is but as from room to room. Come, come, you must not refuse me."

"I cannot go," decisively and repulsively repeated Don Benito.

Renouncing all but the last appearance of courtesy, with a sort of cadaverous sullenness, and biting his thin nails to the quick, he glanced, almost glared, at his guest, as if impatient that a stranger's presence should interfere with the full indulgence of his morbid hour. Meantime the sound of the parted waters came more and more gurglingly and merrily in at the windows; as reproaching him for his dark spleen; as telling him that, sulk as he might, and go mad with it, nature cared not a jot; since, whose fault was it, pray?

But the foul mood was now at its depth, as the fair wind at its height.

There was something in the man so far beyond any mere unsociality or sourness previously evinced, that even the forbearing good-nature of his guest could no longer endure it. Wholly at a loss to account for such demeanor, and deeming sickness with eccentricity, however extreme, no adequate excuse, well satisfied, too, that nothing in his own conduct could justify it, Captain Delano's pride began to be roused. Himself became reserved. But all seemed one to the Spaniard. Quitting him, therefore, Captain Delano once more went to the deck.

The ship was now within less than two miles of the sealer. The whale-boat was seen darting over the interval.

To be brief, the two vessels, thanks to the pilot's skill, ere long in neighborly style lay anchored together.

Before returning to his own vessel, Captain Delano had intended communicating to Don Benito the [smaller][77] details of the proposed services to be rendered. But, as it was, unwilling anew to subject himself to rebuffs, he resolved, now that he had seen the San Dominick safely moored, immediately to quit her, without further allusion to hospitality or business. Indefinitely postponing his ulterior plans, he would regulate his future actions according to future circumstances. His boat was ready to receive him; but his host still tarried below. Well, thought Captain Delano, if he has little breeding, the more need to

---

[77] practical

show mine. He descended to the cabin to bid a ceremonious, and, it may be, tacitly rebukeful adieu. But to his great satisfaction, Don Benito, as if he began to feel the weight of that treatment with which his slighted guest had, not indecorously, retaliated upon him, now supported by his servant, rose to his feet, and grasping Captain Delano's hand, stood tremulous; too much agitated to speak. But the good augury hence drawn was suddenly dashed, by his resuming all his previous reserve, with augmented gloom, as, with half-averted eyes, he silently reseated himself on his cushions. With a corresponding return of his own chilled feelings, Captain Delano bowed and withdrew.

He was hardly midway in the narrow corridor, dim as a tunnel, leading from the cabin to the stairs, when a sound, as of the tolling for execution in some jail-yard, fell on his ears. It was the echo of the ship's flawed bell, striking the hour, drearily reverberated in this subterranean vault. Instantly, by a fatality not to be withstood, his mind, responsive to the portent, swarmed with superstitious suspicions. He paused. In images far swifter than these sentences, the minutest details of all his former distrusts swept through him.

Hitherto, credulous good-nature had been too ready to furnish excuses for reasonable fears. Why was the Spaniard, so superfluously punctilious at times, now heedless of common propriety in not accompanying to the side his departing guest? Did indisposition forbid? Indisposition had not forbidden more irksome exertion that day. His last equivocal demeanor recurred. He had risen to his feet, grasped his guest's hand, motioned toward his hat; then, in an instant, all was eclipsed in sinister muteness and gloom. Did this imply one brief, repentant relenting at the final moment, from some iniquitous plot, followed by remorseless return to it? His last glance seemed to express a calamitous, yet acquiescent farewell to Captain Delano forever. Why decline the invitation to visit the sealer that evening? Or was the Spaniard less hardened than the Jew, who refrained not from supping at the board of him whom the same night he meant to betray? What imported all those day-long enigmas and contradictions, except they were intended to mystify, preliminary to some stealthy blow? Atufal, the pretended rebel, but punctual shadow, that moment lurked by the threshold without. He seemed a sentry, and more. Who, by his own confession, had stationed him there? Was the negro now lying in wait?

The Spaniard behind—his creature before: to rush from darkness to light was the involuntary choice.

The next moment, with clenched jaw and hand, he passed Atufal, and stood [unharmed][78] in the light. As he saw his trim ship lying peacefully [at anchor],[79] and almost within ordinary call; as he saw his household boat, with familiar faces in it, patiently rising and falling

---

[78] unarmed
[79] at her anchor

on the short waves by the San Dominick's side; and then, glancing about the decks where he stood, saw the oakum-pickers still gravely plying their fingers; and heard the low, buzzing whistle and industrious hum of the hatchet-polishers, still bestirring themselves over their endless occupation; and more than all, as he saw the benign aspect of nature, taking her innocent repose in the evening; the screened sun in the quiet camp of the west shining out like the mild light from Abraham's tent; [as charmed][80] eye and ear took in all these, with the chained figure of the black, [clenched][81] jaw and hand relaxed. Once again he smiled at the phantoms which had mocked him, and felt something like a tinge of remorse, that, by [harboring][82] them even for a moment, he should, by implication, have betrayed [an atheist][83] doubt of the ever-watchful Providence above.

There was a few minutes' delay, while, in obedience to his orders, the boat was being hooked along to the gangway. During this interval, a sort of saddened satisfaction stole over Captain Delano, at thinking of the kindly offices he had that day discharged for a stranger. Ah, thought he, after good actions one's conscience is never ungrateful, however much so the benefited party may be.

Presently, his foot, in the first act of descent into the boat, pressed the first round of the side-ladder, his face presented inward upon the deck. In the same moment, he heard his name courteously sounded; and, to his pleased surprise, saw Don Benito advancing—an unwonted energy in his air, as if, at the last moment, intent upon making amends for his recent discourtesy. With instinctive good feeling, Captain Delano, [withdrawing][84] his foot, turned and reciprocally advanced. As he did so, the Spaniard's nervous eagerness increased, but his vital energy failed; so that, the better to support him, the servant, placing his master's hand on his naked shoulder, and gently holding it there, formed himself into a sort of crutch.

When the two captains met, the Spaniard again fervently took the hand of the American, at the same time casting an earnest glance into his eyes, but, as before, too much overcome to speak.

I have done him wrong, self-reproachfully thought Captain Delano; his apparent coldness has deceived me; in no instance has he meant to offend.

Meantime, as if fearful that the continuance of the scene might too much unstring his master, the servant seemed anxious to terminate it. And so, still presenting himself as a crutch, and walking between the two captains, he advanced with them towards the gangway; while

---

80 as his charmed
81 the clenched
82 indulging
83 an almost atheist
84 revoking

still, as if full of kindly contrition, Don Benito would not let go the hand of Captain Delano, but retained it in his, across the black's body.

Soon they were standing by the side, looking over into the boat, whose crew turned up their curious eyes. Waiting a moment for the Spaniard to relinquish his hold, the now embarrassed Captain Delano lifted his foot, to overstep the threshold of the open gangway; but still Don Benito would not let go his hand. And yet, with an agitated tone, he said, "I can go no further; here I must bid you adieu. Adieu, my dear, dear Don Amasa. Go—go!" suddenly tearing his hand loose, "go, and God guard you better than me, my best friend."

Not unaffected, Captain Delano would now have lingered; but catching the meekly admonitory eye of the servant, with a hasty farewell he descended into his boat, followed by the continual adieus of Don Benito, standing rooted in the gangway.

Seating himself in the stern, Captain Delano, making a last salute, ordered the boat shoved off. The crew had their oars on end. The [bowsman][85] pushed the boat a sufficient distance for the oars to be lengthwise dropped. The instant that was done, Don Benito sprang over the bulwarks, falling at the feet of Captain Delano; at the same time calling towards his ship, but in tones so frenzied, that none in the boat could understand him. But, as if not equally obtuse, [three sailors],[86] from three different and distant parts of the ship, splashed into the sea, swimming after their captain, as if intent upon his rescue.

The dismayed officer of the boat eagerly asked what this meant. To which, Captain Delano, turning a disdainful smile upon the unaccountable [Spaniard],[87] answered that, for his part, he neither knew nor cared; but it seemed as if [Don Benito][88] had taken it into his head to produce the impression among his people that the boat wanted to kidnap him. "Or else—give way for your lives," he wildly added, starting at a clattering hubbub in the ship, above which rang the tocsin of the hatchet-polishers; and seizing Don Benito by the throat he added, "this plotting pirate means murder!" Here, in apparent verification of the words, the servant, a dagger in his hand, was seen on the rail overhead, poised, in the act of leaping, as if with desperate fidelity to befriend his master to the last; while, seemingly to aid the black, the three [white][89] sailors were trying to clamber into the hampered bow. Meantime, the whole host of negroes, as if inflamed at the sight of their jeopardized captain, impended in one sooty avalanche over the bulwarks.

---

85 "bowsman" (*Putnam's*) has been chosen over "bowsmen" (*Piazza*) since a few paragraphs on Melville mentions only one bowsman (cf. p. 51, l. 18).
86 three Spanish sailors
87 Benito Cereno
88 the Spaniard
89 Spanish

All this, with what preceded, and what followed, occurred with such involutions of rapidity, that past, present, and future seemed one.

Seeing the negro coming, Captain Delano had flung the Spaniard aside, almost in the very act of clutching him, and, by the unconscious recoil, shifting his place, with arms thrown up, so promptly grappled the servant in his descent, that with dagger presented at Captain Delano's heart, the black seemed of purpose to have leaped there as to his mark. But the weapon was wrenched away, and the assailant dashed down into the bottom of the boat, which now, with disentangled oars, began to speed through the sea.

At this juncture, the left hand of Captain Delano, on one side, again clutched the half-reclined Don Benito, heedless that he was in a speechless faint, while his right foot, on the other side, ground the prostrate negro; and his right arm pressed for added speed on the after oar, his eye bent forward, encouraging his men to their utmost.

But here, the officer of the boat, who had at last succeeded in beating off the [towing sailors],[90] and was now, with face turned aft, assisting the bowsman at his oar, suddenly called to Captain Delano, to see what the black was about; while a Portuguese oarsman shouted to him to give heed to what the Spaniard was saying.

Glancing down at his feet, Captain Delano saw the freed hand of the servant aiming with a second dagger—a small one, before concealed in his wool—with this he was snakishly writhing up from the boat's bottom, at the heart of his master, his countenance lividly vindictive, expressing the centred purpose of his soul; while the Spaniard, half-choked, was vainly shrinking away, with husky words, incoherent to all but the Portuguese.

That moment, across the long-benighted mind of Captain Delano, a flash of revelation swept, illuminating, in unanticipated clearness, [his host's][91] whole mysterious demeanor, with every enigmatic event of the day, as well as the entire past voyage of the San Dominick. He smote Babo's hand down, but his own heart smote him harder. With infinite pity he withdrew his hold from Don Benito. Not Captain Delano, but Don Benito, the black, in leaping into the boat, had intended to stab.

Both the black's hands were held, as, glancing up towards the San Dominick, Captain Delano, now [with scales][92] dropped from his eyes, saw the negroes, not in misrule, not in tumult, not as if frantically concerned for Don Benito, but with mask torn away, flourishing hatchets and knives, in ferocious piratical revolt. Like delirious black dervishes, the six Ashantees danced on the poop. Prevented by their foes from springing into the water, the Spanish boys were hurrying up

90 towing Spanish sailors
91 Benito Cereno's
92 with the scales

to the topmost spars, while such of the few Spanish sailors, not already in the sea, less alert, were descried, helplessly mixed in, on deck, with the blacks.

Meantime Captain Delano hailed his own vessel, ordering the ports up, and the guns run out. But by this time the cable of the San Dominick had been cut; and the fag-end, in lashing out, whipped away the canvas shroud about the beak, suddenly revealing, as the bleached hull swung round towards the open ocean, death for the figure-head, in a human skeleton; chalky comment on the chalked words below, *"Follow your leader."*

At the sight, Don Benito, covering his face, wailed out: " 'Tis he, Aranda! my murdered, unburied friend!"

Upon reaching the sealer, calling for ropes, Captain Delano bound the negro, who made no resistance, and had him hoisted to the deck. He would then have assisted the now almost helpless Don Benito up the side; but Don Benito, wan as he was, refused to move, or be moved, until the negro should have been first put below out of view. When, presently assured that it was done, he no more shrank from the ascent.

The boat was immediately dispatched back to pick up the three swimming sailors. Meantime, the guns were in readiness, though, owing to the San Dominick having glided somewhat astern of the sealer, only the aftermost one could be brought to bear. With this, they fired six times; thinking to cripple the fugitive ship by bringing down her spars. But only a few inconsiderable ropes were shot away. Soon the ship was beyond the gun's range, steering broad out of the bay; the blacks thickly clustering round the bowsprit, one moment with taunting cries towards the whites, the next with upthrown gestures hailing the now dusky [moors][93] of ocean—cawing crows escaped from the hand of the fowler.

The first impulse was to slip the cables and give chase. But, upon second thoughts, to pursue with whale-boat and yawl seemed more promising.

Upon inquiring of Don Benito what fire-arms they had on board the San Dominick, Captain Delano was answered that they had none that could be used; because, in the earlier stages of the mutiny, a cabin-passenger, since dead, had secretly put out of order the locks of what few muskets there were. But with all his remaining strength, Don Benito entreated the American not to give chase, either with ship or boat; for the negroes had already proved themselves such desperadoes, that, in case of a present assault, nothing but a total massacre of the whites could be looked for. But, regarding this warning as coming from one whose spirit had been crushed by misery, the American did not give up his design.

The boats were got ready and armed. Captain Delano ordered

---

[93] expanse

[his]⁹⁴ men into them. He was going himself when Don Benito grasped his arm.

"What! have you saved my life, Señor, and are you now going to throw away your own?"

The officers also, for reasons connected with their interests and those of the voyage, and a duty owing to the owners, strongly objected against their commander's going. Weighing their remonstrances a moment, Captain Delano felt bound to remain; appointing his chief mate—an athletic and resolute man, who had been [a privateer's-man]⁹⁵ —to head the party. The more to encourage the sailors, they were told, that the Spanish captain considered his [ship good]⁹⁶ as lost; that she and her cargo, including some gold and silver, were [worth more than a thousand]⁹⁷ doubloons. Take her, and no small part should be theirs. The sailors replied with a shout.

The fugitives had now almost gained an offing. It was nearly night; but the moon was rising. After hard, prolonged pulling, the boats came up on the ship's quarters, at a suitable distance laying upon their oars to discharge their muskets. Having no bullets to return, the negroes sent their yells. But, upon the second volley, Indian-like, they hurtled their hatchets. One took off a sailor's fingers. Another struck the whale-boat's bow, cutting off the rope there, and remaining stuck in the gunwale like a woodman's axe. Snatching it, quivering from its lodgment, the mate hurled it back. The returned gauntlet now stuck in the ship's broken quarter-gallery, and so remained.

The negroes giving too hot a reception, the whites kept a more respectful distance. Hovering now just out of reach of the hurtling hatchets, they, with a view to the close encounter which must soon come, sought to decoy the blacks into entirely disarming themselves of their most murderous weapons in a hand-to-hand fight, by foolishly flinging them, as missiles, short of the mark, into the sea. But, ere long, perceiving the stratagem, the negroes desisted, though not before many of them had to replace their lost hatchets with handspikes; an exchange which, as counted upon, proved, in the end, favorable to the assailants.

Meantime, with a strong wind, the ship still clove the water; the boats alternately falling behind, and pulling up, to discharge fresh volleys.

The fire was mostly directed towards the stern, since there, chiefly, the negroes, at present, were clustering. But to kill or maim the negroes was not the object. To take them, with the ship, was the object. To do it, the ship must be boarded; which could not be done by boats while she was sailing so fast.

⁹⁴ twenty-five
⁹⁵ a privateer's-man, and, as his enemies whispered, a pirate
⁹⁶ ship as good
⁹⁷ worth upwards of ten thousand

A thought now struck the mate. Observing the Spanish boys still aloft, high as they could get, he called to them to descend to the yards, and cut adrift the sails. It was done. About this time, owing to causes hereafter to be shown, two Spaniards, in the dress of sailors, and conspicuously showing themselves, were killed; not by volleys, but by deliberate marksman's shots; while, as it afterwards appeared, by one of the general discharges, Atufal, the black, and the Spaniard at the helm likewise were killed. What now, with the loss of the sails, and loss of leaders, the ship became unmanageable to the negroes.

With creaking masts, she came heavily round to the wind; the prow slowly swinging into view of the boats, its skeleton gleaming in the horizontal moonlight, and casting a gigantic ribbed shadow upon the water. One extended arm of the ghost seemed beckoning the whites to avenge it.

"Follow your leader!" cried the mate; and, one on each bow, the boats boarded. [Sealing-][98] spears and cutlasses crossed hatchets and hand-spikes. Huddled upon the long-boat amidships, the negresses raised a wailing chant, whose chorus was the clash of the steel.

For a time, the attack wavered; the negroes wedging themselves to beat it back; the half-repelled sailors, as yet unable to gain a footing, fighting as troopers in the saddle, one leg sideways flung over the bulwarks, and one without, plying their cutlasses like carters' whips. But in vain. They were almost overborne, when, rallying themselves into a squad as one man, with a huzza, they sprang inboard, where, entangled, they involuntarily separated again. For a few breaths' space, there was a vague, muffled, inner sound, as of submerged sword-fish rushing hither and thither through shoals of black-fish. Soon, in a reunited band, and joined by the Spanish seamen, the whites came to the surface, irresistibly driving the negroes toward the stern. But a barricade of casks and sacks, from side to side, had been thrown up by the mainmast. Here the negroes faced about, and though scorning peace or truce, yet fain would have [had respite].[99] But, without pause, overleaping the barrier, the unflagging sailors again closed. Exhausted, the blacks now fought in despair. Their red tongues lolled, wolf-like, from their black mouths. But the pale sailors' teeth were set; not a word was spoken; and, in five minutes more, the ship was won.

Nearly a score of the negroes were killed. Exclusive of those by the balls, many were mangled; their wounds—mostly inflicted by the long-edged [sealing-][100] spears, resembling those shaven ones of the English at Preston Pans, made by the poled scythes of the Highlanders. On the other side, none were killed, though several were wounded; some severely, including the mate. The surviving negroes were temporarily

---

98 scaling
99 had a respite
100 scaling

secured, and the ship, towed back into the harbor at midnight, once more lay anchored.

Omitting the incidents and arrangements ensuing, suffice it that, after two days spent in refitting, [the ships][101] sailed in company for Conception, in Chili, and thence for Lima, in Peru; where, before the vice-regal courts, the whole affair, from the beginning, underwent investigation.

Though, midway on the passage, the ill-fated Spaniard, relaxed from constraint, showed some signs of regaining health with free-will; yet, agreeably to his own foreboding, shortly before arriving at Lima, he relapsed, finally becoming so reduced as to be carried ashore in arms. Hearing of his story and plight, one of the many religious institutions of the City of Kings opened an hospitable refuge to him, where both physician and priest were his nurses, and a member of the order volunteered to be his one special guardian and consoler, by night and by day.

The following extracts, translated from one of the official Spanish documents, will, it is hoped, shed light on the preceding narrative, as well as, in the first place, reveal the true port of departure and true history of the San Dominick's voyage, down to the time of her touching at the island of St. Maria.

But, ere the extracts come, it may be well to preface them with a remark.

The document selected, from among many others, for partial translation, contains the deposition of Benito Cereno; the first taken in the case. Some disclosures therein were, at the time, held dubious for both learned and natural reasons. The tribunal inclined to the opinion that the deponent, not undisturbed in his mind by recent events, raved of some things which could never have happened. But subsequent depositions of the surviving sailors, bearing out the revelations of their captain in several of the strangest particulars, gave credence to the rest. So that the tribunal, in its final decision, rested its capital sentences upon statements which, had they lacked confirmation, it would have deemed it but duty to reject.

———

I, DON JOSE DE ABOS AND PADILLA, His Majesty's Notary for the Royal Revenue, and Register of this Province, and Notary Public of the Holy Crusade of this Bishopric, etc.

Do certify and declare, as much as is requisite in law, that, in the criminal cause commenced the twenty-fourth of the month of September, in the year seventeen hundred and ninety-nine, against [the negroes][102] of the ship San Dominick, the following declaration before me was made:

---

101 the two ships
102 the Senegal negroes

Declaration of the first witness, DON BENITO CERENO.

The same day, and month, and year, His Honor, Doctor Juan Martinez de Rozas, Councilor of the Royal Audience of this Kingdom, and learned in the law of this Intendency, ordered the captain of the ship San Dominick, Don Benito Cereno, to appear; which he did in his litter, attended by the monk Infelez; of whom he [received the oath],[103] which he took by God, our Lord, and a sign of the Cross; under which he promised to tell the truth of whatever he should know and should be asked;—and being interrogated agreeably to the tenor of the act commencing the process, he said, that on the twentieth of May last, he set sail with his ship from the port of Valparaiso, bound to that of Callao; loaded with the produce of the country [beside thirty cases of hardware][104] and one hundred and sixty blacks, of both sexes, mostly belonging to Don Alexandro Aranda, gentleman, of the city of Mendoza; that the crew of the ship consisted of thirty-six men, beside the persons who went as passengers; that the negroes were in part as follows:

[*Here, in the original, follows a list of some fifty names, descriptions, and ages, compiled from certain recovered documents of Aranda's, and also from recollections of the deponent, from which portions only are extracted.*]

—One, from about eighteen to nineteen years, named José, and this was the man that waited upon his master, Don Alexandro, and who speaks well the Spanish, having served him four or five years; * * * a mulatto, named Francesco, the cabin steward, of a good person and voice, having sung in the Valparaiso churches, native of the province of Buenos Ayres, aged about thirty-five years. * * * A smart negro, named Dago, who had been for many years a grave-digger among the Spaniards, aged forty-six years. * * * Four old negroes, born in Africa, from sixty to seventy, but sound, calkers by trade, whose names are as follows:—the first was named Muri, and he was killed (as was also his son named Diamelo); the second, Nacta; the third, Yola, likewise killed; the fourth, Ghofan; and six full-grown negroes, aged from thirty to forty-five, all raw, and born among the Ashantees—Matiluqui, [Yau],[105] Lecbe, Mapenda, Yambaio, Akim; four of whom

---

103 received, before Don Jose de Abos and Padilla, Notary Public of the Holy Crusade, the oath

104 "beside thirty cases of hardware" was omitted in the *Putnam* version.

105 It is perhaps too great an editorial liberty to alter "Yan," which appears in both versions of the story, to "Yau"; however, in the source, although some of the natives' names are spelled in different ways (Mure–Muri, Matiluqui–Matinqui), "Yau" appears only in that form.

were killed; * * * a powerful negro named Atufal, who being supposed to have been a chief in Africa, his owner set great store by him.
* * * And a small negro of Senegal, but some years among the Spaniards, aged about thirty, which negro's name was Babo; * * * that he
does not remember the names of the others, but that still expecting the
residue of Don Alexandro's papers will be found, will then take due
account of them all, and remit to the court; * * * and thirty-nine
women and children of all ages.

[[*The catalogue over, the deposition goes on.*]][106]

* * * That all the negroes slept upon deck, as is customary in
this navigation, and none wore fetters, because the owner, his friend
Aranda, told him that they were all tractable; * * * that on the
seventh day after leaving port, at three o'clock in the morning, all the
Spaniards being asleep except the two officers on the watch, who were
the boatswain, Juan Robles, and the carpenter, Juan Bautista Gayete,
and the helmsman and his boy, the negroes revolted suddenly, wounded
dangerously the boatswain and the carpenter, and successively killed
eighteen men of those who were sleeping upon deck, some with hand-
spikes and hatchets, and others by throwing them alive overboard, after
tying them; that of the Spaniards upon deck, they left about seven, as
he thinks, alive and tied, to manœuvre the ship, and three or four
more, who hid themselves, remained also alive. Although in the act
of revolt the negroes made themselves masters of the hatchway, six or
seven wounded went through it to the cockpit, without any hindrance
on their part; that [during][107] the act of revolt, the mate and another
person, whose name he does not recollect, attempted to come up
through the hatchway, [but being quickly wounded, were][108] obliged
to return to the cabin; that the deponent resolved at break of day to
come up the companion-way, where the negro Babo was, being the
ringleader, and Atufal, who assisted him, and having spoken to them,
exhorted them to cease committing such atrocities, asking them, at the
same time, what they wanted and intended to do, offering, himself, to
obey their commands; that notwithstanding this, they threw, in his
presence, three men, alive and tied, overboard; that they told the
deponent to come up, and that they would not kill him; which having
done, the negro Babo asked him whether there were in those seas any
negro countries where they might be carried, and he answered them,
No; that the negro Babo afterwards told him to carry them to Senegal,
or to the neighboring islands of St. Nicholas; and he answered, that this
was impossible, on account of the great distance, the necessity involved

106 [*After the catalogue, the deposition goes on as follows:*]
107 in
108 but having been wounded at the onset, they were

of rounding Cape Horn, the bad condition of the vessel, the want of provisions, sails, and water; but that the negro Babo replied to him he must carry them in any way; that they would do and conform themselves to everything the deponent should require as to eating and drinking; that after a long conference, being absolutely compelled to please them, for they [threatened to kill][109] all the whites if they were not, at all events, carried to Senegal, he told them that what was most wanting for the voyage was water; that they would go near the coast to take it, and thence they would proceed on their course; that the negro Babo agreed to it; and the deponent steered towards the intermediate ports, hoping to meet some Spanish or foreign vessel that would save them; that within ten or eleven days they saw the land, and continued their course by it in the vicinity of Nasca; that the deponent observed that the negroes were now restless and mutinous, because he did not effect the taking in of water, the negro Babo having required, with threats, that it should be done, without fail, the following day; he told him he saw plainly that the coast was steep, and the rivers designated in the maps were not to be found, with other reasons suitable to the circumstances; that the best way would be to go to the island of Santa Maria, where they might [water easily],[110] it being a [solitary][111] island, as the foreigners did; that the deponent did not go to Pisco, that was near, nor make any other port of the coast, because the negro Babo had intimated to him several times, that he would kill all the whites the very moment he should perceive any city, town, or settlement of any kind on the shores to which they should be carried: that having determined to go to the island of Santa Maria, as the deponent had planned, for the purpose of trying whether, [on the passage or near][112] the island itself, they could find any vessel that should favor them, or whether he could escape from it in a boat to the neighboring coast of [Arruco],[113] to adopt the necessary means he immediately changed his course, steering for the island; that the negroes Babo and Atufal held daily conferences, in which they discussed what was necessary for their design of returning to Senegal, whether they were to kill all the Spaniards, and particularly the deponent; that eight days after parting from the coast of Nasca, the deponent being on the watch a little after daybreak, and soon after the negroes had their meeting, the negro Babo came to the place where the deponent was, and told him that he had determined to kill his master, Don Alexandro Aranda, both because he and his companions could not otherwise be sure of their liberty, and

---

109 threatened him to kill
110 water and victual easily
111 desert
112 in the passage or in
113 "Arruco" (both versions) has been allowed to stand even though it is misspelled because here, as in most of this paragraph, Melville is simply quoting his source. Arauco is the correct geographical designation.

that to keep the seamen in subjection, he wanted to prepare a warning of what road they should be made to take did they or any of them oppose him; and that, by means of the death of Don Alexandro, that warning would best be given; but, that what this last meant, the deponent did not at the time comprehend, nor could not, further than that the death of Don Alexandro was intended; and moreover the negro Babo proposed to the deponent to call the mate Raneds, who was sleeping in the cabin, before the thing was done, for fear, as the deponent understood it, that the mate, who was a good navigator, should be killed with Don Alexandro and the rest; that the deponent, who was the friend, from youth, of Don Alexandro, prayed and conjured, but all was useless; for the negro Babo answered him that the thing could not be prevented, and that all the Spaniards risked their death if they should attempt to frustrate his will in this matter, or any other; that, in this conflict, the deponent called the mate, Raneds, who was forced to go apart, and immediately the negro Babo commanded the Ashantee Martinqui and the Ashantee Lecbe to go and commit the murder; that those two went down with hatchets to the berth of Don Alexandro; that, yet half alive and mangled, they dragged him on deck; that they were going to throw him overboard in that state, but the negro Babo stopped them, bidding the murder be completed on the deck before him, which was done, when, by his orders, the body was carried below, forward; that nothing more was seen of it by the deponent for three days; * * * that Don Alonzo Sidonia, an old man, long resident at Valparaiso, and lately appointed to a civil office in Peru, whither he had taken passage, was at the time sleeping in the berth opposite Don Alexandro's; that awakening at his cries, surprised by them, and at the sight of the negroes with their bloody hatchets in their hands, he threw himself into the sea through a window which was near him, and was drowned, without it being in the power of the deponent to assist or take him up; * * * that a short time after killing Aranda, they brought upon deck his german-cousin, of middle-age, Don Francisco Masa, of Mendoza, and the young Don Joaquin, Marques de Aramboalaza, then lately from Spain, with his Spanish servant Ponce, and the three young clerks of Aranda, José [Morairi],[114] Lorenzo Bargas, and Hermenegildo Gandix, all of Cadiz; that Don Joaquin and Hermenegildo Gandix, the negro Babo, for purposes hereafter to appear, preserved alive; but Don Francisco Masa, José Morairi, and Lorenzo Bargas, with Ponce the servant, beside the boatswain, Juan Robles, the boatswain's mates, Manual Viscaya and Roderigo Hurta, and four of the sailors, the negro Babo ordered to be thrown alive into the sea, although they made no resistance, nor begged for anything else but

---

[114] Although "Mozairi" appears in both versions, it has been altered to "Morairi" (Delano's spelling in the source) since Melville follows the source's spelling of all the other Spanish names.

mercy; that the boatswain, Juan Robles, who knew how to swim, kept the longest above water, making acts of contrition, and, in the last words he uttered, charged this deponent to cause mass to be said for his soul to our Lady of Succor: * * * that, during the three days which followed, the deponent, uncertain what fate had befallen the remains of Don Alexandro, frequently asked the negro Babo where they were, and, if still on board, whether they were to be preserved for interment ashore, entreating him so to order it; that the negro Babo answered nothing till the fourth day, when at sunrise, the deponent coming on deck, the negro Babo showed him a skeleton, which had been substituted for the ship's proper figure-head—the image of Christopher Colon, the discoverer of the New World; that the negro Babo asked him whose skeleton that was, and whether, from its whiteness, he should not think it a white's; that, upon [his covering][115] his face, the negro Babo, coming close, said words to this effect: "Keep faith with the blacks from here to Senegal, or you shall in spirit, as now in body, follow your leader," pointing to the prow; * * * that the same morning the negro Babo took by succession each Spaniard forward, and asked him whose skeleton that was, and whether, from its whiteness, he should not think it a white's; that each Spaniard covered his face; that then to each the negro Babo repeated the words in the first place said to the deponent; * * * that they (the Spaniards), being then assembled aft, the negro Babo harangued them, saying that he had now done all; that the deponent (as navigator for the negroes) might pursue his course, warning him and all of them that they should, soul and body, go the way of Don Alexandro, if he saw them (the Spaniards) speak or plot anything against them (the negroes)—a threat which was repeated every day; that, before the events last mentioned, they had tied the cook to throw him overboard, for it is not known what thing they heard him speak, but finally the negro Babo spared his life, at the request of the deponent; that a few days after, the deponent, endeavoring not to omit any means to preserve the lives of the remaining whites, spoke to the negroes [of][116] peace and tranquillity, and agreed to draw up a paper, signed by the deponent and the sailors who could write, as also by the negro Babo, for himself and all the blacks, in which the deponent obliged himself to carry them to Senegal, and they not to kill any more, and he formally to make over to them the ship, with the cargo, with which they were for that time satisfied and quieted. * * * But the next day, the more surely to guard against the sailors' escape, the negro Babo commanded all the boats to be destroyed but the long-

---

115 *Putnam's* "his covering" rather than the *Piazza's* "discovering" not only makes more sense but is also supported, in the same passage, by the fact that all the Spaniards react to Aranda's skeleton in the same way—"each Spaniard covered his face."

116 "of" was omitted in the *Putnam* version.

boat, which was unseaworthy, and another, a cutter in good condition, which knowing it would yet be wanted for [towing][117] the water casks, he had it lowered down into the hold.

* * * * *

[*Various particulars of the prolonged and perplexed navigation ensuing here follow, with incidents of a calamitous calm, from which portion one passage is extracted, to wit:*]

—That on the fifth day of the calm, all on board suffering much from the heat, and want of water, and five having died in fits, and mad, the negroes became irritable, and for a chance gesture, which they deemed suspicious—though it was harmless—made by the mate, Raneds, to the deponent in the act of handing a quadrant, they killed him; but that for this they afterwards were sorry, the mate being the only remaining navigator on board, except the deponent.

* * * * *

—That omitting other events, which daily happened, and which can only serve uselessly to recall past misfortunes and conflicts, after seventy-three days' navigation, reckoned from the time they sailed from Nasca, during which they navigated under a scanty allowance of water, and were afflicted with the calms before mentioned, they at last arrived at the island of Santa Maria, on the seventeenth of the month of August, at about six o'clock in the afternoon, at which hour they cast anchor very near the American ship, Bachelor's Delight, which lay in the same bay, commanded by the generous Captain Amasa Delano; but at six o'clock in the morning, they had already descried the port, and the negroes became uneasy, as soon as at distance they saw the ship, not having expected to see one there; that the negro Babo pacified them, assuring them that no fear need be had; that straightway he ordered the figure on the bow to be covered with canvas, as for repairs, and had the decks a little set in order; that for a time the negro Babo and the negro Atufal conferred; that the negro Atufal was for sailing away, but the negro Babo would not, and, by himself, cast about what to do; that at last he came to the deponent, proposing to him to say and do all that the deponent declares to have said and done to the American captain; * * * that the negro Babo warned him that if he varied in the least, or uttered any word, or gave any look that should give the least intimation of the past events or present state, he would instantly kill him, with all his companions, showing a dagger, which he carried hid, saying something which, as he understood it, meant that that dagger would be alert as his eye; that the negro Babo then announced the plan to all his companions, which pleased them; that he then, the better to disguise the truth, devised many expedients, in

---

117 lowering

some of them uniting deceit and defense; that of this sort was the device of the six Ashantees before named, who were his bravoes; that them he stationed on the break of the poop, as if to clean certain hatchets (in cases, which were part of the cargo), but in reality to use them, and distribute them at need, and at a given word he told them; that, among other devices, was the device of presenting Atufal, his right hand man, as chained, though in a moment the chains could be dropped; that in every particular he informed the deponent what part he was expected to enact in every device, and what story he was to tell on every occasion, always threatening him with instant death if he varied in the least: that, conscious that many of the negroes would be turbulent, the negro Babo appointed the four aged negroes, who were calkers, to keep what domestic order they could on the decks; that again and again he harangued the Spaniards and his companions, informing them of his intent, and of his devices, and of the invented story that this deponent was to tell; charging them lest any of them varied from that story; that these arrangements were made and matured during the interval of two or three hours, between their first sighting the ship and the arrival on board of Captain Amasa Delano; that this happened about half-past seven o'clock in the morning, Captain Amasa Delano coming in his boat, and all gladly receiving him; that the deponent, as well as he could force himself, acting then the part of principal owner, and a free captain of the ship, told Captain Amasa Delano, when called upon, that he came from Buenos Ayres, bound to Lima, with three hundred negroes; that off Cape Horn, and in a subsequent fever, many negroes had died; that also, by similar casualties, all the sea officers and the greatest part of the crew had died.

* * * * *

[*And so the deposition goes on, circumstantially recounting the fictitious story dictated to the deponent by Babo, and through the deponent imposed upon Captain Delano; and also recounting the friendly offers of Captain Delano, with other things, but all of which is here omitted. After* [*the fictitious story*],[118] *etc., the deposition proceeds:*]

* * * * *

—that the generous Captain Amasa Delano remained on board all the day, till he left the ship anchored at six o'clock in the evening, deponent speaking to him always of his pretended misfortunes, under the forementioned principles, without having had it in his power to tell a single word, or give him the least hint, that he might know the truth and state of things; because the negro Babo, performing the office of an officious servant with all the appearance of submission of the

---

[118] fictitious, strange story

humble slave, did not leave the deponent one moment; that this was
in order to observe the deponent's actions and words, for the negro
Babo understands well the Spanish; and besides, there were thereabout
some others who were constantly on the watch, and likewise understood
the Spanish; * * * that upon one occasion, while deponent was standing on the deck conversing with Amasa Delano, by a secret sign the
negro Babo drew him (the deponent) aside, the act appearing as if
originating with the deponent; that then, he being drawn aside, the
negro Babo proposed to him to gain from Amasa Delano full particulars about his ship, and crew, and arms; that the deponent asked
"For what?" that the negro Babo answered he might conceive; that,
grieved at the prospect of what might overtake the generous Captain
Amasa Delano, the deponent at first refused to ask the desired questions, and used every argument to induce the negro Babo to give up
this new design; that the negro Babo showed the point of his dagger;
that, after the information had been obtained the negro Babo again
drew him aside, telling him that that very night he (the deponent)
would be captain of two ships, instead of one, for that, great part of
the American's ship's crew being to be absent fishing, the six Ashantees,
without any one else, would easily take it; that at this time he said other
things to the same purpose; that no entreaties availed; that before
Amasa Delano's coming on board, no hint had been given touching the
capture of the American ship: that to prevent this project the deponent
was powerless; * * * —that in some things his memory is confused,
he cannot distinctly recall every event; * * * —that as soon as they
had cast anchor at six of the clock in the evening, as has before been
stated, the American Captain took leave, to return to his vessel; that
upon a sudden impulse, which the deponent believes to have come
from God and his angels, he, after the farewell had been said, followed
the generous Captain Amasa Delano as far as the gunwale, where he
stayed, under pretense of taking leave, until Amasa Delano should
have been seated in his boat; that on shoving off, the deponent sprang
from the gunwale into the boat, and fell into it, he knows not how,
God guarding him; that—

* * * * *

[*Here, in the original, follows the account of what further happened at the escape, and how the San Dominick was re-taken, and of
the passage to the coast; including in the recital many expressions of
"eternal gratitude" to the "generous Captain Amasa Delano." The
deposition then proceeds with recapitulatory remarks, and a partial
renumeration of the negroes, making record of their individual part in
the past events, with a view to furnishing, according to command of
the court, the data whereon to found the criminal sentences to be
pronounced. From this portion is the following:*]

—That he believes that all the negroes, though not in the first place knowing to the design of revolt, when it was accomplished, approved it. * * * That the negro, José, eighteen years old, and in the personal service of Don Alexandro, was the one who communicated the information to the negro Babo, about the state of things in the cabin, before the revolt; that this is known, because, in the preceding midnight, he used to come from his berth, which was under his master's, in the cabin, to the deck where the ringleader and his associates were, and had secret conversations with the negro Babo, in which he was several times seen by the mate; that, one night, the mate drove him away twice; * * * that this same negro José was the one who, without being commanded to do so by the negro Babo, as Lecbe and Martinqui were, stabbed his master, Don Alexandro, after he had been dragged half-lifeless to the deck; * * * that the mulatto steward, Francesco, was of the first band of revolters, that he was, in all things, the creature and tool of the negro Babo; that, to make his court, he, just before a repast in the cabin, proposed, to the negro Babo, poisoning a dish for the generous Captain Amasa Delano; this is known and believed, because the negroes have said it; but that the negro Babo, having another design, forbade Francesco; * * * that the Ashantee Lecbe was one of the worst of them; for that, on the day the ship was retaken, he assisted in the defense of her, with a hatchet in each hand, [with][119] one of which he wounded, in the breast, the chief mate of Amasa Delano, in the first act of boarding; this all knew; that, in sight of the deponent, Lecbe struck, with a hatchet, Don Francisco Masa, when, by the negro Babo's orders, he was carrying him to throw him overboard, alive, beside participating in the murder, before mentioned, of Don Alexandro Aranda, and others of the cabin-passengers; that, owing to the fury with which the Ashantees fought in the engagement with the boats, but this Lecbe and [Yau][120] survived; that Yau was bad as Lecbe; that Yau was the man who, by Babo's command, willingly prepared the skeleton of Don Alexandro, in a way the negroes afterwards told the deponent, but which he, so long as reason is left him, can never divulge; that Yau and Lecbe were the two who, in a calm by night, riveted the skeleton to the bow; this also the negroes told him; that the negro Babo was he who traced the inscription below it; that the negro Babo was the plotter from first to last; he ordered every murder, and was the helm and keel of the revolt; that Atufal was his lieutenant in all; but Atufal, with his own hand, committed no murder; nor did the negro Babo; * * * that Atufal was shot, being killed in the fight with the boats, ere boarding; * * * that the negresses, of age, were knowing to the revolt, and

---

119 which
120 Cf. footnote 105, p. 56. (All subsequent appearances in the text of "Yan" have been changed to Yau.)

testified themselves satisfied at the death of their [master],[121] Don Alexandro; that, had the negroes not restrained them, they would have tortured to death, instead of simply killing, the Spaniards slain by command of the negro Babo; that the negresses used their utmost influence to have the deponent made away with; that, in the various acts of murder, they sang songs and danced—not gaily, but solemnly; and before the engagement with the boats, as well as during the action, they sang melancholy songs to the negroes, and that this melancholy tone was more inflaming than a different one would have been, and was so intended; that all this is believed, because the negroes have said it. —that of the thirty-six men of the crew, exclusive of the passengers (all of whom are now dead), which the deponent had knowledge of, six only remained alive, with four cabin-boys and ship-boys, not included with the crew; * * * —that the negroes broke an arm of one of the cabin-boys and gave him strokes with hatchets.

[*Then follow various random disclosures referring to various periods of time. The following are extracted:*]

—That during the presence of Captain Amasa Delano on board, some attempts were made by the sailors, and one by Hermenegildo Gandix, to convey hints to him of the true state of affairs; but that these attempts were ineffectual, owing to fear of incurring death, and, furthermore, owing to the devices which offered contradictions to the true state of affairs, as well as owing to the generosity and piety of Amasa Delano incapable of sounding such wickedness; * * * that Luys Galgo, a sailor about sixty years of age, and formerly of the king's navy, was one of those who sought to convey tokens to Captain Amasa Delano; but his intent, though undiscovered, being suspected, he was, on a pretense, made to retire out of sight, and at last into the hold, and there was made away with. This the negroes have since said; * * * that one of the ship-boys feeling, from Captain Amasa Delano's presence, some hopes of release, and not having enough prudence, dropped some chance-word respecting his expectations, which being overheard and understood by a slave-boy with whom he was eating at the time, the latter struck him on the head with a knife, inflicting a bad wound, but of which the boy is now healing; that likewise, not long before the ship was brought to anchor, one of the seamen, steering at the time, endangered himself by letting the blacks remark [some expression][122] in his countenance, arising from [a][123] cause similar to the above; but this sailor, by his heedful after conduct, escaped; * * *

---

121 masters
122 a certain unconscious hopeful expression
123 some

that these statements are made to show the court that from the beginning to the end of the revolt, it was impossible for the deponent and his men to act otherwise than they did;* * * —that the third clerk, Hermenegildo Gandix, who before had been forced to live among the seamen, wearing a seaman's habit, and in all respects appearing to be one for the time; he, Gandix, was killed by a musket ball fired [through mistake from the boats]¹²⁴ before boarding; having in his fright [run]¹²⁵ up the mizzen-rigging, calling to the boats—"don't board," lest upon their boarding the negroes should kill him; that this inducing the Americans to believe he some way favored the cause of the negroes, they fired two balls at him, so that he fell wounded from the rigging, and was drowned in the sea; * * * —that the young Don Joaquin, Marques de Aramboalaza, like Hermenegildo Gandix, the third clerk, was degraded to the office and appearance of a common seaman; that upon one occasion when Don Joaquin shrank, the negro Babo commanded the Ashantee Lecbe to take tar and heat it, and pour it upon Don Joaquin's hands; * * * —that Don Joaquin was killed owing to another mistake of the Americans, but one impossible to be avoided, as upon the approach of the boats, Don Joaquin, with a hatchet tied edge out, and upright to his hand, was made by the negroes to appear on the bulwarks; whereupon, seen with arms in his hands and in a questionable attitude, he was shot for a renegade seaman; * * * —that on the person of Don Joaquin was found secreted a jewel, which, by papers that were discovered, proved to have been meant for the shrine of our Lady of Mercy in Lima; a votive offering, beforehand prepared and guarded, to attest his gratitude, when he should have landed in Peru, his last destination, for the safe conclusion of his entire voyage from Spain; * * * —that the jewel, with the other effects of the late Don Joaquin, is in the custody of the brethren of the Hospital de Sacerdotes, awaiting the [disposition]¹²⁶ of the honorable court; * * * —that, owing to the condition of the deponent, as well as the haste in which the boats departed for the attack, the Americans were not forewarned that there were, among the apparent crew, a passenger and one of the clerks disguised by the negro Babo; * * * —that, beside the negroes killed in the action, some were killed after the capture and re-anchoring at night, when shackled to the ring-bolts on deck; that these deaths were committed by the sailors, ere they could be prevented. That so soon as informed of it, Captain Amasa Delano used all his authority, and, in particular with his own hand, struck down Martinez Gola, who, having found a razor in the pocket of an old jacket of his, which one of the shackled negroes had on, was aiming it at the negro's

---

¹²⁴ through a mistake from the American boats
¹²⁵ ran
¹²⁶ decision

throat; that the noble Captain Amasa Delano also wrenched from the hand of Bartholomew Barlo a dagger, secreted at the time of the massacre of the whites, with which he was in the act of stabbing a shackled negro, who, the same day, with another negro, had thrown him down and jumped upon him; * * * —that, for all the events, befalling through so long a time, during which the ship was in the hands of the negro Babo, he cannot here give account; but that, what he has said is the most substantial of what occurs to him at present, and is the truth under the oath which he has taken; which declaration he affirmed and ratified, after hearing it read to him.

He said that he is twenty-nine years of age, and broken in body and mind; that when finally dismissed by the court, he shall not return home to Chili, but betake himself to the monastery on Mount Agonia without; and signed with his honor, and crossed himself, and, for the time, departed as he came, in his litter, with the monk Infelez, to the Hospital de Sacerdotes.

BENITO CERENO.

DOCTOR ROZAS.

If the [Deposition have][127] served as the key to fit into the lock of the complications which [precede][128] it, then, as a vault whose door has been flung back, the San Dominick's hull lies open to-day.

Hitherto the nature of this narrative, besides rendering the intricacies in the beginning unavoidable, has more or less required that many things, instead of being set down in the order of occurrence, should be retrospectively, or irregularly given; this last is the case with the following passages, which will conclude the account:

During the long, mild voyage to Lima, there was, as before hinted, a period during which [the sufferer][129] a little recovered his health, or, at least in some degree, his tranquillity. Ere the decided relapse which came, the two captains had many cordial conversations—their fraternal unreserve in singular contrast with former withdrawments.

Again and again it was repeated, how hard it had been to enact the part forced on the Spaniard by Babo.

"Ah, my dear [friend],"[130] Don Benito once said, "at those very times when you thought me so morose and ungrateful, nay, when, as you now admit, you half thought me plotting your murder, at those very times my heart was frozen; I could not look at you, thinking of what, both on board this ship and your own, hung, from other hands,

---

127 deposition of Benito Cereno has
128 preceded
129 Don Benito
130 Don Amasa

over my kind benefactor. And as God lives, Don Amasa, I know not whether desire for my own safety alone could have nerved me to that leap into your boat, had it not been for the thought that, did you, unenlightened, return to your ship, you, my best friend, with all who might be with you, stolen upon, that night, in your hammocks, would never in this world have wakened again. Do but think how you walked this deck, how you sat in this cabin, every inch of ground mined into honey-combs under you. Had I dropped the least hint, made the least advance towards an understanding between us, death, explosive death —yours as mine—would have ended the scene."

"True, true," cried Captain Delano, starting, "[you have saved][131] my life, Don Benito, more than I yours; saved it, too, against my knowledge and will."

"Nay, my friend," rejoined the Spaniard, courteous even to the point of religion, "God charmed your life, but you saved mine. To think of some things you did—those smilings and chattings, rash pointings and gesturings. For less than these, they slew my mate, Raneds; but you had the Prince of Heaven's safe-conduct through all ambuscades."

"Yes, all is owing to Providence, I know: but the temper of my mind that morning was more than commonly pleasant, while the sight of so much suffering, more apparent than real, added to my good-nature, compassion, and charity, happily interweaving the three. Had it been otherwise, doubtless, as you hint, some of my [interferences][132] might have ended unhappily enough. [Besides],[133] those feelings I spoke of enabled me to get the better of momentary distrust, at times when acuteness might have cost me my life, without saving another's. Only at the end did my suspicions get the better of me, and you know how wide of the mark they then proved."

"Wide, indeed," said Don Benito, sadly; "you were with me all day; stood with me, sat with me, talked with me, looked at me, ate with me, drank with me; and yet, your last act was to clutch for a [monster],[134] not only an innocent man, but the most pitiable of all men. To such degree may malign machinations and deceptions impose. So far may even the best [man][135] err, in judging the conduct of one with the recesses of whose condition he is not acquainted. But you were forced to it; and you were in time undeceived. Would that, in both respects, it was so ever, and with all men."

"[You generalize],[136] Don Benito; and mournfully enough. But the

---

131 "have" was omitted in the *Putnam* version.
132 interferences with the blacks
133 Besides that
134 villain
135 men
136 I think I understand you; you generalize

past is passed; why moralize upon it? Forget it. See, yon bright sun has forgotten it all, and the blue sea, and the blue sky; these have turned over new leaves."

"Because they have no memory," he dejectedly replied; "because they are not human."

"But these mild trades that now fan [your cheek],[137] do they not come with a human-like healing to you? Warm friends, steadfast friends are the trades."

"With their steadfastness they but waft me to my tomb, Señor," was the foreboding response.

"You are [saved],"[138] cried Captain Delano, more and more astonished and pained; "you are saved: what has cast such a shadow upon you?"

"The negro."

There was silence, while the moody man sat, slowly and unconsciously gathering his mantle about him, as if it were a pall.

There was no more conversation that day.

But if the Spaniard's melancholy sometimes ended in muteness upon topics like the above, there were others upon which he never spoke at all; on which, indeed, all his old reserves were piled. Pass over the worst, and, only to elucidate, let an item or two of these be cited. The dress, so precise and costly, worn by him on the day whose events have been narrated, had not willingly been put on. And that silver-mounted sword, apparent symbol of despotic command, was not, indeed, a sword, but the ghost of one. The scabbard, artificially stiffened, was empty.

As for the black—whose brain, not body, had schemed and led the revolt, with the plot—his slight frame, inadequate to that which it held, had at once yielded to the superior muscular strength of his captor, in the boat. Seeing all was over, he uttered no sound, and could not be forced to. His aspect seemed to say, since I cannot do deeds, I will not speak words. Put in irons in the hold, with the rest, he was carried to Lima. During the passage, Don Benito did not visit him. Nor then, nor at any time after, would he look at him. Before the tribunal he refused. When pressed by the judges he fainted. On the testimony of the sailors alone rested the legal identity of Babo. [   ][139]

Some months after, dragged to the gibbet at the tail of a mule, the black met his voiceless end. The body was burned to ashes; but for many days, the head, that hive of subtlety, fixed on a pole in the Plaza, met, unabashed, the gaze of the whites; and across the Plaza looked

---

137 your cheek, Don Benito

138 saved, Don Benito

139 And yet the Spaniard would, upon occasion, verbally refer to the negro, as has been shown; but look on him he would not, or could not.

towards St. Bartholomew's church, in whose vaults slept then, as now, the recovered bones of Aranda: and across the Rimac bridge looked towards the monastery, on Mount Agonia without; where, three months after being dismissed by the court, Benito Cereno, borne on the bier, did, indeed, follow his leader.

A NARRATIVE OF VOYAGES AND TRAVELS, IN THE
NORTHERN AND SOUTHERN HEMISPHERES:
COMPRISING THREE VOYAGES ROUND THE WORLD,
TOGETHER WITH A VOYAGE OF SURVEY AND
DISCOVERY IN THE PACIFIC OCEAN AND ORIENTAL
ISLANDS (1817)

Amasa Delano

CHAPTER XVIII

*Particulars of the Capture of the Spanish Ship Tryal, at the Island of
St. Maria; with the Documents relating to that affair*

In introducing the account of the capture of the Spanish ship
Tryal, I shall first give an extract from the journal of the ship Perseverance, taken on board that ship at the time, by the officer who had
the care of the log book.

"Wednesday, February 20th, commenced with light airs from the
north east, and thick foggy weather. At six A.M. observed a sail opening
round the south head of St. Maria, coming into the bay. It proved to
be a ship. The captain took the whale boat and crew and went on board
her. As the wind was very light, so that a vessel would not have much
more than steerage way at the time; observed that the ship acted very

The source for Melville's story was discovered by Harold C. Scudder and reprinted in *PMLA*, XLIV (June 1928), 503–529.

About Amasa Delano (1763–1823) not very much is known. Our only sources of
information are his *Narrative* and a biographical sketch appended to his book by
an anonymous friend. He seems to have been both brave and adventurous from an
early age: at eleven he rescued his younger brother from drowning and at fourteen
he enlisted in the Colonial army (he had been turned down at twelve). He first went
to sea on a privateer in 1779; in 1781 he shipped to the West Indies on a merchantman. In 1786, at twenty-three, he received his first command, a schooner to South
America. The following year his ship, the *Jane* ("very meanly furnished"), foundered
off Cape Cod and lost its entire cargo. In an attempt to recoup, Delano tried to
rebuild a ship that had been some time under water, but this only impoverished him
the more. At this low point in his affairs he shipped as second officer on the *Massachusetts*, the largest ship built in the United States to that time. At this point (1790)
the *Narrative* begins. The next twenty years he spent almost wholly at sea. His
declining years were evidently relatively destitute. He was married but childless.

awkwardly. At ten A.M. the boat returned. Mr. Luther informed that Captain Delano had remained on board her, and that she was a Spaniard from Buenos Ayres, four months and twenty-six days out of port, with slaves on board; and that the ship was in great want of water; had buried many white men and slaves on her passage, and that captain Delano had sent for a large boat load of water, some fresh fish, sugar, bread, pumpkins, and bottled cider, all of which articles were immediately sent. At twelve o'clock (Meridian) calm. At two P.M. the large boat returned from the Spaniards, had left our water casks on board her. At four P.M. a breeze sprung up from the southern quarter, which brought the Spanish ship into the roads. She anchored about two cables length to the south east of our ship. Immediately after she anchored, our captain with his boat was shoving off from along side the Spanish ship; when to his great surprise the Spanish captain leaped into the boat, and called out in Spanish that the slaves on board had risen and murdered[318] many of the people; and that he did not then command her; on which manoeuvre, several of the Spaniards who remained on board jumped overboard, and swam for our boat, and were picked up by our people. The Spaniards, who remained on board, hurried up the rigging, as high aloft as they could possibly get, and called out repeatedly for help—that they should be murdered by the slaves. Our captain came immediately on board, and brought the Spanish captain and the men who were picked up in the water; but before the boat arrived, we observed that the slaves had cut the Spanish ship adrift. On learning this, our captain hailed, and ordered the ports to be got up, and the guns cleared; but unfortunately, we could not bring but one of our guns to bear on the ship. We fired five or six shot with it, but could not bring her to. We soon observed her making sail, and standing directly out of the bay. We dispatched two boats well manned, and well armed after her, who, after much trouble, boarded the ship and retook her. But unfortunately in the business, Mr. Rufus Low, our chief officer, who commanded the party, was desperately wounded in the breast, by being stabbed with a pike, by one of the slaves. We likewise had one man badly wounded and two or three slightly. To continue the misfortune, the chief officer of the Spanish ship, who was compelled by the slaves to steer her out of the bay, received two very bad wounds, one in the side, and one through the thigh, both from musket balls. One Spaniard, a gentleman passenger on board, was likewise killed by a musket ball. We have not rightly ascertained what number of slaves were killed; but we believe seven, and a great number wounded. Our people brought the ship in, and came to nearly where she first anchored, at about two o'clock in the morning of the 21st. At six A.M. the two captains went on board the Spanish ship; took with them irons from our ship, and doubled ironed all the remaining men of the slaves who were living. Left Mr. Brown, our second officer, in charge of the ship, the gunner with him as mate, and eight other hands; together with the survivors of the Spanish crew. The captain and chief officer, were removed to our ship, the latter for the benefit of having his wounds better attended to with us, than he could have had them on board his own ship. At nine A.M. the two captains returned,[319] having put everything aright, as they supposed, on board the Spanish ship.

"The Spanish captain then informed us that he was compelled by the slaves to say, that he was from Buenos Ayres, bound to Lima; that he was not from Buenos Ayres, but sailed on the 20th of December last from Valparaiso for Lima, with upwards of seventy slaves on board; that on the 26th of December, the slaves rose upon the ship, and took possession of her, and put to death eighteen white men, and threw overboard at different periods after, seven more; that the slaves had commanded him to go to Senegal; that he had kept to sea until his water was expended, and had made this port to get it; and also with a view to save his own and the remainder of his people's lives if possible, by running away from his ship with his boat."

I shall here add some remarks of my own, to what is stated above from the ship's journal, with a view of giving the reader a correct understanding of the peculiar situation under which we were placed at the time this affair happened. We were in a worse situation to effect any important enterprize than I had been in during the voyage. We had been from home a year and a half, and had not made enough to amount to twenty dollars for each of my people, who were all on shares, and our future prospects were not very flattering. To make our situation worse, I had found after leaving New Holland, on mustering my people, that I had seventeen men, most of whom had been convicts at Botany Bay. They had secreted themselves on board without my knowledge. This was a larger number than had been inveigled away from me at the same place, by people who had been convicts, and were then employed at places that we visited. The men whom we lost were all of them extraordinarily good men. This exchange materially altered the quality of the crew. Three of the Botany-bay-men were outlawed convicts; they had been shot at many times, and several times wounded. After making this bad exchange, my crew were refractory; the convicts were ever unfaithful, and took all the advantage that opportunity gave them. But sometimes exercising very strict discipline, and giving them good wholesome floggings; and at other times treating them with the best I had, or could get, according as their deeds deserved, I managed them without much difficulty during the passage across the South Pacific Ocean; and all the[320] time I had been on the coast of Chili. I had lately been at the islands of St. Ambrose and St. Felix, and left there fifteen of my best men, with the view of procuring seals; and left that place in company with my consort the Pilgrim. We appointed Massa Fuero as our place of rendezvous, and, if we did not meet there, again to rendezvous at St. Maria: I proceeded to the first place appointed; the Pilgrim had not arrived. I then determined to take a look at Juan Fernandez, and see if we could find any seals, as some persons had informed me they were to be found on some part of the island. I accordingly visited that place, as has been stated; from thence I proceeded to St. Maria; and arrived the 13th of February at that place, where we commonly find visitors. We found the ship Mars of Nantucket, commanded by captain Jonathan Barney. The day we arrived, three of my Botany bay men run from the boat when on shore. The next day (the 14th), I was informed by Captain Barney, that some of my convict men had planned to run away with one of my boats, and go over to the main. This information he obtained through the medium of his people. I examined into the affair, and was satisfied as to the truth of it; set five more of the above description of men on shore, making eight in all I had gotten clear of in two days. Captain Barney sailed about the 17th, and left me quite alone. I continued in that unpleasant situation till the 20th, never at any time after my arrival at this place, daring to let my whale boat be in the water fifteen minutes unless I was in her myself, from a fear that some of my people would run away with her. I always hoisted her in on deck the moment I came alongside, by which means I had the advantage of them; for should they run away with any other boat belonging to the ship, I could overtake them with the whale boat, which they very well knew. They were also well satisfied of the reasons why that boat was always kept on board, except when in my immediate use. During this time, I had no fear from them, except of their running away. Under these disadvantages the Spanish ship Tryal made her appearance on the morning of the 20th, as has been stated; and I had in the course of the day the satisfaction of seeing the great utility of good discipline. In every part of the business of the Tryal, not one disaffected word was spoken by the men, but all flew to obey the commands they received; and to their credit it should be recorded, that no men ever behaved[321] better than they, under such circumstances. When it is considered that we had but two boats, one a whale boat, and the other built by ourselves, while on the coast of New Holland, which was very little larger than the whale boat; both of them were clinker built, one of cedar, and the other not much stouter; with only twenty men to board and carry a ship, containing so many slaves, made desperate by their situation; for they were certain, if taken, to suffer death; and when arriving alongside of the ship, they might have staved the bottom of the boats, by heaving into them a ballast stone or log of wood of twenty pounds: when all these things are taken into view, the reader may conceive of the hazardous nature of the enterprise, and the skill and the intrepidity which were requisite to carry it into execution.

On the afternoon of the 19th, before night, I sent the boatswain with the large boat and seine to try if he could catch some fish; he returned at night with but few, observing that the morning would be better if he went early. I then wished him to go as early as he thought proper, and he accordingly went at four o'clock. At sunrise, or about that time, the officer who commanded the deck, came down to me while I was in my cot, with information that a sail was just opening round the south point, or head of the island. I immediately rose, went on deck, and observed that she was too near the land, on account of a reef that lay off the head; and at the same time remarked to my people, that she must be a stranger, and I did not well understand what she was about. Some of them observed that they did not know who she was, or what she was doing; but that they were accustomed to see vessels shew their colours, when coming into a port. I ordered the whale boat to be hoisted out and manned, which was accordingly done. Presuming the vessel was from sea, and had been many days out, without perhaps fresh provisions, we put the fish which had been caught the night before into the boat, to be presented if necessary. Every thing being soon ready, as I thought the strange ship was in danger, we made all the haste in our power to get on board, that we might prevent her getting on the reefs; but before we came near her, the wind headed her off, and she was doing well. I went along side, and saw the decks were filled with slaves. As soon as I got on deck, the captain, mate, people and slaves crowded around me to relate their stories, and to make known their grievances;[322] which could not but impress me with feelings of pity for their sufferings. They told me they had no water, as is related in their different accounts and depositions. After promising to relieve all the wants they had mentioned, I ordered the fish to be put on board, and sent the whale boat to our ship, with orders that the large boat, as soon as she returned from fishing, should take a set of gang casks to the watering place, fill them, and bring it for their relief as soon as possible. I also ordered the small boat to take what fish the large one had caught and what soft bread they had baked, some pumpkins, some sugar, and bottled cider, and return to me without delay. The boat left me on board the Spanish ship, went to our own, and executed the orders; and returned to me again about eleven o'clock. At noon the large boat came with the water, which I was obliged to serve out to them myself, to keep them from drinking so much as to do themselves injury. I gave them at first one gill each, an hour after, half a pint, and the third hour a pint. Afterward, I permitted them to drink as they pleased. They all looked up to me as a benefactor; and as I was deceived in them, I did them every possible kindness. Had it been otherwise there is no doubt I should have fallen a victim to their power. It was to my great advantage, that, on this occasion, the temperament of my mind was unusually pleasant. The apparent sufferings of those about me had softened my feelings into sympathy; or, doubtless my interference with some of their transactions would have cost me my life. The Spanish captain had evidently lost much of his authority over the slaves, whom he appeared to fear, and whom he was unwilling in any case to oppose. An instance of this occurred in the conduct of the four cabin boys, spoken of by the captain. They were eating with the slave boys on the main deck, when, (as I was afterwards informed) the Spanish boys, feeling some hopes of release, and not having prudence sufficient to keep silent, some words dropped respecting their expectations, which were understood by the slave boys. One of them gave a stroke with a knife on the head of one of the Spanish boys, which penetrated to the bone, in a cut four inches in length. I saw this and inquired what it meant. The captain replied that it was merely the sport of the boys, who had fallen out. I told him it appeared to me to be rather serious sport, as the wound had caused the boy to lose about a quart of blood. Several similar instances of[323] unruly conduct, which, agreeably to my manner of thinking, demanded immediate resistance and punishment, were thus easily winked at, and passed over. I felt willing, however, to make some allowance even for conduct so gross, when I considered them to have been broken down with fatigue and long suffering.

The act of the negro, who kept constantly at the elbows of Don Bonito and myself, I should, at any other time, have immediately resented; and although it excited my wonder, that his commander should allow this extraordinary liberty, I did not remonstrate against it, until it became troublesome to myself. I wished to have some private conversation with the captain alone, and the negro as usual following us into the cabin, I requested the captain to send him on deck, as the business about which we were to talk could not be conveniently communicated in presence of a third person. I spoke in Spanish, and the negro understood me. The captain assured me, that his remaining with us would be of no disservice; that he had made him his confidant and companion since he had lost so many of his officers and men. He had introduced him to me before, as captain of the slaves, and told me he kept them in good order. I was alone with them, or rather on board by myself, for three or four hours, during the absence of my boat, at which time the ship drifted out with the current three leagues from my own, when the breeze sprung up from the south east. It was nearly four o'clock in the afternoon. We ran the ship as near to the Perseverance as we could without either ship's swinging afoul the other. After the Spanish ship was anchored, I invited the captain to go on board my ship and take tea or coffee with me. His answer was short and seemingly reserved; and his air very different from that with which he had received my assistance. As I was at a loss to account for this change in his demeanor, and knew he had seen nothing in my conduct to justify it, and as I felt certain that he treated me with intentional neglect; in return I became less sociable, and said little to him. After I had ordered my boat to be hauled up and manned, and as I was going to the side of the vessel, in order to get into her, Don Bonito came to me, gave my hand a hearty squeeze, and, as I thought, seemed to feel the weight of the cool treatment with which I had retaliated. I had committed a mistake in attributing his apparent coldness to neglect; and as soon as the discovery was made, I was happy to rectify it, by a[324] prompt renewal of friendly intercourse. He continued to hold my hand fast till I stepped off the gunwale down the side, when he let it go, and stood making me compliments. When I had seated myself in the boat, and ordered her to be shoved off, the people having their oars up on end, she fell off at a sufficient distance to leave room for the oars to drop. After they were down, the Spanish captain, to my great astonishment, leaped from the gunwale of the ship into the middle of our boat. As soon as he had recovered a little, he called out in so alarming a manner, that I could not understand him; and the Spanish sailors were then seen jumping overboard and making for our boat. These proceedings excited the wonder of us all. The officer whom I had with me anxiously inquired into their meaning. I smiled and told him, that I neither knew, nor cared; but it seemed the captain was trying to impress his people with a belief that we intended to run away with him. At this moment one of my Portuguese sailors in the boat spoke to me, and gave me to understand what Don Bonito said. I desired the captain to come aft and sit down by my side, and in a calm deliberate manner relate the whole affair. In the mean time the boat was employed in picking up the men who had jumped from the ship. They had picked up three, (leaving one in the water till after the boat had put the Spanish captain and myself on board my ship,) when my officer observed the cable was cut, and the ship was swinging. I hailed the Perseverance, ordering the ports got up, and the guns run out as soon as possible. We pulled as fast as we could on board; and then despatched the boat for the man who was left in the water, whom we succeeded to save alive.

We soon had our guns ready; but the Spanish ship had dropped so far astern of the Perseverance, that we could bring but one gun to bear on her, which was the after one. This was fired six times, without any other effect than cutting away the fore top-mast stay, and some other small ropes which were no hindrance to her going away. She was soon out of reach of our shot, steering out of the bay. We then had some other calculations to make. Our ship was moored with two bower anchors, which were all the cables or anchors of that description we had. To slip and leave them would be to break our policy of insurance by a deviation, against which I would here caution the masters of all vessels. It should always[325] be borne in mind, that to do any thing which will destroy the guaranty of their policies, how great soever may be the inducement, and how generous soever the motive, is not justifiable; for should any accident subsequently occur, whereby a loss might accrue to the underwriters, they will be found ready enough, and sometimes too ready, to avail themselves of the opportunity to be released from responsibility; and the damage must necessarily be sustained by the owners. This is perfectly right. The law has wisely restrained the powers of the insured, that the insurer should not be subject to imposition, or abuse. All bad consequences may be avoided by one who has a knowledge of his duty, and is disposed faithfully to obey its dictates.

At length, without much loss of time, I came to a determination to pursue, and take the ship with my two boats. On inquiring of the captain what fire arms they had on board the Tryal, he answered, they had none which they could use; that he had put the few they had out of order, so that they could make no defence with them; and furthermore, that they did not understand their use, if they were in order. He observed at the same time, that if I attempted to take her with boats we should all be killed; for the negroes were such bravos and so desperate, that there would be no such thing as conquering them. I saw the man in the situation that I have seen others, frightened at his own shadow. This was probably owing to his having been effectively conquered and his spirits broken.

After the boats were armed, I ordered the men to get into them; and they obeyed with cheerfulness. I was going myself, but Don Bonito took hold of my hand and forbade me, saying, you have saved my life, and now you are going to throw away your own. Some of my confidential officers asked me if it would be prudent for me to go, and leave the Perseverance in such an unguarded state; and also, if any thing should happen to me, what would be the consequence to the voyage. Every man on board, they observed, would willingly go, if it were my pleasure. I gave their remonstrances a moment's consideration, and felt their weight. I then ordered into the boats my chief officer, Mr. Low, who commanded the party; and under him, Mr. Brown, my second officer; my brother William, Mr. George Russell, son to major Benjamin Russell of Boston, and Mr. Nathaniel Luther, midshipmen; William[326] Clark, boatswain; Charles Spence, gunner; and thirteen seamen. By way of encouragement, I told them that Don Bonito considered the ship and what was in her as lost; that the value was more than one hundred thousand dollars; that if we would take her, it should be all our own; and that if we should afterwards be disposed to give him up one half, it would be considered as a present. I likewise reminded them of the suffering condition of the poor Spaniards remaining on board; whom I then saw with my spy-glass as high aloft as they could get on the top-gallant-masts, and knowing that death must be their fate if they came down. I told them, never to see my face again, if they did not take her, and these were all of them pretty powerful stimulants. I wished God to prosper them in the discharge of their arduous duty, and they shoved off. They pulled after and came up with the Tryal, took their station upon each quarter, and commenced a brisk fire of musketry, directing it as much at the man at the helm as they could, as that was likewise a place of resort for the negroes. At length they drove the chief mate from it, who had been compelled to steer the ship. He ran up the mizen rigging as high as the cross jack yard, and called out in Spanish, "Don't board." This induced our people to believe that he favoured the cause of the negroes; they fired at him, and two balls took effect; one of them went through his side, but did not go deep enough to be mortal; and the other went through one of his thighs. This brought him down on deck again. They found the ship made such headway that the boats could hardly keep up with her, as the breeze was growing stronger. They then called to the Spaniards, who were still as high aloft as they could get, to come down on the yards, and cut away the robings and earings of the topsails, and let them fall from the yards, so that they might not hold any wind. They accordingly did so. About the same time, the Spaniard who was steering the ship, was killed; (he is sometimes called *passenger,* and sometimes *clerk,* in the different depositions,) so that both these circumstances combined rendered her unmanageable by such people as were left on board. She came round to the wind, and both boats boarded, one on each bow, when she was carried by hard fighting. The negroes defended themselves with desperate courage; and after our people had boarded them, they found they had barricadoed the deck by making a breastwork of the water casks which we[327] had left on board, and sacks of matta, abreast the mainmast, from one side of the ship to the other, to the height of six feet; behind which they defended themselves with all the means in their power to the last; and our people had to force their way over this breast work before they could compel them to surrender. The other parts of the transaction have some of them been, and the remainder will be hereafter stated.

On going on board the next morning with hand-cuffs, leg-irons, and shackled bolts, to secure the hands and feet of the negroes, the sight which presented itself to our view was truly horrid. They had got all the men who were living made fast, hands and feet, to the ring bolts in the deck; some of them had part of their bowels hanging out, and some with half their backs and thighs shaved off. This was done with our boarding lances, which were always kept exceedingly sharp and bright as a gentleman's sword. Whilst putting them in irons, I had to exercise as much authority over the Spanish captain and his crew, as I had to use over my own men on any other occasion, to prevent them from cutting to pieces and killing these poor unfortunate beings. I observed one of the Spanish sailors had found a razor in the pocket of an old jacket of his, which one of the slaves had on; he opened it, and made a cut upon the negro's head. He seemed to aim at his throat, and it bled shockingly. Seeing several more about to engage in the same kind of barbarity, I commanded them not to hurt another one of them, on pain of being brought to the gang-way and flogged. The captain, also, I noticed, had a dirk, which he had secreted at the time the negroes were massacreing the Spaniards. I did not observe, however, that he intended to use it, until one of my people gave me a twitch by the elbow, to draw my attention to what was passing, when I saw him in the act of stabbing one of the slaves. I immediately caught hold of him, took away his dirk, and threatened him with the consequences of my displeasure, if he attempted to hurt one of them. Thus I was obliged to be continually vigilant, to prevent them from using violence towards these wretched creatures.

After we had put everything in order on board the Spanish ship, and swept for and obtained her anchors, which the negroes had cut her from, we sailed on the 23rd, both ships in company, for Conception, where we anchored on the 26th. After the common forms were passed, we delivered the ship, and all that was on board her,[328] to the captain, whom we had befriended. We delivered him also a bag of doubloons, containing, I presume, nearly a thousand; several bags of dollars, containing a like number; and several baskets of watches, some gold, and some silver: all of which had been brought on board the Perseverance for safe keeping. We detained no part of this treasure to reward us for the services we had rendered:—all that we received was faithfully returned.

After our arrival at Conception, I was mortified and very much hurt at the treatment which I received from Don Bonito Sereno; but had this been the only time that I ever was treated with ingratitude, injustice, or want of compassion, I would not complain. I will only name one act of his towards me at this place. He went to the prison and took the depositions of five of my Botany bay convicts, who had left us at St. Maria, and were now in prison there. This was done by him with a view to injure my character, so that he might not be obliged to make us any compensation for what we had done for him. I never made any demand of, nor claimed in any way whatever, more than that they should give me justice; and did not ask to be my own judge, but to refer it to government. Amongst those who swore against me were the three outlawed convicts, who have been before mentioned. I had been the means, undoubtedly, of saving every one of their lives, and had supplied them with clothes. They swore everything against me they could to effect my ruin. Amongst other atrocities, they swore I was a pirate, and made several statements that would operate equally to my disadvantage had they been believed; all of which were brought before the viceroy of Lima against me. When we met at that place, the viceroy was too great and too good a man to be misled by these false representations. He told Don Bonito, that my conduct towards him proved the injustice of these depositions, taking his own official declaration at Conception for the proof of it; that he had been informed by Don Jose Calminaries, who was commandant of the marine, and was at that time, and after the affair of the Tryal, on the coast of Chili; that Calminaries had informed him how both Don Bonito and myself had conducted, and he was satisfied that no man had behaved better, under all circumstances, than the American captain had done to Don Bonito, and that he never had seen or heard of any man treating another with so much dishonesty and ingratitude as he had treated the American.[329] The viceroy had previously issued an order, on his own authority, to Don Bonito, to deliver to me eight thousand dollars as part payment for service rendered him. This order was not given till his Excellency had consulted all the tribunals holding jurisdiction over similar cases, except the twelve royal judges. These judges exercise a supreme authority over all the courts in Peru, and reserve to themselves the right of giving a final decision in all questions of law. Whenever either party is dissatified with the decision of the inferior courts in this kingdom, they have a right of appeal to the twelve judges. Don Bonito had attempted an appeal from the viceroy's order to the royal judges. The viceroy sent for me, and acquainted me of Don Bonito's attempt; at the same time recommending to me to accede to it, as the royal judges well understood the nature of the business, and would do much better for me than his order would. He observed at the same time, that they were men of too great characters to be biassed or swayed from doing justice by any party; they holding their appointments immediately from his majesty. He said, if I requested it, Don Bonito should be holden to his order. I then represented, that I had been in Lima nearly two months, waiting for different tribunals, to satisfy his Excellency what was safe for him, and best to be done for me, short of a course of law, which I was neither able nor willing to enter into; that I had then nearly thirty men on different islands, and on board my tender, which was then somewhere amongst the islands on the coast of Chili; that they had no method that I knew of to help themselves, or receive succour, except from me; and that if I was to defer the time any longer it amounted to a certainty, that they must suffer. I therefore must pray that his Excellency's order might be put in force.

Don Bonito, who was owner of the ship and part of the cargo, had been quibbling and using all his endeavors to delay the time of payment, provided the appeal was not allowed, when his Excellency told him to get out of his sight, that he would pay the money himself, and put him (Don Bonito) into a dungeon, where he should not see sun, moon, or stars; and was about giving the order, when a very respectable company of merchants waited on him and pleaded for Don Bonito, praying that his Excellency would favor him on account of his family, who were very rich and respectable. The viceroy remarked that Don Bonito's character[330] had been such as to disgrace any family, that had any pretensions to respectability; but that he should grant their prayer, provided there was no more reason for complaint. The last transaction brought me the money in two hours; by which time I was extremely distressed, enough, I believe, to have punished me for a great many of my bad deeds.

When I take a retrospective view of my life, I cannot find in my soul, that I ever have done anything to deserve such misery and ingratitude as I have suffered at different periods, and in general, from the very persons to whom I have rendered the greatest services.

The following Documents were officially translated, and are inserted without alteration, from the original papers. This I thought to be the most correct course, as it would give the reader a better view of the subject than any other method that could be adopted. My deposition and that of Mr. Luther, were communicated through a bad linguist, who could not speak the English language so well as I could the Spanish, Mr. Luther not having any knowledge of the Spanish language. The Spanish captain's deposition, together with Mr. Luther's and my own, were translated into English again, as now inserted; having thus undergone two translations. These circumstances, will, we hope, be a sufficient apology for any thing which may appear to the reader not to be perfectly consistent, one declaration with another; and for any impropriety of expression.[331]

OFFICIAL DOCUMENTS

A faithful translation of the depositions of Don Benito Cereno, of Don Amasa Delano, and of Don Nathaniel Luther, together with the Documents of the commencement of the process, under the King's Seal.

I Don Jose de Abos, and Padilla, his Majesty's Notary for the Royal Revenue, and Register of this Province, and Notary Public of the Holy Crusade of this Bishoprick, etc.

Do certify and declare, as much as requisite in law, that, in the criminal cause, which by an order of the Royal Justice, Doctor Don Juan Martinez de Rozas, deputy assessor general of this province, conducted against the Senegal Negroes, that the ship Tryal was carrying from the port of Valparaiso, to that of Callao of Lima, in the month of December last. There is at the beginning of the prosecution, a decree in continuation of the declaration of her captain, Don Benito Cereno, and on the back of the twenty-sixth leaf, that of the captain of the American ship, the Perseverance, Amasa Delano; and that of the supercargo of this ship, Nathaniel Luther, midshipman, of the United States, on the thirtieth leaf; as also the Sentence of the aforesaid cause, on the back of the 72nd leaf; and the confirmation of the Royal Audience, of this District, on the 78th and 79th leaves; and an official order of the Tribunal with which the cause and everything else therein continued, is remitted back; which proceedings with a representation made by the said American captain, Amasa Delano, to this Intendency, against the Spanish captain of the ship Tryal, Don Benito Cereno, and answers thereto—are in the following manner—

Decree of the Commencement of the Process.

In the port of Talcahuane, the twenty-fourth of the month of February, one thousand eight hundred and five, Doctor Don Juan

AMASA DELANO/NARRATIVE   83

Martinez de Rozas, Counsellor of the Royal Audience of this Kingdom, Deputy Assessor, and learned in the law, of this Intendency,[332] having the deputation thereof on account of the absence of his Lordship, the Governor Intendent—Said, that whereas the ship Tryal, has just cast anchor in the road of this port, and her captain, Don Benito Cereno, has made the declaration of the twentieth of December, he sailed from the port of Valparaiso, bound to that of Callao; having his ship loaded with produce and merchandize of the country, with sixty-three negroes of all sexes and ages, and besides nine sucking infants; that the twenty-sixth, in the night, revolted, killed eighteen of his men, and made themselves master of the ship—that afterwards they killed seven men more, and obliged him to carry them to the coast of Africa, at Senegal, of which they were natives; that Tuesday the nineteenth, he put into the island of Santa Maria, for the purpose of taking in water, and he found in its harbour the American ship, the Perseverance, commanded by captain Amasa Delano, who being informed of the revolt of the negroes on board the ship Tryal, killed five or six of them in the engagement, and finally overcame them; that the ship being recovered, he supplied him with hands, and brought him to this port.—Wherefore, for examining the truth of these facts, and inflict on the guilty of such heinous crimes, the penalties provided by law. He therefore orders that this decree commencing the process, should be extended, that agreeably to its tenor, the witnesses, that should be able to give an account of them, be examined—thus ordered by his honour, which I attest.— Doctor ROZAS.

Before me, Jose de Abos, and Padilla, his Majesty's Notary of Royal Revenue and Registers.

Declaration of first Witness

Don Benito Cereno

The same day and month and year, his Honour ordered the captain of the ship Tryal, Don Benito Cereno, to appear, of whom he received before me, the oath, which he took by God, our Lord, and a Sign of the Cross, under which he promised to tell the truth of whatever he should know and should be asked—and being interrogated agreeably to the tenor of the act, commencing the process, he said, that the twentieth of December last, he set sail with his ship from the port of Valparaiso, bound to that of Callao; loaded with the produce of the country, and seventy-two negroes of both sexes, and of all ages, belonging to Don Alexandro Aranda,[333] inhabitant of the city of Mendosa; that the crew of the ship consisted of thirty-six men, besides the persons who went passengers; that the negroes were of the following ages,—twenty from twelve to sixteen years, one from about eighteen to nineteen years, named Jose, and this was the man that waited upon his master Don Alexandro, who speaks well the Spanish, having had him four or five years; a mulatto, named Francisco, native of the province of Buenos

Ayres, aged about thirty-five years; a smart negro, named Joaquin, who had been for many years among the Spaniards, aged twenty-six years, and a caulker by trade; twelve full grown negroes, aged from twenty-five to fifty years, all raw and born on the coast of Senegal—whose names are as follow[s],—the first was named Babo, and he was killed,—the second who is his son, is named Muri,—the third, Matiluqui,—the fourth, Yola,—the fifth, Yau,—the sixth Atufal, who was killed,—the seventh, Diamelo, also killed,—the eighth, Lecbe, likewise killed,—the ninth, Natu, in the same manner killed, and that he does not recollect the names of the others; but that he will take due account of them all, and remit to the court; and twenty-eight women of all ages;—that all the negroes slept upon deck, as is customary in this navigation; and none wore fetters, because the owner, Aranda told him that they were all tractable; that the twenty-seventh of December, at three o'clock in the morning, all the Spaniards being asleep except the two officers on the watch, who were the boatswain Juan Robles, and the carpenter Juan Balltista Gayete, and the helmsman and his boy; the negroes revolted suddenly, wounded dangerously the boatswain and the carpenter, and successively killed eighteen men of those who were sleeping upon deck,—some with sticks and daggers, and others by throwing them alive overboard, after tying them; that of the Spaniards who were upon deck, they left about seven, as he thinks, alive and tied, to manoeuvre the ship; and three or four more who hid themselves, remained also alive, although in the act of revolt, they made themselves masters of the hatchway, six or seven wounded, went through it to the cock-pit without any hindrance on their part; that in the act of revolt, the mate and another person, whose name he does not recollect, attempted to come up through the hatchway, but having been wounded at the onset, they were obliged to return to the cabin; that the deponent resolved at break of day to come up the companion-way,[334] where the negro Babo was, being the ring leader, and another who assisted him, and having spoken to them, exhorted them to cease committing such atrocities—asking them at the same time what they wanted and intended to do—offering himself to obey their commands; that notwithstanding this, they threw, in his presence, three men, alive and tied, overboard; that they told the deponent to come up, and that they would not kill him—which having done, they asked him whether there were in these seas any negro countries, where they might be carried, and he answered them, no; that they afterwards told him to carry them to *Senegal*, or to the neighbouring islands of St. Nicolas—and he answered them, that this was impos[s]ible, on account of the great distance, the bad condition of the vessel, the want of provisions, sails and water; that they replied to him, he must carry them in any way; that they would do and conform themselves to every thing the deponent should require as to eating and drinking, that after a long conference, being absolutely compelled to please them, for they threatened him to kill them all, if they were

not at all events carried to Senegal. He told them that what was most
wanting for the voyage was water; that they would go near the coast to
take it, and thence they would proceed on their course—that the negroes
agreed to it; and the deponent steered towards the intermediate ports,
hoping to meet some Spanish or foreign vessel that would save them;
that within ten or eleven days they saw the land, and continued their
course by it in the vicinity of Nasca; that the deponent observed that
the negroes were now restless, and mutinous, because he did not effect
the taking in of water, they having required with threats that it should
be done, without fail the following day; he told them that they saw
plainly that the coast was steep, and the rivers designated in the maps
were not to be found, with other reasons suitable to the circumstances;
that the best way would be to go to the island of Santa Maria, where
they might water and victual easily, it being a desert island, as the
foreigners did; that the deponent did not go to Pisco, that was near, nor
make any other port of the coast, because the negroes had intimated to
him several times, that they would kill them all the very moment they
should perceive any city, town, or settlement, on the shores to which
they should be carried; that having determined to go to the island of
Santa Maria, as the deponent had planned, for the purpose of trying
whether in the[335] passage or in the island itself, they could find any
vessel that should favor them, or whether he could escape from it in a
boat to the neighboring coast of Arruco. To adopt the necessary means
he immediately changed his course, steering for the island; that the
negroes held daily conferences, in which they discussed what was
necessary for their design of returning to Senegal, whether they were
to kill all the Spaniards, and particularly the deponent; that eight days
after parting from the coast of Nasca, the deponent being on the watch
a little after day-break, and soon after the negroes had their meeting,
the negro Mure came to the place where the deponent was, and told
him, that his comrades had determined to kill his master, Don Alexandro Aranda, because they said they could not otherwise obtain their
liberty, and that he should call the mate, who was sleeping, before they
executed it, for fear, as he understood, that he should not be killed with
the rest; that the deponent prayed and told him all that was necessary
in such a circumstance to dissuade him from his design, but all was
useless, for the negro Mure answered him, that the thing could not be
prevented, and that they should all run the risk of being killed if they
should attempt to dissuade or obstruct them in the act; that in this
conflict the deponent called the mate, and immediately the negro Mure
ordered the negro Matinqui, and another named Lecbe, who died in
the island of Santa Maria, to go and commit this murder; that the two
negroes went down to the birth of Don Alexandro, and stabbed him
in his bed; that yet half alive and agonizing, they dragged him on deck
and threw him overboard; that the clerk, Don Lorenzo Bargas, was
sleeping in the opposite birth, and awaking at the cries of Aranda,

surprised by them, and at the sight of the negroes, who had bloody daggers in their hands, he threw himself into the sea through a window which was near him, and was miserably drowned, without being in the power of the deponent to assist, or take him up, though he immediately put out his boat; that a short time after killing Aranda, they got upon deck his german-cousin, Don Francisco Masa, and his other clerk, called Don Hermenegildo, a native of Spain, and a relation of the said Aranda, besides the boatswain, Juan Robles, the boatswain's mate, Manuel Viseaya, and two or three others of the sailors, all of whom were wounded, and having stabbed them again, they threw them alive into the sea, although they made[336] no resistance, nor begged for any thing else but mercy; that the boatswain, Juan Robles, who knew how to swim, kept himself the longest above water, making acts of contrition, and in the last words he uttered, charged this deponent to cause mass to be said for his soul, to our Lady of Succour; that having finished this slaughter, the negro Mure told him that they had now done all, and that he might pursue his destination, warning him that they would kill all the Spaniards, if they saw them speak, or plot any thing against them—a threat which they repeated almost every day; that before this occurrence last mentioned, they had tied the cook to throw him overboard for I know not what thing they heard him speak, and finally they spared his life at the request of the deponent; that a few days after, the deponent endeavored not to omit any means to preserve their lives—spoke to them peace and tranquillity, and agreed to draw up a paper, signed by the deponent, and the sailors who could write, as also by the negroes, Babo and Atufal, who could do it in their language, though they were new, in which he obliged himself to carry them to Senegal, and they not to kill any more, and to return to them the ship with the cargo, with which they were for that satisfied and quieted; that omitting other events which daily happened, and which can only serve to recall their past misfortunes and conflicts, after forty-two days navigation, reckoned from the time they sailed from Nasca, during which they navigated under a scanty allowance of water, they at last arrived at the island of Santa Maria, on Tuesday the nineteenth instant, at about five o'clock in the afternoon, at which hour they cast anchor very near the American ship Perseverance, which lay in the same port, commanded by the *generous captain Amasa Delano,* but at seven o'clock in the morning they had already descried the port, and the negroes became uneasy as soon as they saw the ship, and the deponent, to appease and quiet them, proposed to them to say and do all that he will declare to have said to the American captain, with which they were tranquilized, warning him that if he varied in the least, or uttered any word that should give the least intimation of the past occurrences, they would instantly kill him and all his companions; that about eight o'clock in the morning, captain Amasa Delano came in his boat, on board the Tryal, and all gladly received him; that the deponent, acting then the part of an owner and a free captain[337] of the ship told them that he came from Buenos Ayres, bound to Lima, with that parcel of negroes; that at the cape many had died, that also, all the sea officers and the greatest part of the crew had died, there remained to him no other sailors than these few who were in sight, and that for want of them the sails had been torn to pieces; that the heavy storms off the cape had obliged them to throw overboard the greatest part of the cargo, and the water pipes; that consequently he had no more water; that he had thought of putting into the port of Conception, but that the north wind had prevented him, as also the want of water, for he had only enough for that day, concluded by asking of him supplies; that the *generous captain Amasa Delano* immediately offered them sails, pipes, and whatever he wanted, to pursue his voyage to Lima, without entering any other port, leaving it to his pleasure to refund him for these supplies at Callao, or pay him for them if he thought best; that he immediately ordered his boat for the purpose of bringing him water, sugar, and bread, as they did; that Amasa Delano remained on board the Tryal all the day, till he left the ship anchored at five o'clock in the afternoon, deponent speaking to him always of his pretended misfortunes, under the forementioned principles, without having had it in his power to tell a single word, nor giving him the least hint, that he might know the truth, and state of things; because the negro Mure, who is a man of capacity and talents, performing the office of an officious servant, with all the appearance of submission of the humble slave, did not leave the deponent one moment, in order to observe his actions and words; for he understands well the Spanish, and besides there were thereabout some others who were constantly on the watch and understood it also; that a moment in which Amasa Delano left the deponent, Mure asked him, how do we come on? and the deponent answered them, well; he gives us all the supplies we want; but he asked him afterwards how many men he had, and the deponent told him that he had thirty men; but that twenty of them were on the island, and there were in the vessel only those whom he saw there in the two boats; and then the negro told him, well, you will be the captain of this ship to night and his also, for three negroes are sufficient to take it; that as soon as they had cast anchor, at five of the clock, as has been stated, the American captain took leave, to return to his vessel, and the deponent accompanied[338] him as far as the gunwale, where he staid under pretence of taking leave, until he should have got into his boat; but on shoving off, the deponent jumped from the gunwale into the boat and fell into it, without knowing how, and without sustaining, fortunately, any harm; but he immediately hallooed to the Spaniards in the ship, "Overboard, those that can swim, the rest to the rigging." That he instantly told the captain, by means of the Portuguese interpreter, that they were revolted negroes, who had killed all his people; that the said captain soon understood the affair, and recovered from his surprise, which the leap of the deponent occasioned, and told him, "Be not afraid, be not afraid, set down and be easy," and ordered his sailors to row towards his ship, and before coming up to her, he hailed, to get a cannon ready and run it out of the port hole, which they did very quick, and fired with it a few shots at the negroes; that in the mean while the boat was sent to pick up two men who had thrown themselves overboard, which they effected; that the negroes cut the cables, and endeavoured to sail away; that Amasa Delano seeing them sailing away, and the cannon could not subdue them, ordered his people to get muskets, pikes and sabres ready, and all his men offered themselves willingly to board them with the boats; that captain Amasa Delano wanted to go in person, and was going to embark the first, but the deponent prevented him, and after many entreaties he finally remained, saying, though that circumstance would procure him much honour, he would stay to please him, and keep him company in his affliction, and would send a brother of his, on whom he said he placed as much reliance as on himself; his brother, the mates, and eighteen men, whom he had in his vessel, embarked in the two boats, and made their way towards the Tryal, which was already under sail; that they rowed considerably in pursuing the ship, and kept up a musketry fire; but that they could not overtake them, until they hallooed to the sailors on the rigging, to unbend or take away the sails, which they accordingly did, letting them fall on the deck; that they were then able to lay themselves alongside, keeping up constantly a musketry fire, whilst some got up the sides on deck, with pikes and sabres, and the others remained in the stern of the boat, keeping up also a fire, until they got up finally by the same side, and engaged the negroes, who defended themselves to the last with their weapons, rushing upon the points[339] of the pikes with an extraordinary fury; that the Americans killed five or six negroes, and these were Babo, Atufal, Dick, Natu, Qiamolo, and does not recollect any other; that they wounded several others, and at last conquered and made them prisoners, that at ten o'clock at night, the first mate with three men, came to inform the captain that the ship had been taken, and came also for the purpose of being cured of a dangerous wound, made by a point of a dagger, which he had received in his breast; that two other Americans had been slightly wounded; the captain left nine men to take care of the ship as far as this port; he accompanied her with his own until both ships, the Tryal and Perseverance, cast anchor between nine and eleven o'clock in the forenoon of this day; that the deponent has not seen the twenty negroes, from twelve to sixteen years of age, have any share in the execution of the murders; nor does he believe they have had, on account of their age, although all were knowing to the insurrection; that the negro Jose, eighteen years old, and in the service of Don Alexandro, was the one who communicated the information to the negro Mure and his comrades, of the state of things before the revolt; and this is known, because in the preceding nights he used to come to sleep from below, where they were, and had secret conversations with Mure, in which he was seen several times by the mate; and one night he drove him away twice; that this same negro Jose, was the one who advised the other negroes to kill his master, Don Alexandro; and that this is known, because the negroes have said it; that on the first revolt, the negro Jose was upon deck with the other revolted negroes, but it is not known whether he materially participated in the murders; that the mulatto Francisco was of the band of revolters, and one of their number; that the negro Joaquin was also one of the worst of them, for that on the day the ship was taken, he assisted in the defence of her with a hatchet in one hand and a dagger in the other, as the sailors told him; that in sight of the deponent, he stabbed Don Francisco Masa, when he was carrying him to throw him overboard alive, he being the one who held him fast; that the twelve or thirteen negroes, from twenty-five to fifty years of age, were with the former, the principal revolters, and committed the murders and atrocities before related; that five or six of them were killed, as has been said, in the attack on the ship, and the following remained alive and are prisoners—[340] to wit—Mure, who acted as captain and commander of them, and on all the insurrections and posterior events. Matinqui, Alathano, Yau, Luis, Mapenda, Yola, Yambaio, being eight in number, and with Jose, Joaquin, and Francisco, who are also alive, making the number of eleven of the remaining insurgents; that the negresses of age, were knowing to the revolt, and influenced the death of their master; who also used their influence to kill the deponent; that in the act of murder, and before that of the engagement of the ship, they began to sing, and were singing a very melancholy song during the action, to excite the courage of the negroes; that the statement he has just given of the negroes who are alive, has been made by the officers of the ship; that of the thirty-six men of the crew and passengers, which the deponent had knowledge of, twelve only including the mate remained alive, besides four cabin boys, who were not included in that number; that they broke an arm of one of those cabin boys, named Francisco Raneds, and gave him three or four stabs, which are already healed; that in the engagement of the ship, the second clerk, Don Josi Morairi, was killed by a musket ball fired at him through accident, for having incautiously presented himself on the gunwale; that at the time of the attack of the ship, Don Joaquin Arambaolaza was on one of the yards flying from the negroes, and at the approach of the boats, he hallooed by order of the negroes, not to board, on which account the Americans thought he was also one of the revolters, and fired two balls at him, one passed through one of his thighs, and the other in the chest of his body, of which he is now confined, though the American captain, who has him on board, says he will recover; that in order to be able to proceed from the coast of Nasca, to the island of Santa Maria, he saw himself obliged to lighten the ship, by throwing more than one third of the cargo overboard, for he could not have made that voyage otherwise; that what he has said is the most substantial of what occurs to him on this unfortunate event, and the truth, under the oath that he has taken; —which declaration he affirmed and ratified, after hearing it read to him. He said that he was twenty-nine years of age;—and signed with his honour—which I certify.

BENITO CERENO.

DOCTOR ROZAS.
Before me.—PADILLA.[341]

RATIFICATION

In the port of Talcahuano, the first day of the month of March, in the year one thousand eight hundred and five,—the same Honourable Judge of this cause caused to appear in his presence the captain of the ship Tryal, Don Benito Cereno, of whom he received an oath, before me, which he took conformably to law, under which he promised to tell the truth of what he should know, and of what he should be asked, and having read to him the foregoing declaration, and being asked if it is the same he has given and whether he has to add or to take off any thing,—he said, that it is the same he has given, that he affirms and ratifies it; and has only to add, that the new negroes were thirteen, and the females comprehended twenty-seven, without including the infants, and that one of them died from hunger or thirst, and two young negroes of those from twelve to sixteen, together with an infant. And he signed it with his honour—which I certify.

BENITO CERENO.

DOCTOR ROZAS.
Before me.—PADILLA.

Declaration of DON AMASA DELANO

The same day, month and year, his Honour, ordered the captain of the American ship Perseverance to appear, whose oath his Honour received, which he took by placing his right hand on the Evangelists, under which he promised to tell the truth of what he should know and be asked—and being interrogated according to the decree, beginning this process, through the medium of the interpreter Carlos Elli, who likewise swore to exercise well and lawfully his office, that the nineteenth or twentieth of the month, as he believes, agreeably to the calculation he keeps from the eastward, being at the island of Santa Maria, at anchor, he descried at seven o'clock in the morning, a ship coming round the point;[342] that he asked his crew what ship that was; they replied that they did not know her; that taking his spy-glass he perceived she bore no colours; that he took his barge, and his net for fishing, and went on board of her, that when he got on deck he embraced the Spanish captain, who told him that he had been four months and twenty six days from Buenos Ayres; that many of his people had died of the scurvy, and that he was in great want of supplies —particularly pipes for water, duck for sails, and refreshment for his crew; that the deponent offered to give and supply him with everything he asked and wanted; that the Spanish captain did nothing else, because the ringleader of the negroes was constantly at their elbows, observing what was said. That immediately he sent his barge to his own ship to bring; (as they accordingly did) water, peas, bread, sugar, and fish. That he also sent for his long boat to bring a load of water, and having brought it, he returned to his own ship; that in parting he asked the Spanish captain to come on board his ship to take coffee, tea, and other refreshments; but he answered him with coldness and in-difference; that he could not go then, but that he would in two or three days. That at the same time he visited him, the ship Tryal cast anchor in the port, about four o'clock in the afternoon,—that he told his people belonging to his boat to embark in order to return to his ship, that the deponent also left the deck to get into his barge,—that on getting into the barge, the Spanish captain took him by the hand and immediately gave a jump on board his boat,—that he then told him that the negroes of the Tryal had taken her, and had murdered twenty-five men, which the deponent was informed of through the medium of an interpreter, who was with him, and a Portuguese; that two or three other Spaniards threw themselves into the water, who were picked up by his boats; that he immediately went to his ship, and before reaching her, called to the mate to prepare and load the guns; that having got on board, he fired at them with his cannon, and this same deponent pointed six shots at the time the negroes of the Tryal were cutting away the cables and setting sail; that the Spanish captain told him that the ship was already going away, and that she could not be taken; that the deponent replied that he would take her; then the Spanish captain told him that if he took her, one half of her value would be his, and the other half would remain to the real owners; that thereupon he ordered the people[343] belonging to his crew, to embark in the two boats, armed with knives, pistols, sabres, and pikes, to pursue her, and board her; that the two boats were firing at her near an hour with musketry, and at the end boarded and captured her; and that before sending his boats, he told his crew, in order to encourage them, that the Spanish captain offered to give them the half of the value of the Tryal if they took her. That having taken the ship, they came to anchor at about two o'clock in the morning very near the deponent's, leaving in her about twenty of his men; that his first mate received a very dangerous wound in his breast made with a pike, of which he lies very ill; that three other sailors were also wounded with clubs, though not dangerously; that five or six of the negroes were killed in boarding; that at six o'clock in the morning, he went with the Spanish captain on board the Tryal, to carry manacles and fetters from his ship, ordering them to be put on the negroes who remained alive, he dressed the wounded, and accompanied the Tryal to the anchoring ground; and in it he delivered her up manned from his crew; for until that moment he remained in possession of her; that what he has said is what he knows, and the truth, under the oath he has taken, which he affirmed and ratified after the said declaration had been read to him—saying he was forty-two years of age—the interpreter did not sign it because he said he did not know how—the captain signed it with his honour—which I certify.

AMASA DELANO.

Doctor ROZAS
Before me.—Padilla

RATIFICATION

The said day, month and year, his Honour ordered the captain of the American ship, Don Amasa Delano to appear, of whom his Honour received an oath, which he took by placing his hand on the Evangelists, under which he promised to tell the truth of what he should know, and be asked, and having read to him the foregoing declaration, through the medium of the interpreter, Ambrosio Fernandez, who likewise took an oath to exercise well[344] and faithfully his office—he said that he affirms and ratifies the same; that he has nothing to add or diminish, and he signed it, with his Honour, and likewise the Interpreter.

AMASA DELANO
AMBROSIO FERNANDEZ.

Doctor ROZAS.
Before me.—Padilla

Declaration of Don Nathaniel Luther, *Midshipman*

The same day, month and year, his Honour ordered Don Nathaniel Luther, first midshipman of the American ship Perseverance, and acting as clerk to the captain, to appear, of whom he received an oath, and which he took by placing his right hand on the Evangelists, under which he promised to tell the truth of what he should know, and be asked, and being interrogated agreeably to the decree commencing this process, through the medium of the Interpreter, Carlos Elli, he said that the deponent himself was one that boarded, and helped to take the ship Tryal in the boats; that he knows that his captain, Amasa Delano, has deposed on every thing that happened in this affair; that in order to avoid delay he requests that his declaration should be read to him, and he will tell whether it is conformable to the happening of the events; that if any thing should be omitted he will observe it, and add to it, doing the same if he erred in any part thereof; and his Honour having acquiesced in this proposal, the Declaration made this day by captain Amasa Delano, was read to him through the medium of the Interpreter, and said, that the deponent went with his captain, Amasa Delano, to the ship Tryal, as soon as she appeared at the point of the island, which was about seven o'clock in the morning, and remained with him on board of her, until she cast anchor; that the deponent was one of those who boarded the ship Tryal in the boats, and by this he knows that the narration which the captain has made in the deposition which has been read to him, is certain and exact in all its parts; and he has only three things to[345] add; the first, that whilst his captain remained on board the Tryal, a negro stood constantly at his elbow, and by the side of the deponent, the second, that the deponent was in the boat, when the Spanish captain jumped into it, and when the Portuguese declared that the negroes had revolted; the third, that the number of killed was six, five negroes and a Spanish sailor; that what he has said is the truth, under the oath which he has taken; which he affirmed and ratified, after his Declaration had been read to him; he said he was twenty-one years of age, and signed it with his Honour, but the Interpreter did not sign it, because he said he did not know how—which I certify.

                                        NATHANIEL LUTHER.
DOCTOR ROZAS
Before me.—PADILLA

RATIFICATION

The aforesaid day, month and year, his Honour, ordered Don Nathaniel Luther, first midshipman of the American ship Perseverance, and acting as clerk to the captain, to whom he administ[e]red an oath, which he took by placing his hand on the Evangelists, under the sanctity of which he promised to tell the truth of what he should know and be asked; and the foregoing Declaration having been read to him, which he thoroughly understood, through the medium of the Interpreter, Ambrosio Fernandez, to whom an oath was likewise administ[e]red, to exercise well and faithfully his office, he says that he affirms and ratifies the same, that he has nothing to add or diminish, and he signed it with his Honour, and the Interpreter, which I certify.

                                        NATHANIEL LUTHER
                                        AMBROSIO FERNANDEZ.
DOCTOR ROZAS.
Before me.—PADILLA[346]

SENTENCE

In this city of Conception, the second day of the month of March, of one thousand eight hundred and five, his Honour Doctor Don Juan Martinez de Rozas, Deputy Assessor and learned in the law, of this intendency, having the execution thereof on account of the absence of his Honour, the principal having seen the proceedings, which he has conducted officially against the negroes of the ship Tryal, in consequence of the insurrection and atrocities which they have committed on board of her.—He declared, that the insurrection and revolt of said negroes, being sufficiently substantiated, with premeditated intent, the twenty seventh of December last, at three o'clock in the morning; that taking by surprise the sleeping crew, they killed eighteen men, some with sticks, and daggers, and others by throwing them alive overboard; that a few days afterward with the same deliberate intent, they stabbed their master Don Alexandro Aranda, and threw Don Francisco Masa, his german cousin, Hermenegildo, his relation, and the other wounded persons who were confined in the births, overboard alive; that in the island of Santa Maria, they defended themselves with arms, against the Americans, who attempted to subdue them, causing the death of Don Jose Moraira the second clerk, as they had done that of the first, Don Lorenzo Bargas; the whole being considered, and the consequent guilts resulting from those heinous and atrocious actions as an example to others, he ought and did condemn the negroes, Mure, Matinqui, Alazase, Yola, Joaquin, Luis, Yau, Mapenda, and Yambaio, to the common penalty of death, which shall be executed by taking them out and dragging them from the prison, at the tail of a beast of burden, as far as the gibbet, where they shall be hung until they are dead, and to the forfeiture of all their property, if they should have any, to be applied to the Royal Treasury; that the heads of the five first be cut off after they are dead, and be fixed on a pole, in the square of the port of Talcahuano, and the corpses of all be burnt to ashes. The negresses and young negroes of the same gang shall be present at the execution, if they should be in that city at the time thereof; that he ought and did condemn likewise, the negro Jose, servant to said Don Alexandro, and Yambaio, Francisco, Rodriguez,[347] to ten years confinement in the place of Valdivia, to work chained, on allowance and without pay, in the work of the King, and also to attend the execution of the other criminals; and judging definitively by this sentence thus pronounced and ordered by his Honour, and that the same should be executed notwithstanding the appeal, for which he declared there was no cause, but that an account of it should be previously sent to the Royal Audience of this district, for the execution thereof with the costs.

DOCTOR ROZAS.

Before me.—JOSÉ DE ABOS PADILLA
His Majesty's Notary of the Royal Revenue and Registers

CONFIRMATION OF THE SENTENCE

SANTIAGO, *March the twenty first, of one thousand eight hundred and five.*

Having duly considered the whole, we suppose the sentence pronounced by the Deputy Assessor of the City of Conception, to whom we remit the same for its execution and fulfilment, with the official resolution, taking first an authenticated copy of the proceedings, to give an account thereof to his Majesty; and in regard to the request of the acting Notary, to the process upon the pay of his charges, he will exercise his right when and where he shall judge best.—

There are four flourishes

Their Honours, the President, Regent, and Auditors of his Royal Audience passed the foregoing decree, and those on the Margin set their flourishes, the day of this date, the twenty first of March, one thousand eight hundred and five;—which I certify,

ROMAN.[348]

NOTIFICATION

The twenty third of said month, I acquainted his Honour, the King's Attorney of the foregoing decree,—which I certify,

ROMAN.

OFFICIAL RESOLUTION

The Tribunal has resolved to manifest by this official resolve and pleasure for the exactitude, zeal and promptness which you have discovered in the cause against the revolted negroes of the ship Tryal, which process it remits to you, with the approbation of the sentence for the execution thereof, forewarning you that before its completion, you may agree with the most Illustrious Bishop, on the subject of furnishing the spiritual aids to those miserable beings, affording the same to them with all possible dispatch.—At the same time this Royal Audience has thought fit in case you should have an opportunity of speaking with the Bostonian captain, Amasa Delano, to charge you to inform him, that they will give an account to his Majesty, of the generous and benevolent conduct which he displayed in the punctual assistance that he afforded the Spanish captain of the aforesaid ship, for the suitable manifestation, publication and noticety of such a memorable event.

God preserve you many years.

SANTIAGO, *March the twenty second, of one thousand eight hundred and five.*

JOSÉ DE SANTIAGO CONCHA.

Doctor Don JUAN MARTINEZ De ROZAS,

Deputy assessor, and learned in the Law, of the Intendency of Conception.[349]

I, the undersigned, sworn Interpreter of languages, do certify that the foregoing translation from the Spanish original, is true.

FRANCIS SALES.

Boston, April 15, 1808.

N.B. It is proper here to state, that the difference of two days, in the dates of the process at Talquahauno, that of the Spaniards being the 24th of February and ours the 26th, was because they dated theirs the day we anchored in the lower harbor, which was one day before we got up abreast of the port, at which time we dated ours; and our coming by the way of the Cape of Good Hope, made our reckoning of time one day different from theirs.

It is also necessary to remark that the statement in page 332, respecting Mr. Luther being supercargo, and United States midshipman, is a mistake of the linguist. He was with me, the same as Mr. George Russell, and my brother William, midshipmen of the ship Perseverance.

On my return to America in 1807, I was gratified in receiving a polite letter from the Marquis De CASE YRUSO, through the medium of JUAN STOUGHTON, Esq., expressing the satisfaction of his majesty, the king of Spain, on account of our conduct in capturing the Spanish ship Tryal on the island St. Maria, accompanied with a gold medal, having his majesty's likeness on one side, and on the other the inscription, REWARD OF MERIT. The correspondence relating to that subject, I shall insert for the satisfaction of the reader. I had been assured by the president of Chili, when I was in that country, and likewise by the viceroy of Lima, that all my conduct, and the treatment I had received, should be faithfully represented to his majesty Charles IV, who most probably would do something[350] more for me. I had reason to expect, through the medium of so many powerful friends as I had procured at different times and places, and on different occasions, that I should most likely have received something essentially to my advantage. This probably would have been the case had it not been for the unhappy catastrophe which soon after took place in Spain, by the dethronement of Charles IV, and the distracted state of the Spanish government, which followed that event.

Philadelphia, 8th September, 1806.

SIR,

HIS Catholic Majesty, the king of Spain, my master, having been informed by the audience of Chili of your noble and generous conduct in rescuing, off the island St. Maria, the Spanish merchant ship Tryal, captain Don Benito Cereno, with the cargo of slaves, who had mutinized, and cruelly massacred the greater part of the Spaniards on board; and by humanely supplying them afterwards with water and provisions, which they were in need of, has desired me to express to you, sir, the high sense he entertains of the spirited, humane, and successful effort of yourself and the brave crew of the Perseverance, under your command, in saving the lives of his subjects thus exposed, and in token whereof, his majesty has directed me to present to you the golden medal, with his likeness, which will be handed to you by his consul in Boston. At the same time permit me, sir, to assure you I feel particular satisfaction in being the organ of the grateful sentiments of my sovereign, on an occurrence which reflects so much honour on your character.

I have the honour to be, sir,

Your obedient servant,

(Signed)   MARQUIS DE CASE *YRUSO.*

Captain AMASA DELANO, *of the American Ship Perseverance, Boston.*[351]

Boston, August, 1807.

SIR,

WITH sentiments of gratitude I acknowledge the receipt of your Excellency's much esteemed favour of September 8th, conveying to me the pleasing information of his Catholic Majesty having been informed of the conduct of myself and the crew of the Perseverance under my command. It is peculiarly gratifying to me, to receive such honours from your Excellency's sovereign, as entertaining a sense of my spirit and honour, and successful efforts of myself and crew in saving the lives of his subjects; and still more so by receiving the token of his royal favour in the present of the golden medal bearing his likeness. The services rendered off the island St. Maria were from pure motives of humanity. They shall ever be rendered his Catholic Majesty's subjects when wanted, and it is in my power to grant. Permit me, sir, to thank your Excellency for the satisfaction that you feel in being the organ of the grateful sentiments of your sovereign on this occasion, and believe me, it shall ever be my duty publicly to acknowledge the receipt of such high considerations from such a source.

I have the honour to be

Your Excellency's most obedient

And devoted humble servant,

(Signed)   AMASA DELANO.

His Excellency the Marquis DE CASE YRUSO

Consular Office, 30th July, 1807.

SIR,

UNDER date of September last, was forwarded me the enclosed letter from his Excellency the Marquis DE CASE YRUSO, his Catholic Majesty's minister plenipotentiary to the United States of America, which explains to you the purport of the commission with which I was then charged, and until now have anxiously waited for the pleasing opportunity of carrying into effect his Excellency's orders, to present to you at the same time the gold medal therein mentioned.[352]

It will be a pleasing circumstance to that gentleman, to be informed of your safe arrival, and my punctuality in the discharge of that duty so justly owed to the best of sovereigns, under whose benignity and patronage I have the honour to subscribe myself, with great consideration, and much respect, sir,

Your obedient humble servant,

JUAN STOUGHTON,

Consul of his Catholic Majesty,
Residing at Boston.

AMASA DELANO, *Esq.*

Boston, August 8th, 1807.

SIR,

I FEEL particular satisfaction in acknowledging the receipt of your esteemed favour, bearing date the 30th ult. covering a letter from the Marquis DE CASE YRUSO, his Catholic Majesty's minister plenipotentiary to the United States of America, together with the gold medal bearing his Catholic Majesty's likeness.

Permit me, sir, to return my most sincere thanks for the honours I have received through your medium, as well as for the generous, friendly treatment you have shown on the occasion. I shall ever consider it one of the first honours publicly to acknowledge them as long as I live.

These services rendered his Catholic Majesty's subjects off the island St. Maria, with the men under my command, were from pure motives of humanity. The like services we will ever render, if wanted, should it be in our power.

With due respect, permit me, sir, to subscribe myself,

Your most obedient, and

Very humble servant,

(Signed)   AMASA DELANO.

To Don JUAN STOUGHTON, *Esq., his Catholic*
Majesty's Consul residing in Boston.[353]

Seeing Americanly: The Narrative Point of View

AMASA DELANO'S PLAIN GOOD SENSE

Guy Cardwell

[*Benito Cereno*] falls for nearly all critics into a coherent, orderly pattern of meaning. Don Benito is pure good; Babo is pure evil; and Delano is the genial, insensitive observer. Melville sees the essential nature of the world clearly, and sees it as a perfect dichotomy.

It is true that throughout the long first division of the narrative Delano serves as a center of revelation whose slowness to understand the action is suitable to the deliberate unfolding of a mystery story; but this interpretation simply will not do. It is too neat, too glib, too shallow, and too entirely unlike Melville. A little reflection[161] and our minds stubbornly refuse to canonize Don Benito; we cannot believe that Delano is altogether blind; and we have some sympathy, too, for Babo. In brief, troubled retrospection produces emotions and ideas that will not fit within this apparently tight, final framework.

Fortunately, Melville helps us towards a new interpretation. In two places, and in two places only, he goes behind the characters in *Benito Cereno*. In the first of these instances, in his fourth paragraph, he writes that, to Captain Delano's surprise, the incoming vessel "showed no colors":

Considering the lawlessness and loneliness of the spot, and the sort of stories, at that day, associated with those seas, Captain Delano's surprise might have deepened into some uneasiness had he not been a person of a singularly un-distrustful good nature, not liable, except on extraordinary and repeated incentives, and hardly then, to indulge in personal alarms, any way involving the imputation of malign evil in man. Whether, in view of what humanity is capable, such a trait implies along with a benevolent heart, more than ordinary quickness and accuracy of intellectual perception, may be left to the wise to determine.

From Guy Cardwell, "Melville's Gray Story: Symbols and Meaning in *Benito Cereno,*" *Bucknell Review*, VIII (May 1959), 154–167. Reprinted by permission of the *Bucknell Review* and the author.

This is either an involved, unfavorable reflection on the captain's acuteness or a moderately plain directive, and it can hardly be an adverse reflection. If it is a directive, we have voyaged on tranced, metaphysical sets where the simple, innocent, but not unintelligent Captain Delano is our certified ontologist and axiologist, a philosophical, not a mechanical, center of revelation.

Delano's worth as a mentor obviously depends on his fundamental insights: he does not make too much of evil in man; he is modestly optimistic about man's capabilities. He is not a dialectician, but his silences carry meaning. (Expressive muteness appears often in this story. Atufal carries out his assigned role without a word; Babo's hand, controlling Don Benito, is "mute as that on the wall"; captured, Babo is silent; gibbeted, he meets a "voiceless end.") When Don Benito discourses with Captain Delano on Appearance and Reality and ends in the perfect conviction that Evil is too much for us, we are not surprised that the generous captain should be silent. He has offered consolations—Time and Nature—and he is not given to the refined development of theory.[162]

When we arrive at this view of Delano, the name of his vessel, the *Bachelor's Delight*, is no longer a puzzling, discordant item. In *Moby-Dick* Melville has already introduced a *Bachelor* and a *Delight*. There the *Bachelor*, "glad ship of good luck," her last cask of oil wedged in, was joyously homeward-bound. Her captain had heard of the white whale but did not believe in him. The *Delight*, "most miserably misnamed," lost five men to the whale, and her captain thought the harpoon not yet forged that would kill him. Delano, then, may be related to both the *Bachelor* and the *Delight*: he was acquainted with horror but did not *usually* impute malign evil.

If we seek, we can find additional detailed evidence that Delano was neither the epitome of moral blindness nor an amiable but mechanical figure. What, for example, are his social judgments? How does he view the Negroes, Don Benito, and nature? He pities Spaniards and blacks, although he perceives that suffering has brought out the less good-natured qualities of the Negroes. He considers Negroes to be generally cheerful and tactful. He takes to them, not on theoretical, abolitionist grounds, but naturally, "not philanthropically, but genially, just as other men to Newfoundland dogs." They are, he notes, like animals, both loving and savage. Does this impress us as a foolish stereotype or plain good sense? Are only blacks like animals? We note that a white sailor has the look of a grizzly bear. If these attitudes and opinions seem sensible to us, how do they square with what we know of Melville's conception of human nature? Reviewing Parkman's *Oregon Trail* in 1849, Melville wrote:

We are all of us—Anglo-Saxons, Dyaks, and Indians—sprung from one head, and made in one image.

And wherever we recognize the image of God, let us reverence it, though it hung from the gallows.

In the second passage in which he goes behind his characters, as a preliminary to the shaving scene, Melville comments on the good humor and harmoniousness of the Negro's disposition, extending this observation with the comment:

When to all this is added the docility arising from the unaspiring content-ment of a limited mind, and that susceptibility[163] of blind attachment sometimes inhering in indisputable inferiors, one readily perceives why those hypochondriacs, Johnson and Byron—it may be something like the hypo-chondriac, Benito Cereno—took to their hearts, almost to the exclusion of the entire white race, their serving men, the negroes, Barber and Fletcher.

Mixed with the ironic comparison of captive Don Benito's attitude to that of Johnson and Byron is the writer's own conception of Negro character. Injection of historical instances, Barber and Fletcher, takes the reader outside the story and upholds the recommended, generally favorable stereotype against Benito's helpless horror.

What of Don Benito? Throughout the first division of the story Delano sees in Don Benito both a tortured, sensitive soul and a neurotic representative of a decayed aristocracy. The revelation of Babo's plot hardly serves to cancel out this impression. Don Benito has no "sociality," a trait that the good captain admires. If he represents ex-perience as contrasted with Captain Delano's innocence, it is an ex-perience which debilitates, forcing the sickly Spaniard to a final retreat from reality.

Is it significant that *benito* means "a Benedictine" and the Bene-dictines are Black Monks? Black Friars, as the Negroes are described early in the tale, and a Black Monk together aboard the ruined *San Dominick* seeing nothing but evil in each other! Delano finds whole-some and reassuring the glimpses he has of his jolly whaleboat, his link with the *Bachelor's Delight,* a well-known world where optimism and despair are mixed in normal proportions and kindly authority preserves a friendly order.

Captain Delano, then, is not simply the obtuse observer, a detec-tive-story character who watches the plot unfold. He is in a serious sense—the perceiving center, and in his innocent perceptiveness he reveals kinship to Jack Chase and Billy Budd. With Delano as our guide we see that the world is not neatly dichotomized, does not fall into a simple Manichean dualism. As in "The Encantadas," "Often ill comes from good, as good from ill." As in the "Maldive Shark," one may find "asylum in the jaws of the Fates." Gray—mixed black and white—is now the thematic color of *Benito Cereno.* We see now why it is that at the opening of the story Amasa Delano rises shortly after a gray dawn to examine the[164] strange sail coming into the dun bay; why the sea is sleeked like waved lead, the sky forming a gray surtout; why the *San Dominick* sails through shreds of fog over leaden swells; why gray fowl flit through gray vapors: "Shadows present, foreshadowing deeper shadows to come."

One major puzzling element in the story remains. Why did Melville include the long, mainly unchanged extract from Captain Delano's published account of his affair with the Spanish ship? It involves considerable repetition of what has been told before, and it changes the tone of the story. A recapitulation, some clarifying, some relaxing of tension are clearly in order even if *Benito Cereno* is read as an overly ornate detective story, a kind of television melodrama that divides its characters into unequivocally good guys and bad guys. But when the story is read in this way, the length of the extract must seem tediously excessive to the most tolerant critic. It becomes easy to charge Melville with ineptitude in handling his source (and some ineptitude there may be, a failure in exclusiveness). It becomes easy, too, to suggest that Melville simply failed to rework properly materials he had thought of expanding to book length or to say that he padded the story by one-fourth because he was paid space rates by *Putnam's*. But as soon as *Benito Cereno* is read as a gray story, the long extract is seen in new perspective.

We have been in the world of the mystery thriller, but that is not the world in which Melville intends to leave us. The extract adds verisimilitude in a very important way: as the brief reference to Barber and Fletcher persuades us that genuine affection may exist between Negroes and Englishmen, so the long extract imposes the sanction of reality upon the total meaning of the story. By expanding the story to include the world of fact, Melville forces the reader to contemplate its web of ideas in the light of corollary, existential problems. Among the problems would inevitably be questions about the nature of freedom and slavery. In 1855 these questions were urgently in the minds of all his readers. They had been dealt with frequently, most popularly only four years earlier by Mrs. Stowe.

Benito Cereno is not to be thought of as an anti-antislavery piece, and by our final interpretation Melville shows no signs of wishing to emulate Mrs. Stowe in reverse, that is by creating a [165] Christlike white man to match against her black, martyred Uncle Tom. Don Benito is not a deeply perceptive martyr: the hypochondriac dies of his own inadequacy, of his inability to face or transcend the horror of life. On the other hand, by the interpretation urged here, *Benito Cereno* speaks to the burning issue of slavery as, knowing Melville, we would expect it to.

The relationship between master and slave in Latin America was not so different from that in the United States as to encourage Melville to suppose the whites all good, the blacks appropriate symbols of evil. (Slavery and the slave trade carried their typical ills with them to both continents. Some of the images that Melville attaches to the *San Dominick* remind us that the Brazilians called slave ships from Angola *tumbeiros,* floating coffins.) The fictional world and the real world come into close congruence when, in the extract from Delano's narrative, Melville represents white Spaniards as attempting to stab shackled slaves after the capture of the *San Dominick. Benito Cereno,* we see, is by the man who at a time when calmness was needed pleaded for understanding treatment of the South in his supplement to *Battle-Pieces* (1866) but classed himself among those "who always abhorred slavery as an atheistical iniquity." It is by the man who, in a more heated moment, wrote in *Mardi* (1849):

"Pray, heaven!" cried Yoomey, "they may yet find a way to loose their bonds without one drop of blood. But hear me, Oro! were there no other way, and should their master not relent, all honest hearts must cheer this tribe of Hamo on: though they cut their chains with blades thrice edged and gory to the haft!"

Comparison of the extract with Captain Delano's original *Narrative of Voyages and Travels* reveals that Melville went to great trouble to revise his source. Although the moral meaning of the source is comparable to the moral meaning of the story, the source is too crassly candid and too naively pessimistic to suit Melville. In the source, Don Benito, himself, is caught in the act of stabbing a shackled slave; he proves to be dishonest in money matters and practices gross ingratitude towards Delano. In the source Delano takes a crudely pessimistic, juvenile view of life's moral mysteries; he cannot find it in his soul that he has ever deserved the miseries or the ingratitude he has experienced.[166]

Modified, made more complex and mature, the moral view of Delano in the source becomes that which Melville distils into the story. The sins and confusions that the living Yankee captain recognized in life are drawn by Melville into his tale. For life's ultimate moral mysteries he had no solution, but he struggled to bring us into their presence. In the end, to select merely one example, the wound on Babo's face is not a horrid, Gothic detail, nor is it evidence of iron-willed satanism. Though self-inflicted, it may betoken cruelties visited on Babo's race by the whites. Beyond this, it may be emblematic of those psychic wounds that each man inflicts on himself or on his fellow. Babo's character is like all character, deeply mysterious. Nature, human and external, is neither Locke's state of unmixed peace and good will nor Hobbes' *bellum omnium contra omnes.*

Read for the second time *Benito Cereno* is, like a Greek tragedy, an exercise in dramatic irony. On first reading the irony is retrospective: the revelation of the entire ironic situation breaks upon the reader after the action of the story is completed. Consequently, the fundamental, weighty ironies of the story have little to do with maintaining interest and integrating the story structurally for first readers. But these ironies do lend unifying strength to the structure when viewed retrospectively.

Admittedly, Melville made unusual demands on his readers. We must deal with shifting symbols, reflexive structure, and ambiguity of moral vision. Admittedly he placed a sudden and heavy burden on a slender framework, the conventional mystery-and-key organization. There is, moreover, the "technical" difficulty that Melville's key opens a succession of obstinate doors and that our task as readers is unfinished until we stand beyond the last one. Then apparently disjointed or senseless parts fall into their due places. Then we contemplate the ambivalence of a writer who took a mixed (if not undecided) view of reality. This view of reality is at least akin to that of our century and excites our sympathy. If not profoundly tragic, it is, nonetheless, far removed from the common optimism of Melville's time, whether transcendental or scientific.[167]

ʃʃʃ

CAPTAIN DELANO AND THE PROBLEM OF AUTHORITY

Nicholas Canaday, Jr.

. . .

The qualities in Captain Delano that show the ease with which he maintains his own command make possible his mistaken notion about the state of affairs aboard the *San Dominick*. Melville's initial view of Don Benito's loss of authority is through the eyes of Captain Delano, and thus it is a view that ostensibly does not take into account the fact that a mutiny has occurred. That the American captain's mistake is not only credible but indeed natural and inevitable is assured by Melville's presentation of the character of Amasa Delano. He is accustomed to instant and exact obedience to his own commands. This dominance is illustrated by the action of his own crew throughout the narrative, especially by the hearty alacrity with which they undertake the dangerous mission of recapturing the *San Dominick*. It is the nature of Delano's authority, accepted without question by his men and assumed automatically by himself, that makes it impossible for him to imagine a captain aboard a ship who does not exercise the same sway. As if this were not enough to ensure credibility in his adventure, Melville carefully discloses an important trait of his

From Nicholas Canaday, Jr., "A New Reading of Melville's *Benito Cereno,*" *Studies in American Literature,* Waldo McNeir and Leo B. Levy, eds. (Baton Rouge, 1960), 49–57. Reprinted by permission of the Louisiana State University Press.

character in the beginning of the narrative when Delano first sights the disheveled *San Dominick* sailing into the harbor without a flag. The American has heard of lawlessness occurring in such lonely spots, but he is merely surprised by the approach of the strange ship, not in the least distrustful. This surprise does not turn into uneasiness because, according to Melville, he is "a person of singularly undistrustful good nature, not liable, except on extraordinary and repeated incentives, and hardly then, to indulge in personal alarms, any way involving the imputation of malign evil in man." To this analysis Melville adds the ambiguous remark: "Whether, in view of what humanity is capable, such a trait implies, along with a benevolent heart, more than ordinary quickness and accuracy of[54] intellectual perception, may be left to the wise to determine." Such a trait, combined with the ease with which Delano assumes and exercises his own authority, makes inevitable the type of appraisal he gives to the situation aboard the *San Dominick* and the conclusion that he draws from what he witnesses there. Although Melville does not overtly refer to the inevitability of Captain Delano's conclusion, it is implied in Melville's remark that "to have beheld this undemonstrative invalid [Benito Cereno] gliding about, apathetic and mute, no landsman could have dreamed that in him was lodged a dictatorship beyond which, while at sea, there was no earthly appeal." However incredible it might seem to the observer uninitiated in the ways of the sea, inexorable seafaring tradition forced Captain Delano to the conclusion that absolute authority resided in the person of Benito Cereno despite all evidence to the contrary.

Until the moment in the narrative when Don Benito escapes from the *San Dominick,* the story has been told from the point of view of Amasa Delano. The authority of a ship captain has been examined in its various aspects based upon the assumption that this captain is actually in command of his ship. Once this mistaken notion is dispelled, the entire affair is described from a second point of view. The concluding portion of the tale is dealt with on the basis of the fact that the Negroes are in revolt, and many of the incidents that occurred prior to Don Benito's escape from his ship are re-examined.

In the lengthy extracts from the testimony of Benito Cereno, who gives his deposition during the trial of the mutineers, Melville clearly distinguishes between authority and power. The drawing of this distinction is revealed in the many cruel and barbarous acts of the mutineers. During the time the Negroes were in command of the ship, power was exercised without authority. The mutineers, led by the wily Babo, have the power to act as they do after their successful revolt, but they have no authority, even though they have temporarily made ineffectual the authority of their captain. Don Benito's authority is based upon legal right; the Negroes' power is based upon force. Babo has led them in a reign of terror that tortured or killed progressively more Spaniards every time the Negroes' power was challenged. It is revealed that[55] their final act of cruelty was the killing of the owner of the slaves and the nailing of his skeleton to the prow. They had led each white man to view the skeleton—and the motto they had inscribed beneath it, "Seguid vuestro jefe" (Follow your leader)—in an attempt to intimidate the Spaniards once and for all. Later when it became necessary for the mutineers to allow Captain Delano to board the ship, the use of the six hatchet-polishers to survey the scene was a naked display of power. Such devices are typical of the use of power without authority.

Although it is not possible to transfer authority by force, the authority of Don Benito and his officers was made ineffectual by their loss of power. The Spaniards were forced to submit to the rebelling slaves. Melville recognizes that once a captain's authority is overthrown it can only be replaced by the same agency that originally established it. Had the Americans arrived during the mutiny and aided in putting it down, the end of the narrative could have been different. Once the revolt was successful, only Spanish law could return the ship's government to order. In *Benito Cereno* the force represented by Captain Delano could only destroy the power of the mutineers. It became the task of the courts to restore authority.

The function of the law in relation to authority is demonstrated by Melville's conclusion to the tale. The law is an expression of the authority of the state. The law cannot command a ship, but the captain who does so derives his authority from maritime or naval law. When a captain's authority is destroyed, the law replaces it with that of another. Because of this traditional "chain of command," Melville's story involves mutiny without the death of the ship's captain. Benito Cereno's death would have removed him as a commander, but at the same time his authority would have passed to another of the Spanish officers. When he is held captive, dressed in the regalia of his office but stripped of his authority, Melville creates a situation in which the law is inoperative. The captain's loss of command is symbolized by the empty scabbard that he still wears: "And that silver-mounted sword, apparent symbol of despotic command, was not, indeed, a sword, but the ghost of one. The scabbard, artificially stiffened, was empty." The power vacuum aboard the ship is temporarily filled,[56] not by law but by the naked force employed by the mutineers to command obedience. When the power of the mutineers has in turn been overcome, the Spanish courts are in a position to restore legal power and authority to the *San Dominick* in the person of a new captain.

Benito Cereno is unique among Melville's tales and novels because it deals with a ship captain who has lost his command. This story alone illustrates certain aspects of Melville's general concept of the authority of the ship captain—a theme that appears in each of his novels dealing with the sea. Through his dual approach to the affair aboard the *San Dominick*, Melville demonstrates two things: first, the result of Don Benito's status as a ship captain without the power to enforce his commands; and, secondly, the misuse of power by usurping Negroes who rule without authority. The American captain, combining both authority and power, illustrates the ease with which command can be exercised under normal conditions. Chaos and disorder are the inevitable results of authority functioning without power and of power exercised without authority.[57]

〰〰〰

AMASA DELANO, REALIST

James E. Miller, Jr.

. . .

Melville's drama of evil emerges in the old familiar patterns. And Captain Delano is his maskless man, a man frank and sincere in his basic nature, quick with his help for others, kind and forgiving out of a spontaneously generous heart—but not so naïve in his understanding of the human scene as to be unable, when convinced of the necessity, to cope with evil. His is a practical virtue, neither too much nor too little of this world. At least so it turns out. For the whole length of the story, however, the issue is uncertain as Delano's good nature seems to render him incapable of distinguishing innocence from its disguise.

Captain Amasa Delano, from Duxbury, Massachusetts, is Melville's Western Man, with all of his most noble traits. He is endowed with a "singularly undistrustful good nature, not liable, except on extraordinary and repeated incentives, and hardly then, to indulge in personal alarms, any way involving the imputation of malign evil in man." Melville poses a question which he declines at the outset to answer: "Whether, in view of what humanity is capable, such a trait implies, along with a benevolent heart, more than ordinary quickness and accuracy of intellectual perception, may be left to the wise to determine." As always in Melville, the crucial question revolves about the balance of[154] heart and mind. An imbalance, as in Ahab or Billy Budd, courts disaster. A perfect balance, as in Jack Chase, achieves the ideal. Captain Delano may seem at first to suffer from an excess of the one and a deficiency of the other—but in the showdown, when action is crucial, he acts.

It is Captain Delano's basic good nature and generous heart which

Reprinted from "Benito Cereno," A Reader's Guide to Herman Melville by James E. Miller, Jr. (New York, 1962), pp. 152–159. By permission of Farrar, Straus & Giroux, Inc. Copyright © 1962 by James E. Miller, Jr.

impel him when he first sights the crippled ship to offer his assistance, and it is these same noble traits which force him to forgive so easily the apparently ungrateful and even rude recipients of his aid. Numerous small incidents momentarily arouse the suspicions of Captain Delano, but he invariably and ingeniously lulls the suspicions to rest. Even when Captain Benito Cereno is shaved, at his Negro's reminder, during Delano's visit in the middle of the day, and trembles so violently that the "servant" Babo draws blood, the serene American Captain cannot yet sustain his suspicions. He reflects—"But then, what could be the object of enacting this play of the barber before him? At last, regarding the notion as a whimsy, insensibly suggested, perhaps, by the theatrical aspect of Don Benito in his harlequin ensign, Captain Delano speedily banished it." Captain Delano is constantly seeking a rational explanation for the evil he fleetingly imagines, and when he can find none, he dismisses the suspicion as "whimsy."

In the exciting climax of the story, when first Don Benito Cereno and next Babo leap into Captain Delano's boat before it can part from the crippled ship, Delano can still not sense the presence of evil, and for a moment it appears that he will never awaken to the distraught state of affairs aboard the San Dominick. But finally he spots Babo in the boat with a dagger at his master's heart: "That moment, across the long-benighted mind of Captain Delano, a flash of revelation swept, illuminating, in unanticipated clearness, his host's whole mysterious demeanor, with every enigmatic event of the day, as well as the entire past voyage of the San [155] Dominick." Captain Delano's insight has the speed and scope of a sudden vision as he sees in a flash behind the multitudinous masks of innocence which have so long and dangerously betrayed him: "Captain Delano, now with scales dropped from his eyes, saw the negroes, not in misrule, not in tumult, not as if frantically concerned for Don Benito, but with mask torn away, flourishing hatchets and knives, in ferocious piratical revolt." As the discarding of the "masks" confirms his insight, Captain Delano acts—and acts swiftly and positively. Though reluctant to recognize evil, he is not slow to confront it; though hesitant in naming it, he does not hesitate to cope with it. Unlike either Ahab or Billy Budd, Captain Delano can deal with evil in a practical and effective manner, for in him mind and heart are held in balance. His great and generous heart, although it leads him near to disaster, does not push him over the edge. He releases Don Benito, binds Babo, picks up the other Spanish sailors who have leaped from their captivity, and, when he returns to his ship, dispatches a whaling boat in successful pursuit of the fleeing San Dominick. By this immediate and courageous action Captain Delano demonstrates that his notable generosity is kept within "human" bounds by a strong, instinctive sense of realism.

If Captain Delano is the maskless man of the tale, Benito Cereno is the subtly masked man, presenting one face to society, another to himself—neither of which, as he perhaps recognizes subconsciously, is the true Don Benito. In his occasional and gloomy glimpses into his own dark interior, he is like Pierre peering at times into his own deep soul; in his unwillingness to confront evil and his final withdrawal to a monastery, he is like Billy Budd responding whimsically as a child to the world's sin. Benito Cereno contrasts markedly with Amasa Delano, captain from the New World of America. His ship is no *Bachelor's Delight* (like Delano's) but the stately reminder of the past, the *San Dominick*.[156] Don Benito himself is a Spanish Catholic, both his country and his religion steeped in compelling traditions. In his weakness in the face of danger and in his final withdrawal from life, Don Benito seems to be the representative of a proud but nearly exhausted civilization, one on the brink of disintegration and decay. His inability to cope with the Negroes is not so much a failure of intellect or strength as a failure of will. Though the victim of black evil, Don Benito seems himself to emanate a darkness of his own.

Don Benito's outermost mask, removed only by his leap into Captain Delano's boat, is forced upon him by his captors. Beneath this mask lies the mask of innocence. When Captain Delano confesses that he at first believed, when Don Benito leaped, that Benito was signaling the launching of a plot against Delano and his crew, Don Benito replies: "You were with me all'day; stood with me, sat with me, talked with me, looked at me, ate with me, drank with me; and yet, your last act was to clutch for a monster, not only an innocent man, but the most pitiable of all men. To such degree may malign machinations and deceptions impose." Innocent of the plot imagined by Captain Delano—Don Benito certainly was. But he is not, as he says, an innocent man; indeed, the experience brings to him an acute sense of his heritage of guilt. In Babo, who appears symbolically as his double (they are of the same age, have many similar characteristics), Don Benito vividly perceives his own—and man's—evil, and the knowledge undoes him.

His irrational fear, compounded in part of an insane hate, causes him when he is rescued by Captain Delano to refuse to come on deck of the *Bachelor's Delight* until the securely bound Babo is removed from sight, and he refuses ever after, even at the trial, to endure the presence of the Negro. He carefully notes in his deposition the reversal of the barbarism, the attack on the blacks (after they have been captured and shackled) by the Spanish sailors—a[157] number were killed, others saved by Captain Delano just as the razor was aimed at the throat, the dagger at the heart. This reversal impresses clearly on Don Benito the universality of the savage impulse. And in the closing lines of the story, he reveals his inability to accept the human fate. When Captain Delano cries out to Don Benito to forget—"See, yon bright sun has forgotten it all, and the blue sea, and the blue sky; these have turned over new leaves"—Don Benito quietly replies: "Because they

have no memory . . . because they are not human." Captain Delano
asks Don Benito the cause of his dejection, and receives in simple
reply: "The negro." In his withdrawal and subsequent death, Don
Benito deliberately severs his link in the common human chain: he
refuses any longer to bear the responsibility of his *humanhood*.

Among the rebelling Negroes, two provide the necessary leader-
ship—Babo the intellect, Atufal the brute strength. It is Babo who not
only has masterminded the mutiny but also has conceived the fantastic
plot of deceiving Captain Delano as to the true state of affairs aboard
the *San Dominick*. Babo is a colored confidence man, a bit more sinister, perhaps, but reveling like the common racketeer in an ingenious
and complicated plot fiendishly calculated to hurt as well as to fleece.
Babo obviously enjoys evil for itself alone. This perverted joy is most
clearly demonstrated in the relish with which he murders Don Benito's
friend, Don Alexandro Aranda, the owner of the slaves on board, and
mounts his bleached skeleton in place of the figure of Christopher Columbus as the *San Dominick's* figurehead. With this constant reminder
of his cruelty on conspicuous display, Babo "teases" the remnant of
the Spanish crew and Don Benito about the whiteness of the skeleton.
One by one, he asks each sailor whether he cannot affirm, from the
whiteness of the bones, that they belong to a white man. This is but one
of several small incidents which testify to the depth of[158] Babo's
"negro slave" resentment against the "master" white race.

Babo's silent accomplice, the magnificently built Atufal, is another reminder of the seething rebelliousness of the black man. Once
a chief of his tribe in Africa, he has had thrust upon him the indignities
of slavery by men physically inferior who, ironically, espouse a religion
of charity and love. Though the cruelties of the Negroes are extreme,
they are not without precedents among white men, and they well up
spontaneously from a confusion of fear and hate only dimly (if at all)
understood by the perpetrators. But Babo and his followers are clever
enough to understand that evil is most likely to succeed when it
masquerades as innocence: they are as diligent in conceiving their
naïve drama of deception as they are in executing their acts of violence.

In *Benito Cereno* Melville uses the drama of the masks to generate
suspense. The deceptions in this story in a real sense *are* the story, for
the deceptions capture the imagination of author and reader. The
fate of the characters at the end is in part a dramatic reflection of their
attitudes. Captain Delano, the maskless man, endures, and will continue his direct and frank confrontation of life. The clever Babo, once
deprived of his ingenious mask, refuses to speak a word either at his
trial or on any other occasion; but his severed head, "that hive of
subtlety," is displayed in public where it meets, "unabashed, the gaze
of the whites." And Benito Cereno, three months after the trial, is
borne from his monastery on a bier as he makes the ultimate withdrawal from the human scene. Captain Delano welcomes life; Benito
Cereno welcomes death; Babo seems to scoff defiantly at both.[159]

ひ々ひ

"THE GOOD CAPTAIN": AMASA DELANO,
AMERICAN IDEALIST

Barry Phillips

. . .

The critics of *Benito Cereno* fail for the same reason Amasa Delano fails. They place the problems of the story in the realm of concepts when all the concepts of the story point to the primary problem of perception. They assign absolute values when the only values are relative. They find objective meaning in experiences whose main significance is the ambiguous, multi-leveled, mysterious nature of experience, and the subjective, albeit emphatically empirical, nature of the only real meaning. A central emphasis in *Benito Cereno* is the focus on the elusive, ambiguous nature of reality, "actual," independent reality, the reality of the natural world.

The most persistent symbol in the story is the *San Dominick* itself, the scene of most of the action. As a symbol, it is most striking in its anonymity, on the one hand, and in its ambiguity, on the other. It remains characterless at the same time that it suggests and contains a mysterious multiplicity of characteristics. The deathlike, decaying, "pipe-clayed aspect" of its crowded, crudded decks variously suggests "a white-washed monastery after a thunderstorm," "London streets in the time of the plague," a deserted Venetian palace, a royal Egyptian tomb, "Ezekiel's Valley of Dry Bones."

Her cargo, crew, and captain are no less multiple and mysterious than her decks. She contains blacks, whites, mulattoes; Africans and Europeans; primitives and moderns; slaves and masters; evil and good. If she contains the decayed and deathlike, she can also contain life— the virile hatchet-polishers, the buoyant Delano, the powerful Atufal, the indestructible Babo. "The world's a ship on its passage out," Ishmael observed. And surely the *San Dominick,* in its inclusive diversity, is no less the ship of the world than the *Pequod.* But in symbolizing the world, her main function is to symbolize life's mysterious and ambiguous character. / She is a world where meanings are relative, inverted, multiple, and hidden. Slaves freely strike their masters, a

From Barry Phillips, " 'The Good Captain': A Reading of *Benito Cereno,*" *Texas Studies in Literature and Language,* IV (Summer 1962), 188–197. Reprinted by permission of *Texas Studies in American Literature and Language* and the author.

captain has no control, a king is in chains he can loosen at any moment, time is chimed off the hour. The ship has wandered from obscure origins into unknown waters, pursuing an uncertain journey and an unattainable destination.

The ubiquitousness of the grey decay and of the dark primitives makes more insistent the mysterious appearances and the unknown forces. Babo, the most important of the blacks, is not, ultimately, the embodiment of natural human depravity—a Claggart or, as A. L. Vogelback sees him, an Iago.[1] Claggart and Iago act with timeless,[189] motiveless, impersonal and impervious purity. Cereno's faithful servant never transcends the implied confines of an historical context and a personal rationale which render him impure and susceptible. Thus, in the context of tragedy, he is both a fascinating and a sympathetic character. Dark and inscrutable, Babo is the mysterious subterranean potential lurking beneath all natural human surface, potential which, when suppressed, does spring back on its suppressor.

The natural unknown which Babo symbolizes informs the story at many points. Specific scenes and objects intensify, not the meaning of mystery, but the mystery of all meaning. "The old man [who] looked like an Egyptian priest, making Gordian knots for the temple of Ammon," and the knot he ties, are significant only because of their inextricability:

> "What are you knotting there, my man?"
> "The knot," was the brief reply, without looking up.
> "So it seems; but what is it for?"
> "For someone else to undo," muttered back the old man.

But the knot is not undone; it is tossed overboard to sink to whatever fate awaits beneath the dark surface of the sea. The six hatchet-polishers are significant not for any one thing they specifically suggest so much as for their very suggestiveness. The "sphynx-like" oakum-pickers are meaningful because of their apparent meaninglessness. Even the shaving scene finds its primary significance in the terrifying irresolution that arises from its multiple perplexing possibilities.

Perhaps the key symbol in *Benito Cereno* is the ship's sternpiece, "a dark satyr in a mask, holding his foot on the prostrate neck of a writhing figure, likewise masked." We may interpret the satyr as natural force and the prostrate figure as natural (fallen) man; but what is important is that they are masked. The meaning of both is undisclosed. The bow-piece, the ship's figurehead, is hidden throughout most of the story by a canvas cover. When the figure is finally unmasked, it turns out to be but another symbolic suggestion of the unknown: the skeleton of the murdered Aranda.

The oppressive presence of the seeming unknown, looming over the deck of the *San Dominick*, is not, however, completely unfathom-

---

[1] "Shakespeare and Melville's 'Benito Cereno'," *MLN*, LXVII (February 1952), 113–116.

able. This is the natural world, the historical world, fallen but real; and, at the least, there are lessons to be had from it.

But to the natural world, to say nothing of the lessons it can teach, Amasa Delano, the prosperous optimist and determined American idealist, "the good captain" of the *Bachelor's Delight,* is as brazenly blind as the detached head of the executed Babo, "fixed on a pole in the Plaza,[190] [meeting], unabashed, the gaze of the whites." He cannot even recognize the mask for what it is. "Be they heroic or pathetic, noble or ludicrous," Milton Stern emphasizes, "Melville's idealists are all finally fools. . . . [They] present the kind of belief which, in varying degrees of appearance and reality, represents a nation one of whose mottoes is, 'In God we trust'," a nation, he might have added, which stamps that motto on its currency.[2] Delano transcends this formula only in its "finally": Delano from the very first is exclusively a fool. And he would be exclusively ludicrous were he not at times something worse. Constantly he refers to the *San Dominick*— the world of experience, nature, life, and death—as "the stranger." Indeed, the natural world is a stranger to the American idealist.

When he first sees the *San Dominick* pull into harbor, a strange ship, flying no colors, sailing in pirate waters, "Captain Delano's surprise might have deepened into some uneasiness had he not been a person of a singularly undistrustful good nature, not liable, except on extraordinary and repeated incentives, and hardly then, to indulge in personal alarms, any way involving the imputation of malign evil in man." Once on board the *San Dominick,* he is either blind to aspects of the ship's ominous suggestiveness or he dismisses suspicion as unreal: "He began to feel a ghostly dread of Don Benito [and he's mistaken in that]. And yet, when he roused himself, dilated his chest, and coolly considered it—what did all these phantoms amount to? . . . 'I dare say, Spaniards are as good folks as any in Duxbury, Massachusetts.' . . . Mistrust would yet be proved illusory."

The good captain emerges as a blind buffoon. But he is something worse than just a buffoon. Delano displays in his faulty vision a smugness of which only the self-righteous are capable. The irony of his harping on Cereno's pride (which is not pride) makes Melville's condemnation all the heavier. The smug American, priggish, prudent, patronizing, feels perfectly free to criticize the lack of discipline and lack of decency on another captain's ship. Through the very last, he looks upon himself as the superior but genial bearer of Cereno's salvation.

Amasa Delano, the typically American idealist, is benevolent. But, Melville makes explicit, this benevolence is not simply naive: it is so treacherously stupid and so insidiously self-congratulating that, even after it does finally confront an evil, it cannot recognize and accept it.

---

2 *The Fine Hammered Steel of Herman Melville* (Urbana, 1957), pp. 11, 13. This essay owes to Stern the conceptual framework in which it views Melville.

Delano alone, against the wishes of the escaped Cereno and the advice
of his own mates, insists on risking his crew's lives in giving chase to
the[191] *San Dominick.* He doesn't want to kill the Negro mutineers:
he wants only to capture them and bring them to trial. The good captain cannot live with the thought that somewhere evil does exist; he
insists on rounding it up, to be dispensed with by legal justice. He does
not realize that there is no justice, much less legal justice, which can
dispense with natural realities.

What completes Melville's satiric portrait is the fact that this
picture is in large part but the actual presentation of an actual person.
The real Delano, the man who penned the journal on which *Benito
Cereno* is based, is almost precisely the smug buffoon who appears in
Melville's fictional amplification. . . . The satiric thrust is but a stab
with the man's own pen. Melville is not amiss in saying the captain
was "incapable of irony": snug in his own adolescent idealism, the
actual Delano is as empty of self-perception as of worldly perception.
His self-portrait, for all purposes, is complete in its own unwary self-
condemnation.

Lest we underestimate the real contempt Melville must have felt
when he first read Captain Delano's *Narrative* or the significance he
must have attached to Delano as a "representative man," we may recall
the reaction Melville pressed into the margins of Emerson's more intelligent idealism:

Emerson: The good, compared to the evil which [man] sees, is as his own
good to his own evil.
Melville: A perfectly good being, therefore, would see no evil.—But what did
Christ see?—He saw what made him weep.—However, too, the "Philan-
thropist" must have been a very bad man—he saw, in jails, so much evil. To
annihilate all this nonsense read the Sermon on the Mount, and consider
what it implies.

.   .   .

Emerson: Trust men, and they will be true to you.
Melville: God help the poor fellow who squares his life according to this.

.   .   .

Melville: [Emerson's] gross and astonishing errors & illusions spring from a
self-conceit so intensely intellectual and calm that at first one hesitates to call
it by its right name. Another species of Emerson's errors, or rather, blindness,
proceeds from a defect in the region of the heart.[3]

Critics may object to Melville's reading of Emerson, but the significant thing here is that, for Melville, Emerson exhibited the same
defects in his vision of the world and of providence as Delano displayed in his.[192] In Amasa Delano, more than in any other of his
major characters, Melville concentrated his contempt for the optimism
of the American idealist.

Benito Cereno himself, though given more stature than Delano,

---

[3] The marginalia are provided by Jay Leyda, *The Melville Log* (New York,
1951), II, 648–649. I have corrected *it's,* in the last citation, to *its.*

is secondary to him in the story. In Cereno, Melville created a man who, whatever his past inexperience, could learn something from the historical world. It is reasonable to assume that, as a young representative of a decadent nobility, supported by the ordered belief and orthodox ritual of his religion, accustomed to enslaving and trading freely upon the black primitives, Cereno before the uprising had been as out of touch with reality as Delano. But like a Pip fallen into the dark drowning sea, Cereno was surrounded, pushed down, and defeated by the dark natural forces. Like a Pip, Cereno learned from the experience and was spiritually exhausted, if not suffocated, by it. What he learned of life was a lesson too large for him to live with.

We can believe him when he says that he was motivated to jump ship not to save his own life but to save Delano's. Cereno was already spiritually dead, and he knew it, completely unable to cope with the realities—not just with Babo, but with all that Babo represented. After the recapture of the Negroes, even before the ordeal of the trial, Cereno had become "so reduced as to be carried ashore in arms." A religious order gave him refuge, "and a member of the order volunteered to be his one special guardian and consoler, by night and by day." He refused at the trial, as at all times, even to look at Babo, and when pressed to do so by the judges, "he fainted. On the testimony of the sailors alone rested the legal identity of Babo." Cereno died a short three months after the trial.

"There is a wisdom that is woe and ... a woe that is madness." At the same time that it enlightened his intellect, the shadow of "the negro," the darkness on Benito's brain, worked on him like a spiritual frontal lobotomy.

The contrast between the sad, mad, wise Cereno and the glad, healthy, obtuse Delano comes to a tense and heavily resonant climax near the story's close. Delano speaks first:

"... the past is passed; why moralize upon it? Forget it. See, yon bright sun has forgotten it all, and the blue sea, and the blue sky; these have turned over new leaves."

"Because they have no memory," he dejectedly replied; "because they are not human."

"But these mild trades that now fan your cheek, do they not come with a human-like healing to you? Warm friends, steadfast friends are the trades."[193]

"With their steadfastness they but waft me to my tomb, Señor," was the foreboding response.

"You are saved," cried Captain Delano, more and more astonished and pained; "you are saved: what has cast such a shadow upon you?"

"The negro."

There was a silence, while the moody man sat, slowly and unconsciously gathering his mantle about him, as if it were a pall.

Only the determined ignorance in which Delano is wrapped is more deadly than Cereno's mantle of sad wisdom. . . .[194]

The Cast Shadow: *Benito Cereno* and the Negro Problem

MELVILLE AND THE NEGRO PROBLEM: *BENITO CERENO*

Charles I. Glicksberg

A writer's attitude toward what may loosely be called the Negro problem is caused by a complex variety of forces. It is conditioned by his early upbringing, the views of his parents and neighbors in the community, the cultural compulsives of his time and land, his temperament, his experiences, and his subsequent intellectual development. In the case of a writer of fiction, what complicates matters is that it is not easy to disentangle his own views from those he puts into the mouths of his characters. Implicit in the warp and woof of a novel is not only a writer's *Weltanschauung* but also his social values, his conception of human nature, his estimate of man, whether white or colored, Christian or heathen. In this connection, what is of particular significance in his work, however, is not only his overtly formulated system of ethics or his humanitarianism but also his hidden and often unconscious valuations: the things he tends to take for granted, the beliefs he projects as a matter of course. In short, the writer's language and plot, his symbols and his images betray him just as a dream, when interpreted, reveals the repressed but dynamic wishes of the dreamer.

No one, so far as I know, has yet made a detailed study of Melville's attitude toward the Negro. The reason, obviously, is that Melville did not play a conspicuous part in the Abolition movement nor did he openly champion the cause of the Negro people. Though he protested against the activities of the missionaries in the South Sea islands, he was not by nature a reformer or propagandist, whereas we can find plenty of stirring and defiant attacks on the evils of slavery in such writers as Thoreau, Emerson, Bryant, Whittier, James Russell Lowell, and Walt Whitman. An analysis of ... *Benito Cereno* ..., however, will indicate that Melville, as artist and man, was more closely implicated in the fate of the Negro in the United States than we would offhand suspect.

From Charles I. Glicksberg, "Melville and the Negro Problem," *Phylon*, XI (Autumn 1950), 207–215. Reprinted by permission of *Phylon* and the author.

In his introduction to the *Short Novels of the Masters,* Charles Neider points out that Melville, in basing his story of *Benito Cereno* on the accounts published by Captain Amasa Delano, *Voyages and Travels,* departed strangely from the documented account of the original source. In his factual narration of the mutiny aboard the Spanish ship, Captain Delano was filled with genuine sympathy for the plight of the slaves, the cruel conditions which they had to bear under Spanish oppression, though he does not, of course, condone their act of mutiny. Nevertheless, he makes it clear that the Spaniards were unconscionable butchers and [207] paints the character of Cereno in no flattering terms, revealing the uglier side of his nature. The editor, in short, charges that "Melville glosses over extenuating circumstances in his effort to blacken the blacks and whiten the whites, to create poetic images of pure evil and pure virtue. The result is sometimes unfortunate in the feelings it arouses against the Negro."

This is a serious charge. It is all the more difficult to explain in light of the fact that Melville, in *Moby Dick,* evinced a profound and consistent sympathy and admiration for the Negro as being at heart more noble, less corrupt, less eaten through with the acids of bigotry and intolerance, than the whites. For in *Moby Dick* we have among the seamen aboard the ship an international congregation, representatives of almost every land, and particularly such types as Lascars, Chinese, Danes, Malaysians, Tahitians, and Negroes. As Van Wyck Brooks puts it, Melville always drew the Negroes

with a special delight and tenderness, full of admiration as he was for their 'great gift of good humor.' He liked to speak of little Pip's 'pleasant, genial, jolly brightness' and the coolness, indifference and easiness of the gigantic Daggoo, who made a white man standing before him seem like a white flag that had come to beg truce of a fortress. Without abasing the strong and the proud, he exalted the humble, as did Whitman, the cannibal Queequeg, above the rest, the 'soothing savage' whose honest heart restored Ishmael's faith in a wolfish world.

In a footnote Brooks compares this with Whitman's admiring references to the Negro in *Leaves of Grass,* but the comparison, however interesting in a literary sense, is invalidated by one important consideration. What Whitman, by and large, discovered in the Negro is his picturesqueness, his polished and perfect limbs, his graceful stature, his calm glance, and while he loved him he loved him as a Negro. Though he conceded his humanity, he did not instinctively acknowledge his equality as a man. Melville, however, was deeply disturbed over the problem of slavery in the middle of the nineteenth century.

In *Benito Cereno,* Melville has written a compelling story of horror and suspense. Captain Amasa Delano, when he boards the slave ship, has no suspicion that anything is seriously wrong; though occasionally he is tormented by doubt and feels uneasy, he is so generous by nature that he throws off such suggestions of evil. Here is this vessel, a Spanish merchantman, carrying Negro slaves. The story, written in

1855, deals with events that took place in 1799. When Captain Delano comes aboard, he is struck by the sight of the Negroes on deck, especially four elderly, grizzled Negroes picking the junk into oakum and accompanying their work with a low, monotonous chant. Apparently the men on board, the Negroes and the Spaniards, had suffered privation, lack of food and water, and the Captain attributed the lack of order and authority on board to[208] the long period of suffering these men had endured. At every turn, however, the Spanish captain, Don Benito, is attended by a most faithful, seemingly devoted slave, Babo. All this is seen through the eyes of Captain Delano, who considers himself a hearty, tolerant New Englander, a native of Duxbury, Massachusetts. So that in portraying the Negroes and in passing judgment on their actions, Melville is himself not taking sides, though the sympathies of the reader are weighted in favor of the whites and against the cruelty and ferocity of the blacks.

Yet, there are enough passages to warrant the surmise that Captain Delano is intended as a satiric portrait, a composite reflection of the righteous stereotyped attitudes prevalent at the time. Captain Delano is sentimentally touched by the sight of Babo ministering so affectionately to the wants of his master, and it is this affectionate zeal, he thinks, which has gained for the Negro the reputation of making the best and most pleasing servant in the world. The New England captain derives "humane" satisfaction from observing the steady good conduct of Babo as compared to the rowdiness and indocility of the blacks in general. Captain Delano, however, observes too many suspicious signs to be entirely at ease, and begins to speculate on what sinister plots may be on foot. Could Don Benito, perhaps, be in conspiracy with the blacks? Then comes this significant reflection: "But they were too stupid. Besides, who ever heard of a white so far a renegade as to apostatize from his very species almost, by leaguing against it with Negroes?" Here we have the expression of an attitude characteristic of an entire culture. The values that Captain Delano holds as a matter of course are revealing—and damning. His reflections bring out the innate prejudices he harbors against the Negro.

While watching Don Benito being shaved by Babo, the New England captain muses:

> There is something in the negro which, in a peculiar way, fits him for avocations about one's person. Most negroes are natural valets and hairdressers; taking to the comb and brush congenitally as to the castanets, and flourishing them apparently with almost equal satisfaction.

He notes their tact, their graceful briskness of manner, and particularly their great gift of good humor. Not the clownish grin or laugh but an easy-going cheerfulness, "harmonious in every glance and gesture; as though God had set the whole negro to some pleasant tune." Now in view of what was then actually happening on board ship, this observation takes on richly ironic overtones. These reflections are given dramatic intensity by the reader's perception that Don Benito, while being shaved, is also being menaced, held under a grim threat of death. The guileless Captain Delano, however, suspects nothing, and continues to admire the docility of the Negroes, which arises, he naively supposes, "from the unaspiring[209] contentment of a limited mind, and that susceptibility of blind attachment sometimes inhering in indisputable inferiors. . . ."

There is abundant food for irony in these complacent cogitations when one considers that the slaves on board had revolted, killed off most of the officers, and kept Don Benito alive in order that he might steer them to their native land. There is, too, a source of ironic tension in the fact that Captain Delano is made out to be an essentially humane, kindly, tolerant man.

At home, he had often taken rare satisfaction in sitting at his door, watching some free man of colour at his work or play. If on a voyage he chanced to have a black sailor, invariably he was on chatty and half-gamesome terms with him. In fact, like most men of a good, blithe heart, Captain Delano took to negroes, not philanthropically, but genially, just as other men to Newfoundland dogs.

This, if we are alert to such subtly interpolated clues, gives the game away. Here for the first time we see that Captain Delano, far from echoing Melville's own sentiments or beliefs, is intended as a dramatic device, a mirror reflecting the prejudices of New Englanders of a certain type. Captain Delano has a "weakness" for Negroes, he prides himself on his humanity and kindliness, though he clearly feels most kindly disposed toward them when he beholds them in a menial position, devotedly tending to the needs of their master. This is a consummate portrait of unconscious, hypocritical righteousness. For example, the Captain, we learn, refuses to believe the current stereotype that a mulatto with a regular European face is bound to turn out a devil. It were strange indeed, he tells Don Benito, "and not very creditable to us white skins, if a little of our blood mixed with the African's, should, far from improving the latter's quality, have the sad effect of pouring vitriolic acid into black broth; improving the hue, perhaps, but not the wholesomeness." Not a word about the moral aspect of this vicious, brutally enforced system of miscegenation! Could anything be better calculated to betray the "enlightened" state of the Captain's mind?

Insubordinate as the Negroes appear, they respond readily enough to the commands of their own leaders, working with a will, ready to die in defense of their liberty. It is important to recognize that Melville was willing to develop this theme, which underlines what we now know to be true, namely, that the Negroes, far from being contented and docile under slavery, engaged in frequent revolts. Only at the very end do we get the full story of the uprising on board, the massacre, with Babo taking command and using terrorism to keep the Spaniards still alive subservient to his will, as he bids Don Benito set sail for Senegal. Babo displays a remarkable gift for acting, for devising plans, for commanding the ship, though he knows no navigation. When the slave ship is finally captured and brought into port and the black pirates "properly" punished, Captain Delano tells Don Benito to cease brooding on the affair.[210] Why moralize about it? Best forget it. Don Benito, however, feels that he is doomed. When Captain Delano asks him what has cast such a shadow upon him, the broken-hearted Don Benito replies: "The negro."

Thus the story winds to a close. Babo, once apprehended, refuses to utter a word and Don Benito refuses to look at him, even at the trial; even after Babo has been dragged to the gibbet at the tail of a mule and the head fixed on a pole in the Plaza; but the severed head met, unabashed, says Melville, the gaze of the whites. From the tone of the tale, from the cumulative internal evidence, the inference must be drawn that Melville did not attempt to blacken the blacks and whitewash the whites. Far from arousing feelings of hatred against the Negro, the incarnate image of evil, he presents a complex, artistically balanced story, which arouses mixed emotion. Though we sympathize with the plight of Don Benito, we admire the steadfast courage and indomitable spirit of Babo, a born leader, just as we admire the capacity for self-rule and the heroic resolution of the Negroes on board. If they went to extremes of butchery in their desperate bid for freedom, who shall presume to pass final judgment upon them? But the important consideration is that Melville is thoroughly consistent and honest in his limning of the race problem. . . .[211]

§§§

THE SLAVERY ISSUE IN *BENITO CERENO*

Joseph Schiffman

...dreadful insurrections...have been made when opportunity offered.
—Absolom Jones and Richard Allen, Negro leaders, 1794.

. . . Williams[1] early in his paper reminds us that the meaning of *Benito Cereno* still eludes us, and expresses agreement with Ellery

From Joseph Schiffman, "Critical Problems in Melville's *Benito Cereno*," *Modern Language Quarterly*, XI (September 1950), 317–324. Reprinted from *Modern Language Quarterly* by permission of the editor and the author.
[1] See Bibliography, p. 200.

Sedgwick that we "must know all of his [Melville's] books to comprehend his mind, of which each is a 'profile.' " Yet Williams does not take
Sedgwick's good advice, for he makes little attempt in his article to
cast the mystery of *Benito Cereno* against the light that Melville's
other books afford us, and so comes to the mistaken conclusion that
Babo is evil. Williams says: "[Natural] to Babo . . . is hatred for the
happiness of hatred, evil for the sake of evil . . . [his is] a motiveless
malignity. . . ."

This is a customary misinterpretation, for Babo's malignity is not
motiveless. He was leading a rebellion of slaves in their fight for
freedom, and all his acts of cruelty were dictated by this purpose. He
ordered the killing of the slave owner, Don Alexandro, "because he
and his companions could not otherwise be sure of their liberty." And
Don Alexandro's skeleton was nailed to the ship's masthead with the
words "Follow Your Leader" under it as a warning to the Spanish
captain and crew that, unless the slaves were returned to free Senegal,
each Spaniard would follow his leader to death. Babo is evil because
of an evil world.

Almost all critics who insist that Babo is evil refuse to discuss the
question of slavery. Rosalie Feltenstein,[2] for example, says that Babo's
condition of servitude is outside the boundaries of discussion since
Melville does not take it into account.

Melville could not felicitously discuss slavery within the framework of the short story, but aside from this problem, Miss Feltenstein's[318] refusal to consider slavery in Babo's case raises other critical
problems. The critic is not confined within limits set by the author. If
this were so, there would be no true criticism. As Taine said, "It is a
mistake to study the document as if it were isolated. This were to
treat things like a simple scholar, to fall into the error of the biblio-
maniac." Surely a discussion of Melville's attitudes toward slavery and
the Negro would throw valuable light on Babo's actions in *Benito
Cereno.*

What did slavery mean to Melville? In *Mardi* he makes his position clear. In his allegorical trip through the southern part of Vivenza
(the United States of America) he is shocked by the sight of slaves in
the land of liberty. The travelers cannot believe their eyes when, on
close scrutiny of the tribe of Hamo, they discover they are slaves—and
yet men!

Throughout Melville's books there is warm understanding and
sympathy shown for the Negro. In *Redburn* Melville speaks of the
freedom Negro sailors enjoy in Liverpool as contrasted with the restrictions on them in their own country. In *Moby Dick* Melville hits a
high-water mark in his presentation of Negro characters as people. The
only Negro in the book who betrays any kind of neurosis is young

---

2 See pp. 146–152 of this book.

Pip, who shrinks from life after a nightmare experience in chasing a whale. Melville significantly refers to him as "Poor Alabama boy." The other people of color in the book, except Old Fleece, have never lived under slavery, and they show themselves to be the equals of their white mates. It is in keeping with Melville's philosophy that Babo as a human being would desire freedom.

The human desire for freedom is something Melville always understood and admired in men. Gabriel says that for Melville, all positions save two were tentative. The only two absolutes were "the eternal dualism between good and evil, and man's destiny to make war upon wrong." Certainly, to Melville, Babo was warring on wrong.

Thirty years after *Benito Cereno*, Melville made clear his attitude towards rebellion. In the Preface to *Billy Budd* he speaks of the French Revolution in these words:

The opening proposition made by the Spirit of that Age involved rectification of the Old World's hereditary wrongs. In France, to some extent, this was bloodily effected. But what then? Straightway the Revolution itself became a wrongdoer, one more oppressive than the kings.... During those years not the wisest could have foreseen that the outcome of all would be what to some thinkers apparently it has since turned out to be—a political advance along nearly the whole line for Europeans.[319]

Melville knew that "the rectification of wrongs" does not always come pleasantly. *Benito Cereno* shows that. This is the answer Melville's whole lifework gives to the riddle of good and evil.

Miss Feltenstein has attempted to discover factual meanings in the rich symbolism of *Benito Cereno*. But, like Williams, she comes to the faulty conclusion that Babo signifies evil, and that through him Cereno comes to understand "the blackness at the center of life." Miss Feltenstein says that "blackness and darkness are Melville's predominant symbols of evil, and Babo is blackness, not simply a Negro ... [hence] he is pure evil. . . ."

It is true that for most people of the Western Hemisphere black symbolizes evil and white symbolizes good. But this does not hold for Melville. He was a rebel against his age and culture,[3] such a deep-

---

3 Melville said " 'No' in an age which demanded that all good citizens should say 'Yes.' " From the *Introduction to Herman Melville: Representative Selections*, by Willard Thorp (New York, 1938), p. xcvii. Note especially the section of the Introduction entitled "Melville's Social Ideas," pp. xcvii–xcix, for a discussion of Melville's attitudes toward slavery, Christian missions, primitive man, etc. Information such as the following is very important to a proper understanding of *Benito Cereno*. "He [Melville] seems, indeed, to be unique among his contemporaries in his freedom from zeal and prejudice."

Many modern critics of Melville do not match his tolerant attitudes. For example, Arthur Hobson Quinn speaks of the attraction of *Benito Cereno* in these terms: "It is the picture of one man [Cereno], of our own race, alone amid the hostile strangers who are waiting to strike, that appeals so strongly." See his *American Fiction: An Historical and Critical Survey* (New York, 1936), p. 155.

going rebel that even his symbolism became unorthodox. To Melville white was evil, harsh, ugly—the unknown. Moby Dick, the White Whale, had to be killed if the tragic crew of the *Pequod* were to find rest. Ishmael (Melville) speaks of white in these terms:

It was the whiteness of the whale that above all things appalled me. But how can I hope to explain myself here; and yet, in some dim, random way, explain myself I must, else all these chapters might be naught . . . consider that the mystical cosmetic which produces every one of her hues, the great principle of light, for ever remains white or colorless in itself, and if operating without medium upon matter, would touch all objects, even tulips and roses, with its own blank tinge—pondering all this, the palsied universe lies before us a leper; and like wilful travellers in Lapland, who refuse to wear colored and coloring glasses upon their eyes, so the wretched infidel gazes himself blind at the monumental white shroud that wraps all the prospect around him. And of all these things the Albino Whale was the symbol. Wonder ye then at the fiery hunt?

And at another point in *Moby Dick* Melville raises his dark and white symbolism to the level of human coloring. The sailors are seated about at ease:

OLD MANX SAILOR
. . . This is the sort of weather when brave hearts snap ashore, and keeled hulls split at sea. Our captain has his birth-mark; look yonder, boys, there's another in the sky—lurid-like, ye see, all else pitch black.[320]

DAGGOO
What of that? Who's afraid of black's afraid of me! I'm quarried out of it!

SPANISH SAILOR
(*Aside.*) He wants to bully, ah!—the old grudge makes me touchy. (*Advancing.*) Aye, harpooneer, thy race is the undeniable dark side of mankind—devilish dark at that. No offence. . . .

5TH NANTUCKET SAILOR
What's that I saw—lightning? Yes.

SPANISH SAILOR
No; Daggoo showing his teeth.

DAGGOO [*Springing*]
Swallow thine, mannikin! White skin, white liver.

Symbolism becomes meaningful only when analyzed in the light of the author's mind, or within the context in which it is used. Williams overlooks this point in attempting to ascribe moral values to the name "Babo." Williams says, "Babo, after all, as perhaps his name suggests, is just an animal, a mutinous baboon." That the name Babo had any special symbolic meaning for Melville is unlikely. He found the name in Delano's *Narrative,* the source of his *Benito Cereno.* The name

Babo can be explained only in the role Babo plays. Though he was mutinous, as Williams says, he was no baboon. Instead he was a forceful, clever, courageous leader of his fellow slaves. If the name Babo connotes evil, what do the names Daggoo and Queequeg connote? These strange names are given to respected harpooneers on the *Pequod*, sworn enemies of Moby Dick, and the best-paid men in the crew. Only in such terms can "symbolism" in Daggoo and Queequeg be discussed. Similarly, the name Babo, like any other piece of "symbolism," derives its significance from the role the character plays. To attempt to interpret symbols in any fixed, isolated manner is to indulge in mysticism, not criticism.

Within the demands of the short-story form, how does Melville betray his sympathies? It is important to observe that *Benito*[321] *Cereno* as a story flows from two sources: first, from Don Alexandro's mistaken belief that his slaves were tractable, and, second, from Delano's inability to perceive that a slave rebellion was occurring under his very eyes. Had Don Alexandro not mistakenly advised Cereno that his slaves were content and could be transported without chains, there could have been no slave revolt. And had Delano been able to understand that Negroes could revolt successfully, there would have been no *Benito Cereno*. In depicting the short-sightedness of those who thought slavery was acceptable to other people, Melville was condemning slavery.

Practically all of *Benito Cereno* is told through the eyes of one person, Captain Delano. Melville remains carefully in the background. Delano is referred to as "The American" by Melville, and since he is the only American who takes an appreciable part in the story, one can believe that Melville intends Delano perhaps as a microcosm of American attitudes of the time toward Negroes. If this is so, Melville has given us a mind that rings historically true.

Delano suffers a mental block in looking at Negroes. He cannot conceive of them as fully rounded people. To him, they are simple, lovable, sub-human beings, quite happy as slaves and servants. This is the fulcrum on which the whole story is based. Had Delano, the American, been able to understand that here was a shipload of Negroes who had successfully revolted, had he understood that Atufal was really not in chains but that he was periodically reconquering Cereno, had he understood that the "unsophisticated" hatchet polishers and "drooling" Negroes were part of an elaborate control system, there could have been no story.[4] So despite a strange atmosphere about the ship, Delano cannot perceive that the slaves are in rebellion. Feeling uneasy, he suspects Cereno. He looks everywhere but in the right

---

4 Delano's inability to comprehend the Negro's reaction to slavery is characteristic of many white American historians. John Fiske, James Schouler, and Ulrich B. Phillips, for example, all believe that the Negro, as an "inferior" being, was docile

place for an answer to the mysterious conduct of Cereno and the whole ship. And so Delano and the reader feel these "currents spin [their] heads around almost as much as they do the ship." A hundred little conflicts lash at Delano and the reader—action and repose, suspicion and reassurance, prickling and balm; and through it all Babo's role mocks the white man's low estimate of the Negro. For Delano "took to negroes . . . genially, just as other men to Newfoundland[322] dogs." A grand hoax is put over on him, to be dispelled only by Cereno's desperate plunge into the rowboat.

In some ways *Benito Cereno* is a fossil relic of the stress and strain that America experienced over the slavery issue in the 1850's. In answer to *Uncle Tom's Cabin*, fourteen pro-slavery novels were published between 1852 and 1854. These novels argued that the Negro "is not fit for freedom, knows himself an inferior, and in the majority of cases prefers to remain a slave." In these ante-bellum tracts, "A thinking Negro is unusual, a Negro expressing himself on slavery is unaccountable...."[5] It was in this climate of controversy that *Benito Cereno* appeared.

Melville did not intend *Benito Cereno* as an abolitionist tract. He wanted primarily to write a "good story," one that would sell. But in selecting a theme of slave rebellion, and in treating Babo and his fellow slaves as able, disciplined people, as capable of evil as the white man, he treated the Negro as an individual. Both subject and treatment were conditioned by the 1850's, and both subject and treatment marked advances for American literature.[6]

---

under slavery. See Herbert Aptheker, *American Negro Slave Revolts* (New York, 1943). Aptheker says: "The data herein presented make necessary the revision of the generally accepted notion that his [the American Negro slave's] response [to slavery] was one of passivity and docility. The evidence, on the contrary, points to the conclusion that discontent and rebelliousness were not only exceedingly common, but, indeed, characteristic of American Negro slaves" (p. 374).

The slave leaders' quote used at the beginning of this paper is taken from Aptheker, p. 14.

[5] See Jeannette Reid Tandy, "Pro-Slavery Propaganda in American Fiction of the Fifties," *South Atlantic Quarterly*, XXI (January, April 1922), 40–50, 170–178.

[6] It is interesting to note that one writer, significantly a Negro, comes closest to an understanding of the social implications of *Benito Cereno*. Sterling Brown says: "The contrast between the reputed gentleness of Negroes . . . and the fierceness with which they fight for freedom [in *Benito Cereno*] is forcibly driven home. Certain Negroes stand out: Babo who . . . engineered the revolt with great skill . . . ; Francesco, the mulatto barber; Don José, personal servant to a Spanish Don; and Atufal. . . . All bear witness to what Melville recognized as a spirit that it would take years of slavery to break . . . although the mutineers are bloodthirsty and cruel, Melville does not make them into villains; they revolt as mankind has always revolted. . . . [He] comes nearer the truth in his scattered pictures of a few unusual Negroes than do the other authors of this period." See Sterling Brown, *The Negro in American Fiction* (Washington, D.C., 1937), pp. 12–13. While Brown's analysis of *Benito Cereno* is the best I have seen, he misses the point of Babo's moral victory at the end.

Babo emerges the moral victor in *Benito Cereno*. Cereno can never return to the slave trade after his experience with Babo. He remains depressed and disconsolate. Delano cannot understand Cereno's depression, since Babo is bound and out of harm's way. Delano asks Cereno: "... you are saved; what has cast such a shadow upon you?" To which the beaten Cereno replies, "The negro." And at the trial, Cereno cannot be made to face Babo.

Babo is sentenced to death by the law courts of Lima. His head is stuck upon a pole and his body is burned to ashes:

... for many days, the head [of Babo], that hive of subtlety, fixed on a pole in the Plaza, met, unabashed, the gaze of the whites; and across the Plaza looked ... toward the monastery, on Mount Agonia without; where, three months [later] ... Benito Cereno, did, indeed, follow his leader.[323]

Babo's head gazed "unabashed" as Benito Cereno, who would trade in flesh, does "indeed follow his leader." What an indictment of slavery! Melville's thinking, artistically sublimated in form, shines through *Benito Cereno*.[324]

இ இ இ

RACISM IN *BENITO CERENO*

Joseph Schiffman

Irony is rooted in Delano's superficial appraisal of Babo and his fellow Negroes. To him, they are simple, subhuman beings, quite happy as slaves and servants; Delano "took to negroes ... genially, just as other men to Newfoundland dogs." Here is the fulcrum on which the whole story turns. Had Delano been able to understand that Negroes desire freedom, had he understood that Atufal was really not in chains, that the "unsophisticated" hatchet polishers and "drooling" Negroes were part of an elaborate control system, there could have been no story. So, despite a strange atmosphere about the ship, Delano cannot perceive that the slaves are in rebellion. Feeling uneasy, he suspects Cereno.[233] He looks everywhere but in the right place for an answer to the mysterious conduct of Cereno and others on the ship, and through it all Babo's stoical role mocks Delano's patronizing attitude. Cereno's desperate plunge into the rowboat finally shatters

From Joseph Schiffman's note to *Benito Cereno* in *Three Shorter Novels of Herman Melville* (New York, 1962), pp. 230–235. Copyright © 1962 by Harper & Brothers. Reprinted with the permission of Harper & Row, Publishers.

the stereotype of the Negro, but it fails to teach unperceptive Delano that slavery is abhorrent as a way of life.

Delano's obtuseness contrasts with Cereno's sensitivity. Through suffering, Cereno attains understanding of the horror of slavery and of its power to destroy owner, trader, and slave. After his experience with Babo, Cereno can never return to the slave trade, and remains depressed and disconsolate. Delano cannot understand Cereno's depression, since Babo is bound and out of harm's way. Delano asks Cereno: "... you are saved; what has cast such a shadow upon you?" To which the beaten Cereno replies, "The negro." At the trial, Cereno cannot be made to face Babo. Although the slave leader is sentenced to death by the law courts of Lima and his body burned to ashes, his head "fixed on a pole in the Plaza, met, unabashed, the gaze of the whites; and across the Plaza looked ... toward the monastery, on Mount Agonia without; where, three months [later] ... Benito Cereno ... did, indeed, follow his leader."

All this raises a question as to Melville's attitude toward Negroes. In *Benito Cereno* Negroes are generally depicted as barbarous primitives, sadists, "ferocious pirates." Their leader, Babo, is revealed as cleverly malign, engaging in practices more cruel than those he himself endured as a slave. And yet Melville's writings prior to *Benito Cereno* display warm understanding, sympathy, and frequent admiration for the Negro. In *Redburn*, he speaks glowingly of the freedom Negro sailors enjoy in Liverpool as contrasted with restrictions upon them in their own country. *Moby-Dick* is notable in American literature for its presentation of Negro characters as splendid shipmates. The only Negro in the book betraying any kind of neurosis is young Pip, who naturally shrinks from life after a nightmare experience in chasing a whale. Melville significantly refers to him as "Poor Alabama boy." The[234] other colored people in the book, except Old Fleece, have never lived under slavery, and they prove themselves the equals of their white mates.

What did Negro slavery itself mean to Melville? *Mardi* makes his position clear. Melville's travelers, in their allegorical trip through the southern part of Vivenza (the United States), are shocked by the sight of slaves in the land of liberty. Yoomy, the poet, cries out: "... hear me, Oro! [God] were there no other way, and should their masters not relent, all honest hearts must cheer this tribe of Hamo on; though they cut their chains with blades thrice edged, and gory to the haft! 'Tis right to fight for freedom, whoever be the thrall." To which Babbalanja, the philosopher, replies: "... for these serfs you would cross spears; yet I would not. Better present woes for some, than future woes for all." Here Melville's ambivalent attitudes toward Negro slavery are fully debated.

Benito Cereno was written by Melville in a period of personal depression, when he feared "the primeval savageness which ever slumbers in human kind." Writing in the violent decade just before the Civil War, when panic over slave insurrections was mounting, Melville, with characteristic ambivalence, treated slavery and the rebellion against it as a sign of evil in the universe. In high-lighting the savagery of the rebellion, Melville sullied his tale with racism—an element which detracts from the stature of *Benito Cereno*.[235]

♫♫♫

BENITO CERENO AND THE AMERICAN NATIONAL SIN

Sidney Kaplan

. . .

Reluctantly, very reluctantly—for it is with a special sadness that we are forced to repudiate any portion of the "usable past" in the classic figures of our American Renaissance—it must be ventured that the image of Melville as subtle abolitionist in *Benito Cereno* may be a construction of generous wish rather than hard fact. Just as Melville cautioned his readers that they must discriminate between what was indited as Pierre's and what was indited concerning him, so here care must be had to discriminate the thoughts that Melville indites in *Benito Cereno* from what the reader may hope these thoughts to be. The events of a story by themselves do not always clearly reveal the writer's judgment on those events; bare plot does not mechanically provide its interpretation.

As Melville once wrote to Hawthorne, he liked "a skeleton of actual reality to build about with fulness & veins & beauty." Now, Delano's *Narrative* was such "a skeleton of actual reality." Taken as incident, as a news-item reported with horror by a pro-slavery writer in the Southern press, to a John Brown or Ralph Waldo Emerson the revolt of the Negroes against their white masters of the *San Dominick* might seem a healthy and heartening thing (indeed, the *Liberator* is full of such joyful items); conversely, reported by a Frederick Douglass or a Sojourner Truth in the abolitionist press of the North, to a Calhoun, a Simms or a Poe the same revolt would be an illustration of the last evil. Thus, Glicksberg's query—"If they went to extremes of[12]

_____

From Sidney Kaplan, "Herman Melville and the American National Sin," *Journal of Negro History*, XLI (October 1956), 311–338, XLII (January 1957), 11–37. Reprinted by permission of the Association for the Study of Negro Life and History, Inc., and the author.

butchery in their desperate bid for freedom, who shall presume to pass final judgment upon them?"—is in a sense a meaningless one; nor is Schiffman to the point when he contends that the anti-slavery intention of *Benito Cereno* is shown by Melville's mere choice of the *subject* of slave-revolt, even at a time when pro-slavery novelists, in order to rebut Mrs. Stowe, were busy turning out caricatures of contented slaves. The fact is that Melville's intention must be determined mainly by what he did with his plot, how he veined and fleshed it, and in part how he manipulated his source. His mere telling of the story, while it will reveal something about that intention, will not by its bare outline establish Babo as hero or Cereno as villain.

Let us try to clarify this point. To begin with, it seems highly improbable that Melville in writing *Benito Cereno* was not thinking within the framework of the cultural concerns of his time as well as in a timeless region of universal truth. His technique was often to expand a current and concrete context into eternal abstractions, but this technique rarely excluded judgment on the concrete. Now, *Benito Cereno* was written at the mid-point of the hottest decade of the anti-slavery struggle prior to the Civil War, when to many the conflict seemed both irrepressible and impending. Nor was it a struggle fought solely in legislative halls, in the press, in the lyceum circuit, in the pulpit. The threat of a black Spartacus waiting to rise in the South pervaded the decade of the fifties; it was John Brown's idea precisely to raise up such leaders. The names of Gabriel, Vesey, Turner and Douglass were familiar names in American households. One modern historian, Harvey Wish, looking back on the period, has written of what he calls "the slave insurrection panic of 1856"—the year that *The Piazza Tales* came off the press.[1] [13]

Nor were slave revolts on the plantations of the South the only items of Negro unrest that Americans could read about either in their daily press or in the pamphlet literature of the slavery controversy. Black mutiny on the high seas was also a familiar thing. Although by the mid-century, Captain Amasa Delano's original *Narrative* was apparently unknown to contemporary readers of *Benito Cereno,* the mutiny described in it was no antique chronicle either for them or for Melville. Such mutinies, a part of the living tissue of American life, had

---

[1] Nor was the panic confined to the United States. Herbert Aptheker [*American Negro Slave Revolts*] writes: "...the American envoys to England, France, and Spain...meeting in Ostend in 1854, let the world know that...Cuba ought to belong to the United States. An important argument for this, they declared, lay in the possibility that the slaves of the Pearl of the Antilles might emulate their brethren of St. Domingo. [Was Melville thinking of St. Domingo when he changed the real Cereno's *Tryal* to the *San Dominick?*] Were that prize within the strong hand of the United States, she would not permit the flames to extend to our neighboring shores, seriously to endanger or actually to consume the fair fabric of our Union."

probably begun not long after Captain John Hawkins had pioneered the slave trade in his good ship, *The Jesus*.[2]

In Melville's young manhood, two famous slave mutinies filled the press—the first on the Spanish blackbird *Amistad* in the summer of 1839, the second on the brig *Creole* two years later. Four nights out of Havana en route to Port Principe the fifty-four slaves on the *Amistad* murdered its captain, sailed the ship north and ultimately surrendered to the authorities at Montauk Point after ascertaining that they were in a "free country." As described in New York[14] and New England newspapers, the appearance of the *Amistad* is strangely reminiscent of the *San Dominick's:*

Her sides were covered with barnacles and long tentacles of seaweed streamed from her cable and her sides at the water line. Her jibs were torn and big rents and holes appeared in both foresail and mainsail as they flapped in the gentle breeze. Most of the paint was gone from the gunwails and rail—over which [peered] coal-black African faces.

The *Amistad* case became a *cause célèbre* of the abolitionists, who hired Rufus Choate to defend the Negroes against the claims of the Spaniards. Kali, one of the mutineers, travelled throughout the North on a speaking tour, while on the New York stage the event was dramatized in *The Black Schooner,* whose protagonist was Joseph Cinquez, leader of the mutiny. Cinquez, reported to be the son of an African prince, "of magnificent physique, commanding presence, forceful manners and commanding oratory," reminds one of Atufal, a prince in his own country.

Every step in the progress of the case was followed by the Northern press. The abolitionist campaign was a strong one, and two years later, as Melville was shipping for the South Seas, Justice Story delivered the opinion of the Supreme Court—a historic decision which stated legally for the first time that black men, carried from their homes as slaves, had the right, when seeking liberty, to kill anyone who tried to deprive them of it. In the North there was great sympathy for the mutineers of the *Amistad* and much hostility against the Spaniards who, claiming indemnity for their lost slaves, called them "pirates who,

---

2 To cite a few: in 1731 and 1747, on Rhode Island slavers returning from the Guinea coast the Negroes killed all the whites in one instance, and spared the captain and his son in the other; in 1732, on a New Hampshire slaver, they murdered captain and crew; in 1735, slaves broke into the powder room of the *Dolphin* of London and blew her up off the African coast; in 1761, a Boston slaver lost forty of its Negroes in an insurrection. The trials of the conspirators in the Denmark Vesey plot of 1822 revealed that they had sent a letter asking for help to the president of the Republic of San Domingo. The letter was carried by a Negro cook on board a Northern schooner. The press of the 1850's is full of reports of battles between slave-runners and the authorities; such battles were the frequent subjects of popular juvenile and adult literature.

by revolt, murder, and robbery, had deprived" owners of their property.

The case of the *Creole* received even wider publicity. In the fall of 1841, the brig had set sail from Hampton Roads for New Orleans with a cargo of tobacco and 135 slaves. One Sunday night nineteen of the slaves led by one Madison Washington—a fugitive who had returned from Canada to[15] rescue his wife, had been captured, and was being returned to bondage—rose up, killed a slavedealer on board, wounded the captain, cowed the passengers, and forced the crew to sail the ship to free Nassau. There, although the British authorities held the nineteen on charges of mutiny, the rest, despite the protest of the American consul, were freed. The indignation of Southerners in Congress was violent, and Daniel Webster, then Secretary of State, supported them, for which action Garrison, Channing and Sumner excoriated him. For a dozen years the case was in and out of the papers, and it was only two years before *Benito Cereno* was written that the quarrel between the Americans and the British was finally arbitrated by the Englishman, Joshua Bates, whom Melville had dined with in London in 1849. Some years later, Frederick Douglass wrote a short story, whose hero was Madison Washington.

It was in the atmosphere of the slave insurrection panic of the middle fifties, of the mounting tension of the slavery controversy (in which Melville's relatives and friends took varying positions), of the *Amistad* and *Creole* mutinies, that *Benito Cereno* was conceived and written.

Is it credible, then, that Melville meant *Benito Cereno* to have little or nothing to do with slavery and rebellion, or with the character of the Negro as slave and rebel? . . .

The most central and completely described character of *Benito Cereno* is Amasa Delano, through whose temperament filters most, although not all, of the action of the tale. On Delano both schools of interpretation concur in at least one respect: in the Yankee captain Melville meant to paint a satiric portrait. An important question, however, still remains to be answered: What is satirized? What in Delano is the target of Melville's irony? That the duped Delano[16] was meant to be simple, even stupid, both schools agree. It is at the point where agreement stops and divergence begins that we find the crux of the problem of *Benito Cereno*, for whereas one school holds that Delano was naive because he could not discern the motiveless malignity in Babo and his fellows, it is the contention of the other that his stupidity lay in his blindness to the innate and heroic desire of the Negroes for freedom, to their dignity as human beings.

Which side is right? What did Melville mean?

The major premise for the development of Delano's character is given quite clearly in Melville's first assessment of it: Delano was "a person of a singularly undistrustful good-nature, not liable, except on extraordinary and repeated incentives, and hardly then, to indulge in personal alarms, any way involving the imputation of malign evil in man." Thus Melville declares that Delano is blind—not to goodness or courage or the love of freedom in anybody—but to the "malign evil in man." Delano is trusting. Is he intelligent? Not at all. That he is a good-natured fool Melville points up in the ironic sentence that follows: "Whether, in view of what humanity is capable, such a trait implies, along with a benevolent heart, more than ordinary quickness and accuracy of intellectual perception, may be left to the wise to determine." Now, the tale that follows is precisely the parable by which the wise may so determine; by it readers are to be educated; in it Captain Delano is to be educated. Yet, as we shall see, the final truth that Delano will learn is that Babo is the embodiment of "malign evil," Cereno of goodness maligned. For Delano to learn this new truth, he must unlearn the old errors of his period of delusion.

What are these old errors about Negroes in general and about those of the *San Dominick* in particular that Delano must unlearn? He thinks that they are all jolly, debonair, "sight-loving Africans," who invariably love bright colors and fine shows; that their gentleness peculiarly fits them to[17] be good body servants and that they possess the "strange vanity" of faithful slaves; that they sing as they work because they are uniquely musical; that they are generally stupid, the white being the shrewder race; that mulattoes are not made devilish by their white blood and that the hostility between mulattoes and blacks will not allow them to conspire against whites; that yellow pirates could not have committed the cruel acts rumored of them. And of all these beliefs he is disabused. He is a man who has had "an old weakness for negroes"; who has always been "not only benign, but familiarly and humorously so" to them; who has been fond of watching "some free man of color at work or play," and if on a voyage he chanced to have a black sailor, had inevitably been on "chatty and half-gamesome terms with him." He is a man who, "like most men of good, blithe heart... took to negroes, not philanthropically, but genially, just as other men to Newfoundland dogs," and who on the *San Dominick* speaks a "blithe word" to them; who admires the "royal spirit" of Atufal and pities his chains; who suspects that Don Benito is a hard master and that slavery breeds ugly passions in men—and in every item he will be proven blind.

To Delano, in short, Negroes are jolly primitives, uncontaminated nature, simple hearts, people to be patronized. The "uncivilized" Negro women aboard the *San Dominick* are "tender of heart"; as the "slumbering negress" is awakened by her sprawling infant, she catches the child up "with maternal transports," covering it with kisses. "There's naked nature, now; pure tenderness and love," thinks Captain Delano, "well pleased." Gazing at the kindly sea and sky, he is sorry for betraying an atheist doubt about the goodness of Providence.

All these things Delano has believed—and they are all to be proven false in fact, masquerades behind which lurk "ferocious pirates," barbarous sadists, both male and female, shrewd wolves, devilish mulattoes. In the course of[18] events he must learn what Cereno already knows, and Cereno it is who rams the lesson home, generalizing what the obtuse Yankee has been constitutionally unable to comprehend. His last words are, "The negro." Delano has no answer; it is the silence of agreement. "You were undeceived," Cereno had said to him, "would it were so with all men." Delano has been stripped of his delusions; he is wiser. But wiser in what respect? In that he now knows that Negroes are courageous lovers of freedom? Not at all; rather wiser in that he has at last discerned the blacks to be wolves in the wool of gentle sheep.

The shock of recognition makes brothers of Delano and Cereno; they now can speak with "fraternal unreserve"; indeed, there was never any real basic opposition between them. Delano was no philanthropic abolitionist; he was not even anti-slavery—he offered to buy Babo; for him the San Dominick carries "negro slaves, amongst other valuable freight"; he intends his sugar, bread and cider for the whites alone, the wilted pumpkins for the slaves; he orders his men to kill as few Negroes as possible in the attack, for they are to divide the cargo as a prize; he stops a Spanish sailor from stabbing a chained slave, but for him the slaves are "ferocious pirates" and he says no word against their torture and execution, far more cruel than the machinations of Babo. Like Cereno he too has been "a white noddy, a strange bird, so called from its lethargic, somnambulistic character, being frequently caught by hand at sea." No more will he be a somnambulist in the presence of evil. Meeting another San Dominick he will not again be duped.

And Cereno? He is the good man, the religious man, whose nobility may be seen in his hidalgo profile, in health, perhaps, something like the graceful Spanish gentry who listened to Ishmael tell his Town-Ho story, the real aristocrat that the superficial democrat, Delano, had wrongly suspected. Everywhere Melville pruned the Cereno of Delano's Narrative to vein and flesh him with altruism and goodness.[19] In life, he was a swindler, a liar, the scorn of his friends, the stabber of a helpless Negro slave; as Lewis Mumford justly declares, in the original narrative, Cereno is "far more cruel, barbarous, and unprincipled than the forces he contends against." All this is gone in the tale. Pathetic and beaten he is, done to death by his experience, but only because he has been an altruist and trusted the slaves as tractable; the good man's illusions of goodness have been fatally overthrown. At the last Cereno reminds one of Bartleby the scrivener, who has rejected life as a blank and monstrous wall he cannot pierce. Whereas in Bartleby the wall is the enigma of life, in Cereno it is Babo.

And what of Babo? Let us forget that objectively he is a maritime

Nat Turner. What was he for Melville—for the tale? He is the "malign evil" that Delano at first cannot comprehend—and all his brothers and sisters are that evil too. The fact that for *us*, the heirs of Lincoln, his cunning ruthlessness is worthily motivated is not an issue *within the story;* to Melville "faithful" Babo is an "honest" Iago; to Delano and Cereno he is a ferocious pirate, not a black David. A pirate has motives; his motives are malign—a fact not necessary to discuss.

Babo is more like a minor character of *Omoo,* one Bembo, than like Jackson or Bland. Did Melville, finding Babo in Delano's *Narrative,* remember the "swart" Mowree Bembo, harpooneer of the *Julia?* "Unlike most of his countrymen," Bembo was short and "darker than usual." It was whispered that he was a cannibal, so fearless and blood-thirsty was he in his desire to kill whales. Extremely sensitive to slight, he would not tolerate joshing from Sydney Ben: "Bembo's teeth were at his throat." Thrown down on the deck by Ben's friends, Bembo was "absolutely demoniac; he lay glaring, and writhing on the deck without attempting to rise." In revenge he plots to wreck the ship.[20] Thwarted, Bembo "never spoke one word. . . . His only motive could have been a desire to revenge the contumely heaped upon him the night previous, operating upon a heart irreclaimably savage, and at no time fraternally disposed toward the crew."

True Melville found the name Babo in Delano's *Narrative,* but the Babo of *Benito Cereno* is actually a composite of two characters in the source, Babo and Mure. Melville chose Babo—the baboon, ring-leader of the Negroes who are primitives, beasts.[3] The imagery connected with Babo and the other Negroes throughout the tale is strictly from the bestiary. The *San Dominick's* headpiece is a dark satyr in a mask, trampling the neck of a writhing figure, likewise masked. It is, of course, Babo trampling on Don Benito: Babo is the satyr, a lecherous sylvan deity, sensual, part beast. He is the "lion rampant" in the white field of the flag of Spain. The four grizzled junk-into-oakum pickers are "sphynx like"—silent, inscrutable, anti-human, part beast; the "ebon flights of naked boys and girls, three or four years old, darting in and out of the den's mouth," are "like a social circle of bats, sheltering in some friendly cave. . . ." Babo "snakishly writhes" to kill Benito— the image is Satanic and is associated with Babo's "central purpose." The Negro women are leopardesses, the nursing mother a doe whose

---

3 Is there an echo here too of Baubo, obscene leader of the witches in Goethe's *Faust,* which Melville possibly was reading while writing his story? And was a writer in the issue of *Putnam's* that carried the final installment of *Benito Cereno* alluding to Babo when in an article "About Niggers" he had this to say: "But with all this charming jollity and waggishness, the nigger has terrible capacities for revenge and hatred (which opportunity may develope, as in St. Domingo), and which ought to convince the skeptic that he is a man, not a baboon . . . our Southern partners will learn that they are no joke. The nigger is no joke, and no baboon; he is simply a black man, and I say: Give him fair play and let us see what he will come to."

fawn sprawls at its dam's lapped breasts, its paws searching, its mouth and nose rooting for the mark, while it grunts. As the *San Dominick* gives way before the onslaught of the *Bachelor's Delight,* the retreating Negroes[21] are "cawing crows"; during the fight on deck, they are "black-fish" among which swordfish run amok; their "red tongues drool wolf-like from their black mouths" (while the white sailors fight with pale set faces); to the source account Melville adds a strong hint that Aranda's skeleton has been cannibalistically prepared. Most of these are Melville's direct images—not Delano's. Moreover, to show that neither Christianity nor white blood can redeem this beastliness there is the "mulatto, named Francesco, the cabin steward, of a good person and voice, having sung in the Valparaiso churches"—all this added by Melville to Cereno's original deposition. It is Francesco, "just before a repast, in the cabin," who proposes "to the negro Babo, poisoning a dish for the generous Captain Amasa Delano."[4]

Is there anything in the color imagery of *Benito Cereno* to refute this analysis of character and plot? Schiffman maintains that the reversal of conventional black-white symbolism in *Moby-Dick* is applied also in *Benito Cereno* and is proof positive that white Cereno is an image of evil. The opposite is the case. In *Moby-Dick,* the traditional equation is rejected so that in the new equation black may equal virtue and white evil. In *Benito Cereno* the traditional equation is merely transposed so that black (delusively virtuous or harmless to early Delano) may equal blacker (incarnate iniquity to later Delano), while white (delusively evil and suspiciously malign to early Delano) may equal whiter (tragically victimized virtue to later Delano). Beyond this, within the color schema of *Benito Cereno* wherever black and white are used for ambiguous or foreboding effects, the[22] aim is simply conventional deception that builds up wrong leads in order to contrive mechanical suspense and a trick finale. Is Cereno's *real* whiteness (conventional) anything like the whiteness of the whale? Is Babo's blackness (conventional) anything like Pip's "lustrous ebony, panelled in King's cabinets"? Again let us go to the text.

As the *San Dominick* swings into view, the opening tone is gray—an appropriate mixture of white and black portending ambiguity, uncertainty, shadows ahead—and the grayness lingers throughout the tale. The *San Dominick* shows "no colors"; what light there is on the ship streams "equivocally enough" from the cabin, "much like the sun" (Cereno), which through "low, creeping clouds" (the Negroes) shows

---

[4] Note also Dago, another invention, "who had been for many years a grave-digger among the Spaniards...." Was Melville reversing his conception of Daggoo in *Moby-Dick,* who was ready to dig a grave for his Spanish tormenter? As we have pointed out, there is more than a hint in the forecastle tableau of *Moby-Dick* that Melville's choice of the Spanish sailor to quarrel with Daggoo was based on the old conflict between Spaniard and Moor.

like a Lima intriguante's one sinister eye through the Indian loop-hole of her "dusk" saya-y-manta. The flawed bell of the *San Dominick* has a muted gray sound. The ship is "pipe-clayed"—a grayish white; later it is "bleached." And it is wreathed with "dark festoons of sea-grass."

Don Benito himself is "dusked by ill-health." When Delano suspects him most, he is "the dark Spaniard," who sulks in "black vapours," or in "dark spleen." Conventional black-white pairing is seen in Melville's comment: "There was a difference between the idea of Don Benito's darkly preordaining Captain Delano's fate, and Captain Delano's lightly arranging Don Benito's"; again, when Delano suspects Cereno and Atufal of complicity, he thinks of the "Spaniard behind—his creature before." Says Melville: "to rush from darkness to light was his involuntary choice." In assessing a Spanish sailor Delano associates black with evil: "If, indeed, there be any wickedness on board this ship, thought Captain Delano, be sure that man has fouled his hand in it, even as he now fouls in it the pitch." The mahogany chair and settee of Babo's shaving salon are suitably black and Babo follows his nicking of Don Benito's neck with a "dusky comment of silence."[23]

At every opportunity conventional black imagery is worked into the story as symbol, lure and pun. Cereno's "gloomy disdain" is interpreted by Delano: "as if, forced to black bread themselves," he deemed it but equity to make his associates eat the same. Again, Delano, admiring Don Benito's aristocratic profile, reproaches himself for his suspicion: "In short, to the Spaniard's black-letter text, it was best, for awhile, to leave open margin." How hard and consciously Melville worked at this may be seen in a revision of the *Putnam's* printing that he made for *The Piazza Tales*: in *Putnam's* the "cawing crows," as they attempt their flight, hail "the now dusky expanse of ocean"; in the revision, they hail "the now dusky moors of ocean."

The house or ship as symbolic image, so often employed by Poe, Hawthorne, Twain and other writers of the century, is joined to conventional black-white symbolism in the tale. Thus one of the first images of the *San Dominick* is of a "white-washed monastery after a thunder-storm" inhabited by dark-cowled Black Friars who turn out to be black dominies of Dis. Like the House of Usher with its cracked wall, the "strange house" of the *San Dominick* is a ruined mansion, whose rotten balustrade is partly stained with hell's pitch, as is the "purple-black" (Dante's black) "tarred-over panel of its state-cabin door."

Where then *within the story* does Melville use black-white symbolism in the manner of *Moby-Dick?* The reverse-symbolism of *Moby-Dick*, it must be concluded, is simply not present in *Benito Cereno*, nor indeed, will it ever appear again in Melville's fiction, except, perhaps, in a brief interlude on the first page of *Billy Budd*. How different really are seemingly like images in the two works. In *Moby-Dick*, when little Flask is held up by giant Daggoo, Melville tells us—perhaps unnecessarily, but he does not want the point to be missed—that the bearer was nobler than the rider. In *Benito Cereno:* "As master and man stood before him, the black upholding the white, Captain Delano could not but[24] bethink him of the beauty of that relationship which presented such a spectacle of fidelity on the one hand and confidence on the other." The reality, of course, is the negation of fidelity and confidence, and the satire is clear: the true picture is that of satyr trampling on innocence, of black headsman with white head on block, of "Nubian sculptor finishing off a white statue-head." How different the conflict between Daggoo and the Spaniard on the *Pequod* and that between the slave and the Spanish boy on the *San Dominick*.

No, there is no ambiguity about the meaning of black in *Benito Cereno*. "The negro"—Don Benito's last words—whether read as Spanish abstract noun for "blackness" or "darkness," as English concrete noun with abstract connotations, as Swedenborgian emblem, Emersonian correspondence, Bushnellian logos, or simply as synonym for Babo and his fellows,[5] is the wise man's final answer to that question which at the start of the parable was "left to the wise to determine." And the answer of Melville, the wise author, is clear. "I think I understand," says Delano in the conversation that ushers in the close of the tale: "You generalize, Don Benito, and mournfully enough." But Delano does not yet understand, for he thinks the good man's gloom proceeds only from the memory of the time when the American thought him a monster, from the ambiguities of life. Banish that memory, he counsels, "yon bright sun has forgotten it all." When Cereno rejects nature's balm, Delano cannot fathom him: "You are saved: what has cast such a shadow upon you?" The question recalls the opening adumbration of the tale: "Shadows present, foreshadowing deeper shadows to come." Don Benito[25] must spell out the full answer; it is—"The negro." Delano, wiser now, has nothing more to say; he knows finally that "malign evil" exists—and where. "There was no more conversation that day." It is the finality of the closing lines of Poe's *Narrative of Arthur Gordon Pym,* where the essential evil of black men in their darkness is written in the black waters and on the ageless rocks. To ignore the Negro in *Benito Cereno,* as some have done, is to do what Wolf Mankowitz has done in his critique of Eliot's *Gerontion,* omitting the Jew in order to praise the piece's "enduring significance."

Is it possible, then, to go along with Schiffman when he says that

---

5 That Melville, on the concrete level at least, meant "The negro" to mean Babo, may be seen in a redundant sentence he deleted from the penultimate paragraph of the first printing: "And yet the Spaniard could, upon occasion, verbally refer to the negro, as has been shown; but look upon him he would not, or could not."

Melville meant Don Benito's last words to be a villain's final concession
of defeat by the heroic will to freedom of the Negro people? Once more
it must be said, however regretfully, that such a view is the outcome of
generous hope. It is Babo, the prototype of innate depravity, who,
like an unrepentant villain, an Iago indeed, gazes "unabashed" from
his death's head of unfathomably malign subtlety at the goodness he
has murdered. For Melville, in his story, Babo was a victor in the malign
sense only.

   True it is, of course, that Melville, even in his failures, is almost
always an adroit artist, and as many have noted, there are moments
of undeniable power in *Benito Cereno*. But looked at objectively, the
tale seems a plummet-like drop from the unconditionally democratic
peaks of *White-Jacket* and *Moby-Dick*—an "artistic sublimation" not,
as Schiffman maintains, of anti-slaveryism, but rather of notions of
black primitivism dear to the hearts of slavery's apologists, a sublimation in fact of all that was sleazy, patronizing, backward and fearful in
the works that preceded it. It is to put the matter too mildly perhaps to
say, as Charles Neider does, that "Melville glosses over extenuating circumstances in his effort to blacken the blacks and[26] whiten the
whites, to create poetic images of pure evil and pure virtue," so that
the result is "sometimes unfortunate in the feelings it arouses against
the Negro," or to say, as Matthiessen does, that "the embodiment of
good in the pale Spanish captain and of evil in the mutinied African
crew, though pictorially and theatrically effective, was unfortunate in
raising unanswered questions."[6] When Melville, at a certain point in
his development, repudiated his superficial, old notions (which
were Delano's too) about the innately jolly, minstrel, religious nature
of Negroes, it was, sadly enough, not to perceive the free spirit of the
Tawneys and the Daggoos as the reality behind the masks. Instead,
in *Benito Cereno,* the fear and doubt of slave-revolt proclaimed in
Mardi and implied in *White-Jacket* were to be transmuted into hatred
of the "ferocious pirates" of the *San Dominick*—as were demoniac
Bembo into demoniac Babo; lordly Daggoo into Atufal, prince of hell;
the "poor mulatto," Rose-Water, into the sinister mulatto, Francesco;
the good slavemaster—Randolph of Roanoke, the purser of the *Never-
sink,* the slaveholder of Vivenza who was not an insensate Nulli—into
Don Benito Cereno. . . .[27]

---

[6] Matthiessen continues: "Although the Negroes were savagely vindictive and
drove a terror of blackness into Cereno's heart, the fact remains that they were
slaves and that evil had thus originally been done to them. Melville's failure to
reckon with this fact within the limits of his narrative makes its tragedy, for all
its prolonged suspense, comparatively superficial." Matthiessen's judgments on
Benito Cereno are curiously contradictory. Our point, of course, is that Melville
did "reckon with this fact within the limits of his narrative" (*American Renaissance*
[New York, 1941], p. 508).

〰〰〰

BABO AND THE DESTRUCTION OF THE STEREOTYPE
Warren D'Azevedo

. . .
As for Babo, "whose brain . . . had schemed and led the revolt," Melville writes:

. . . sensing all was over, he uttered no sound, and could not be forced to. His aspect seemed to say: since I cannot do deeds, I will not speak words. . . . Some months after, dragged to the gibbet at the tail of a mule . . . [he] . . . met his voiceless end. The body was burned to ashes; but for many days, the head, that hive of subtlety, fixed on a pole in the Plaza, met, unabashed, the gaze of the whites, and across the Plaza looked toward St. Bartholomew's church, in whose vaults slept then, as now, the recovered bones of Aranda; and across the Rimac bridge looked toward the monastery, on Mount Agonia without; where, three months after being dismissed by the court, Benito Cereno, borne on the bier, did, indeed, follow his leader.

It is inconceivable that any critic should so miss the obvious implications of Melville's concluding lines[137]. . . . To argue that a condemnation of Negro slavery in the South was Melville's main intent would be fruitless. On the other hand, it is shocking that there has been so thorough an underestimation of the profound insight into the issue of human bondage which Melville brought to bear on the characterizations and theme of this story. Withdrawal and introspection may have been an important aspect of Melville's personality, but for all his discomfiture over the practical demands of social unrest in his time, he does not deviate ever from his hatred of human oppression. Unable as he was to accept the solutions posed by the Abolitionists in terms of action (even satirizing their militancy in his earlier works), he asserted without equivocation that slavery was "a blot, foul as the crater-pool of hell." With the great creative experience of *Moby Dick* behind him, and confronted with the increasing political agitation of the day, Melville had, in *Benito Cereno,* returned once again to the straight narrative tale with a new and fuller understanding of his craft.

That this story did not achieve the popular success that Melville might well have expected is accountable for a number of reasons. The most popular stories of the pre-Civil War period were militantly partisan. The imagination of the public had been fired by the Abolitionist

From Warren D'Azevedo, "Revolt on the *San Dominick,*" *Phylon,* XVII (June 1956), 129–140. Reprinted by permission of *Phylon.*

cause and the pitch of indignation steadily heightened as, at last, a slow realization of conditions in the South began to dawn. The most poorly written, sentimental fiction was avidly read as long as it portrayed the southern planter as a personification of evil, the slave as the submissive victim of luridly described cruelties, and the northern white as the avenging angel. Except for the many actual accounts by fugitive slaves themselves, the Negro was either portrayed as a wordy philosopher in chains, full of northern white sentiments, or a cringing pathetic waiting to be rescued by his protectors of the North. Before this time the Negro had appeared mainly as a picturesque or ludicrous character in the fiction of Irving, Cooper, Simms, Poe and others. Not until much later was there any evidence, little as it was, that white writers were beginning to understand the Negro people as an extremely vital influence upon American culture.

In this context *Benito Cereno* is an unusually outstanding work. It strikes close to us today now that we have valuable experience to look back upon and the issues are clearer. Nowhere in the story can the[138] reader detect any condescension toward the Negro characters, except in the thoughts of Captain Delano, whose personality and background are clearly defined for us by Melville. They are juxtaposed against the characters of Delano and Don Benito with equal dignity and forcefulness. He does not use dialect or broken speech which had begun to be a popular device in fiction. This is noteworthy because it indicates he was in some way aware that to do so in his time, before a general development of such usages had taken place in literature, would distort his characters. Through Captain Delano at the beginning of the story we receive the conventional view of Babo and the other Negroes on the ship. But by the end of the story they are intelligent and determined human beings fighting their way out of slavery.

Babo stands out as one of the great Negro figures created by white authors in American fiction. Melville wisely did not presume, as did many writers, to know a Negro slave's innermost mind or the complex structure of his personality. He shows us Babo, instead, through the eyes and accounts of the other characters. We learn about him by what he does. He is the awesomely brilliant leader of a revolt under appalling conditions. He has masterminded a plan so exacting that it almost succeeds. He is only sinister to the degree that the reader identifies with the characters and prejudices of Delano or Cereno. His motive is to free himself and his companions from slavery and to return to "any negro country." His performance in victory and defeat is heroic, a man who "if he cannot do deeds . . . will not speak words." He acts never in desperation, even during the violence of the revolt, but always as one keeping clearly in mind the main objective. His keen intelligence, Atufal's magnificent dignity, and the compact unity of all the Negroes on the ship, leave an impression on the reader achieved by few white writers even to this day.

Both Captain Delano and Don Benito are "decent" men. They are bound by circumstances the basis of which they had never before questioned. It is this fundamental decency and sensitivity of Don Benito that leads to his torment in the end. The mutiny, and the dynamic authority wielded by Babo, has not only struck a deep blow at his own concept of white supremacy and personal prestige, but has thrown his whole being into moral confusion. His close friend Aranda, of whom we know little, has received the full brunt of consequences as the owner of slaves. Once released from the actual dominance of Babo, Cereno cannot react with anger or revenge, but remains immobilized under a tremendous pall of guilt and horror. His world is "honeycombed" beneath his feet.

Captain Delano, on the other hand, reacts just as one would expect him to do within the scope of Melville's portrayal. Once he has overcome the shock that his mind has totally "deceived" him, he takes command[139] of the situation, gives chase to the mutineers and returns them to a tribunal of justice. Never does he question that the issue is more than one of law and order. His duty done, everything as it should be, he is sympathetic but uncomprehending before Don Benito's depression.

The theme of the story, the psychological impact of slavery and revolt upon Delano and particularly Don Benito is one which had no precedent in Melville's time, nor has this fact been adequately recognized since. The redundant emphasis upon Melville as an aloof and tormented mystic has been cosily entrenched in profuse romantic criticism of his work, and has been employed more or less to divert attention from the disturbing and profounder implications of the story. Where the great hopelessness and defeat of Don Benito, as a pawn of a system, may not have been direct enough for Melville's contemporaries, it may be too direct for some of ours. Where the withering irony created by Captain Delano's patronizing good will might have been too close to satire for the comfort of many northern whites of the mid 1800's, it is a finger of accusation today. And where Babo would not have fit into the picture of the pleading slave waiting for deliverance, we, today, have seen his proud "unabashed" face more and more frequently among us.

In every way *Benito Cereno*, as a story of the relationship between Negroes and whites, is far in advance of its time. Sterling Brown sums it up well in his study, *The Negro Character in American Fiction,* when he writes:

Although opposed to slavery Melville does not make *Benito Cereno* into an abolitionist tract; he is more concerned with a thrilling narrative and character portrayal. But although the mutineers are bloodthirsty and cruel, Melville does not make them into villains; they revolt as mankind has always revolted. Because Melville was unwilling to look upon men as 'Isolatoes,' wishing instead to discover the 'common continent of man,' he came nearer to the truth in his scattered pictures of a few unusual Negroes than do the other authors of the period.[140]

〽〽〽

IN DEFENSE OF BABO

Allen Guttmann

. . .

The story opens with a three-paragraph "prologue" leading to the section in which Captain Delano acts as "central intelligence."[1] This prologue sets the scene for Melville's persistent theme of moral ambiguity. Color symbolism dominates:

Everything was mute and calm; everything gray. The sea, though undulated into long roods of swells, seemed fixed, and was sleeked at the surface like waved lead that has cooled and set in the smelter's mould. The sky seemed a gray surtout. Flights of troubled gray fowl, kith and kin with flights of troubled gray vapours among which they were mixed, skimmed low and fitfully over the waters. . . . Shadows present, foreshadowing deeper shadows to come.

The comparison of the sea with molten and then solidified lead fuses connotations of fixity and heaviness with those of grayness. The emphasized grayness is—as Guy A. Cardwell notes in his excellent discussion of the tale's color symbolism—a parallel for the moral ambiguity which will confound Captain Delano. Melville has been accused of unimaginative borrowing, but this grayness is a transformation of the *Narrative of Voyages and Travels* of Captain Amasa Delano, wherein we find merely a ship without an ensign. The fourth paragraph, with its repeated reference to "Captain Delano's surprise," introduces the innocent Yankee as the central intelligence, the Jamesian reflector who will mirror not reality but a constant parade of contradictory images. Delano's role is continually stressed. Almost every paragraph contains verbs such as "seem" or "appear." Consider, for example, the description of the sea (quoted above) or the paragraph which introduces another of Melville's transformations of the original source, the pattern of religious imagery. To Delano, the[40] strange ship (formerly the *Tryal,* now renamed the *San Dominick*)

From Allen Guttmann, "The Enduring Innocence of Captain Amasa Delano," *Boston University Studies in English,* V (Spring 1961), 35–45. Reprinted by permission of *Boston University Studies in English* and the author.

1 If the concept of "central intelligence" seems anachronistic, one need only recall the pains taken in *Moby-Dick* to differentiate the views of Ishmael and Ahab and Stubb and Starbuck. For instance, the first sentence of Chapter XLII, "What the White Whale was to Ahab has been hinted; what, at times, he was to me [Ishmael] remains unsaid."

appeared like a whitewashed monastery after a thunder-storm, seen perched upon some dun cliff among the Pyrenees. But it was no purely fanciful resemblance which now ... *almost led Captain Delano to think* that nothing less than a ship-load of monks was before him. Peering over the bulwarks were *what really seemed*, in the hazy distance, throngs of dark cowls; while, fitfully revealed through the open port-holes, other dark moving figures were dimly descried, *as* of Black Friars pacing the cloisters (my italics).

Delano's role is further underscored by constant references to his "impressions," "observations," "thoughts": "This poor fellow now, *thought the pained American*, is the victim of ... sad superstition," and, on the same page, "This is some mulish mutineer, *thought Captain Delano*" (my italics). Delano continually changes his general interpretation of what he observes; although he has a "singularly undistrustful good-nature," he alternates between absolute trust and a suspicion that, under Don Benito's "aspect of infantile weakness, the most savage energies might be couched—those velvets of the Spaniard but the silky paws to his fangs." (Note the use of animal imagery to describe the white man.) Captain Delano speculates: "The man was an imposter. Some low-born adventurer, masquerading as an oceanic grandee; yet so ignorant of the first requisites of mere gentlemanhood as to be betrayed into the present remarkable indecorum." Captain Delano fears that Don Benito is really a pirate, he lists reasons for doubting the appearances of things, and he resolves his doubts only to doubt again. Captain Delano's tendency is to admire the Negroes: "His attention had been drawn to a slumbering negress ... with youthful limbs carelessly disposed, under the lee of the bulwarks, like a doe in the shade of a woodland rock." When the Negress kisses her child, Delano thinks of this as "pure tenderness and love," and he feels that the Negresses aboard are all "unsophisticated as leopardesses; loving as doves." Their naturalness contrasts with Don Benito's tawdry artificiality. Atufal is seen as an imposing and a regal figure. He resembles the *Pequod's* Daggoo, "a gigantic, coal-black negro-savage, with a lion-like tread—an Ahasuerus to behold." As Ishmael was struck by Daggoo, so Captain Delano is struck by the silence and the kingliness of Atufal, "a gigantic black." Delano surveys, "not without a mixture of admiration, the colossal form of the negro."[41] He exclaims, "Upon my conscience, then, he has a royal spirit in him, this fellow." Atufal's royal spirit contrasts with Don Benito's effeteness and effeminacy. Nevertheless, all these impressions are, in an instant, reversed when Babo attacks Don Benito: "Captain Delano, now with scales dropped from his eyes, saw the negroes, not in misrule, not in tumult, not as if frantically concerned for Don Benito, but with mask torn away, flourishing hatchets and knives, in ferocious piratical revolt. Like delirious black dervishes, the six Ashantees danced on the poop." What reason have we for assuming that this vision of ferocious pirates and delirious dervishes is any *more* accurate a reflection of reality than the vision of kingliness and primitive felicity? What reason have we for assuming that we have found the key to the symbolic padlock which intrigued Captain Delano, that we have untied the symbolic knot that puzzled him? We have *Don Benito's testimony,* as recorded in the long deposition attested to by "Don José de Abos and Padilla, His Majesty's Notary for the Royal Revenue, and Register of this Province, and Notary Public of the Holy Crusade of this Bishopric...." Newton Arvin, echoing G. W. Curtis's complaint over the "dreary documents," objects to Melville's "failure" in not rewriting the "drearily prosaic prose,"[2] but further thought suggests that Melville *wanted* the prose official and dreary because the official and attested view of the matter, the view put forth by Don Benito and ingenuously accepted by Captain Delano, is *the very thing which Melville is subverting.* With its legalistic pretensions of objectivity, the deposition misses the truth as widely as did Delano in his completest innocence. Captain Delano is, again and again, "generous Captain Delano," and each action of the Negroes is interpreted as further evidence of a preternaturally diabolical depravity. The Negresses, for instance, murdered, incited to murder, "testified themselves satisfied at the death of their master," and "sang melancholy songs to the negroes" before and during the struggle for possession of the ship. These melancholy songs were, intentionally, "more inflaming" than other songs would have been. One wonders what kind of song[42] would have proved more desirable. . . . Finally, to revert once more to the aged canard that seems to migrate from one critique to another, Melville *did* rewrite the deposition, and the changes he made serve to increase the importance, to raise the stature, of Babo. In the original version, Babo was killed in the taking of the ship by the Americans. Don Benito testifies, in Melville's tale, that "the negro Babo was he who traced the inscription . . . that the negro Babo was the plotter from first to last; he ordered every murder, and was the helm and keel of the revolt." The *Narrative* reprints the court sentence condemning "the negroes, Mure, Matinqui, Alazase, Yola, Joaquin, Luis, Yau, Mapenda, and Yambaio, to the common penalty of death...." In rewriting this, as in rewriting in *White-Jacket* the fall of Nathaniel Ames, Melville focuses attention on fundamentals. The "common penalty of death" disappears: Babo dies alone.

Benito Cereno ends with a three-paragraph "epilogue" which represents Melville's recovery of the stage from his departed "central intelligence." In this epilogue Benito Cereno expires weakly; Babo dies bravely: "Seeing all was over, [Babo] uttered no sound, and could not be forced to. His aspect seemed to say, since I cannot do deeds, I will not speak words." In this Babo is like Atufal, who had "mounted the steps of the poop, and, like a brave prisoner, brought up to receive sentence, stood in unquailing muteness before Don Benito...." Babo has often been compared to Iago; he seems much more akin to his fellow slave, Epictetus, who had remarked, "I must die. But must I die groan-

---

2 Newton Arvin, *Melville* (New York, 1950), p. 239.

ing? I must be imprisoned.[43] But must I whine as well?"[3] So powerful is Babo's impassivity that, as when confronted by Atufal, Don
Benito turns away. "When pressed by the judges, he fainted." The final
paragraph represents the triumph of Babo's sheer and literally dis-
embodied will:

Some months after, dragged to the gibbet at the tail of a mule, the black met
his voiceless end. The body was burned to ashes; but for many days, the
head, that hive of subtlety, fixed on a pole in the Plaza, met, unabashed, the
gaze of the white; and across the Plaza looked towards St. Bartholomew's
church, in whose vaults slept then, as now, the recovered bones of Aranda:
and across the Rimac bridge looked towards the monastery, on Mount Agonia
without; where, three months after being dismissed by the court, Benito
Cereno, borne on the bier, did, indeed, follow his leader.

All the themes of the story are involved in the ironic conclusion: animal
imagery, barely hinted in the metaphor of the hive, reminds us once
more of the distance between the primitive and the decadent; Christianity, which once provided hope of salvation for the chattel slaves of the
Roman era, is once again associated with death and decay, and Babo,
whose continued and unabashed silence is a victory over mortality
itself, "sees" *his* motto, *his* ironic advice—the "Follow Your Leader"
inscribed beneath the figure-head skeleton of Don Alexandro—carried
out by the corpse of the utterly defeated Don Benito Cereno.

If . . . Don Benito is unheroic, it is because he is not intended as
the hero. Babo, for all his ruthlessness and savagery, is the one person
in the story to struggle against a moral wrong and, in a sense, by his
stoicism conquer it. He was right to rebel. This reading, while not
dependent on Melville's other work, seems truer to the spirit of the man
who wrote admiringly to Hawthorne, "There is the grand truth about
Nathaniel Hawthorne. He says No! in thunder; but the Devil himself
cannot make him say *yes*. For all men who say *yes* lie. . . ."[4] The most
extended analysis of Melville's treatment of Negroes is incomplete if
we forget that the creator of Babo is also the man whose greatest
creation is Captain Ahab: "How can the prisoner reach outside except
by thrusting[44] through the wall? . . . Talk not to me of blasphemy,
man; I'd strike the sun if it insulted me."

Surely it is unnecessary to asume that, in this story, Melville "re-
treated from the advanced position of his earlier works." Captain
Delano's understanding of Babo's mutiny is as inadequate as Starbuck's
understanding of Captain Ahab's quest; the innocent Yankee captain
never does fathom the moral complexities; his "epiphany" is an ironic
revelation of only so much as the "Bishopric's Notary Public" could
see; he remains as unenlightened as the Jamesian hero of *The Aspern
Papers*. His failure is a failure to understand that all men are involved

---

3 Arrian, *Discourses of Epictetus,* tr. P. E. Matheson, in *The Stoic and Epicurean
Philosophers,* ed. Whitney J. Oates (New York, 1957), p. 225.
    4 Eleanor Metcalf, *Herman Melville: Cycle and Epicycle* (Cambridge, 1953),
p. 105.

in evil, that *all men* are subject to the ambiguous "power of blackness" which Harry Levin sees most vividly embodied in this tale.[5] Captain Amasa Delano never realizes what W. H. Auden's[45] schoolchildren realize:

> Those to whom evil is done
> Do evil in return.

---

[5] See *The Power of Blackness* (New York, 1958), pp. 189–190, 196–197. Levin holds the standard interpretation: "Melville was to make a conventionally sinister presentation of darker breeds in the mutinous slaves of *Benito Cereno*," p. 209.

Source, Symbol, and Theme

BENITO CERENO: FROM SOURCE TO SYMBOL

Rosalie Feltenstein

. . .

One of the best ways to see Melville's mastery of technique is to examine his treatment of his source. *Benito Cereno* is no exception to the rule that everything he wrote, with the possible exclusion of *Pierre,* had some foundation in fact, for, as Mr. Harold H. Scudder was the first to show,[1] the story is based upon the eighteenth chapter of Captain Amasa Delano's *Narrative of Voyages,* published in Boston in 1817. Melville's transforming powers reach their culmination in *Benito Cereno,* for the real Delano's narrative is a flatly matter-of-fact account, written with as much artistry and emotion as one would find in a weather report. Delano emerges as a brave, shrewd sea captain, who gives his crew plenty of good, wholesome whippings and who is less interested in the nature of evil than in the Spanish captain's efforts to deprive him of salvage rights. The whole point of the original tale seems to be that Americans should be very cautious in their dealings with foreigners.

So complete is Melville's transmutation of the source that it is far from accurate to say, as Mr. Scudder does, that he found his story ready-made in Delano's book, so that "he merely rewrote this chapter,

---

From Rosalie Feltenstein, "Melville's *Benito Cereno*," *American Literature,* XIX (November 1947), 245–255. By permission of *American Literature* and the author.

[1] "Melville's *Benito Cereno* and Captain Delano's 'Voyages,'" *PMLA,* XLII (1928), 502–532.

including a portion of one of the legal documents appended, suppressing a few items, and making some small additions."[2] . . .[246]

The statement that Melville found his story ready-made is surely contradicted by the extent of the list of his alterations. He changes the names of the two ships from the *Perseverance* and the *Tryal* to the *Bachelor's Delight* and the *San Dominick;* he invents the oakum pickers and the hatchet polishers, the shaving of Cereno by Babo, the appearance of the giant Atufal in chains, the luncheon aboard the Spanish ship, the attack of the two Negroes upon the Spanish seaman, the glimpse of the sailor with the jewel, the incident of the sailor and the knot, and finally, Don Benito's death in a monastery. He also makes Babo, the leader of the revolt, the Spaniard's devoted servant, rather than one Muri, and extends the period of Delano's isolation aboard the Spanish vessel. Instead of suppressing "just a few items," he omits the whole second half of the narrative, which deals with the quarrel between the two captains.

This large omission is part of the procedure by which Melville everywhere elevates the character of Benito Cereno, who, in the source, is as heartless and savage as the slaves, and by which he turns Babo into a manifestation of pure evil. In connection with this process, Melville makes some further alterations. In the source it is the bloodthirsty Cereno himself who, with a hidden dirk, tries to stab one of the slaves and is restrained by Delano. Transferred entirely to Babo, this action provides the crisis of the story and adds a final touch to the portrait of the slave's malignity. The choice of[247] Babo as villain, rather than Muri, is also related to this effort to transfer sympathy entirely to the Spanish captain since it concentrates the source of evil in one person and intensifies the drama of the situation by making the murderous leader of the revolt the same man as the supposedly devoted servant of the victim of the revolt.[3] Melville is everywhere consistent in altering the source to emphasize Babo as the origin of evil. For example, in the legal documents, wherever guilt is laid upon certain slaves or upon the Negroes in general, Melville substitutes "the negro Babo."

There are also some small but very important and significant changes which show how deliberately Melville shaped the rambling source into a beautiful design. In the *Narrative of Voyages,* Delano always refers to the Spanish captain as *Bonito,* although in the appended legal documents he is called *Benito.* The explanation of Melville's choice of one name rather than the other is not clear until one recalls that in Spanish *benito* means "Benedictine [monk]" (*bonito,* of course, means "pretty"). In this change of a single letter lies the clue to many aspects of the story, such as the constant description of the

---

[2] *Ibid.,* p. 502.

[3] Scudder, p. 515, accounts for this alteration by saying that Melville must have felt a "certain sinister suggestiveness" in the name "Babo," which was lacking in "Muri."

Spanish ship and its crew in similes drawn from monastic life, something otherwise inexplicable. At first glimpse, the ship looked like a "white-washed monastery after a thunderstorm," and Captain Delano thought a shipload of monks was before him, for he saw in the hazy distance what seemed to be "throngs of dark cowls" and "other dark moving figures . . . as of Black Friars pacing the cloisters." Babo, in his ragged clothing and with his "composed, deprecatory air," looked "something like a begging friar of Saint Francis"—a purely ironic simile, as one discovers. In the end, Don Benito, with the monk, Infelez ("unhappy," "luckless"), retires to die in a monastery on Mount Agonia.

The change of the name of the Spanish ship from the *Tryal* to the *San Dominick* is also made clear. The Dominicans are known as the Black Friars, whom Delano momentarily thinks he sees aboard the ship, so that the name is not only appropriate for a shipload of Negroes, but also hints of the blackness with which the[248] story is filled. The Dominicans, moreover, are especially associated with the Inquisition in all countries, so that the name is most meaningfully linked with Don Benito's experience. The very first reference to monasticism foreshadows Cereno's withdrawal from the world, overcome by the evil in it. This thread of allusions to monks and monasteries thus leads directly to the center of the story, so that the end is implicit in the beginning, and, running through the tale as it does, it is another means by which Melville ties all together. The results of such apparently trifling alterations of the source show that nothing happens by accident in this story and suggest that one cannot pay too much attention to what Melville is doing.

The rechristening of the American ship, *Perseverance*, as the *Bachelor's Delight* is also very important. At first the original name of the ship may seem more appropriate, at least in connection with Delano, but not when one relates the name to two of the ships met by the *Pequod*. The *Bachelor* was a glad, holiday sort of ship, filled with oil and good luck, homeward bound, and her captain had heard of the white whale but did not believe in it. The *Delight*, "most miserably misnamed," was reduced to wreckage by the whale; and her captain thought that the harpoon had not been forged that would kill the monster. The combination of these two names in the name of Delano's ship is rich in suggestion. On one level, the *Bachelor* has a symbolical relationship to Delano, who was a man "not liable, except on extraordinary and repeated excitement, and hardly then, to indulge in personal alarms in any way involving the imputation of malign evil in man," and who, even after his experience on the *San Dominick*, bids the Spaniard forget the vision of evil, as the sun and the waves do. Cereno, like the *Delight*, has been wrecked by evil and has no hope of resisting its power. Extend the significance of the two captains and the two ships further, and you have an effort to describe through symbols the relationships of human life to evil.

The episodes which Melville adds to the source have several functions. Like some of the alterations, they increase the helpless purity of Don Benito and the wickedness, subtle in its action and[249] brutal in its result, of Babo and his cohorts. They deepen the central mystery, intensify the sinister atmosphere, and increase the suspense, since each incident reveals another facet of the one problem about which Delano speculates as he becomes more and more lost in a labyrinth of suspicion and fear. This material is also the source of powerful irony— the mighty Atufal in chains, Babo's watching all the movements of his master with doglike devotion—which increases the drama of the story.

Benito Cereno, like almost all of Melville's other work, has both an elementary factual level and a level of symbolic extension. With as much power as in *Moby-Dick*, though within narrower limits, Melville again explores the relation of matter and spirit, and through symbolism bridges the inner and outer worlds. Just as, when Ishmael and Queequeg weave a mat, the identification of their actions with the operation of fate and free will in life is so complete that it is finally a "ball of free will" that Ishmael drops, so in *Benito Cereno* the whole factual story is identified with a wider range of consciousness and has more than one mode of being.

By his use of the symbol, Melville presents "even more reality than life itself can show." He does much more than simply follow the Emersonian doctrine that natural facts correspond to spiritual facts. He never loses his firm hold on immediate experience in such a way that material existence drifts away in a transcendental vapor, nor does he present his symbols merely as the correspondence or equation of one object with another. "It is with fiction as with religion," Melville wrote in *The Confidence Man;* "it should present another world, yet one to which we feel the tie." Through solid and detailed physical description, we learn the state of the *San Dominick,* and through such description we are led to realize its spiritual significance. Because Melville establishes the possibility that matter and spirit are one, his symbols are much more[250] complex and subtle than Hawthorne's, for example, which are simply the substitution of one object for another.

Because of this complexity, it is difficult to discuss Melville's symbols outside of their context. In *Benito Cereno* the symbolism is especially resistant to analysis, especially hard to separate from its vehicle, because it is so consistently subordinated to the concrete expression and nowhere emerges as bare abstraction, nor does Melville offer comments and interpretations as he often does in other works. Another difficulty lies in the nature of the symbol of metaphor itself, for, since it tries to express what would otherwise be inexpressible, when one tries to translate it into anything other than itself, one is bound to tell some lies.

Since a "great author is of one substance and often of one theme, and the relation between his various creations is bound to be recipro-cal, even mutual,"[4] it is not surprising that symbols of *Benito Cereno* are all recurrent ones. Again there is a ship, conceived as a microcosm, as in *White-Jacket, Billy Budd,* and *Moby-Dick.* Again it is at sea that men meet unknown and incomprehensible terrors, and on land that things are known and perceptions can be ruled by judgment, as in the law courts of Lima. But the most powerful symbols are related to the two themes that obsessed Melville: the nature of evil and the ambiguity of appearances, especially as related to evil. These themes are the core of *Moby-Dick,* of *Pierre, or the Ambiguities,* of *The Confidence Man: His Masquerade,* and even of such minor pieces as "The Lightning-Rod Man." In *Benito Cereno* the discrepancy between appearance and truth is so complete that every person and every incident appear as their opposites. Again, "pasteboard masks" are the symbol of this am-biguity, and, like the two masked figures on the stern piece, Don Benito, seemingly a villain, and Babo, seemingly a good and faithful servant, are disguised until the moment of revelation. It is this heart-rending ambiguity, this impossibility of valid judgments except by accident, that helps to destroy Don Benito, much more than any physical pain. In his last conversation with Captain Delano, the Spaniard says sadly:

> "You were with me all day; stood with me, sat with me, talked with[251] me, looked at me, ate with me; and yet, your last act was to clutch for a villain, not only an innocent man, but the most pitiable of all men. To such a degree may malign machinations and deceptions impose, so far may even the best man err, in judging the conduct of one with the recesses of whose condition he is not acquainted. But you were forced to it; and you were in time undeceived. Would that, in both respects, it was so ever, and with all men."

The most baffling ambiguities arise in relation to evil, and in Melville's conception of evil lies the central power of this story. In most fiction, evil is not very impressive, since it is usually very vaguely sketched, or involves only some social misconduct, or has no function except to push along the plot, or else it is simply laughed away, for, as Screwtape remarks, devils are predominantly comic figures in the modern imagination.[5] With Melville, evil is a mighty living force, at once physical and metaphysical, an identification which gives his con-ception great strength and makes it seem much closer to what may be reality than one finds in most writers. Because of his identification, just as it is false to equate Melville's symbols with any one object, it is false to say that evil is in Babo, or that Babo is like evil. The closest one can come to an accurate statement is to say that Babo is evil, for Melville makes no divisions between the symbol and the thing symbolized.

---

[4] R. P. Blackmur, "The Craft of Herman Melville," *Virginia Quarterly Review,* XIV (1938), 274.

[5] C. S. Lewis, *The Screwtape Letters* (New York, 1942), p. 40.

In *Benito Cereno* Melville is no longer asking why evil should exist and be so mighty. Instead he is examining in the actions of the Negroes how evil operates and, in Don Benito and Delano, what its effects are. The fundamental evil of men is freed to act because Don Benito has confidence; he trusts the Negroes and allows them liberty aboard ship. Like Pierre, he is led by his own good intentions into unspeakable horrors and to his destruction. He belongs to that group of "good, harmless men and women" of whom Isabel [in *Pierre*] speaks, "human things placed at cross-purposes in a world of snakes and lightnings, in a world of horrible and inscrutable inhumanities."

Like all the Melville heroes, Benito Cereno is destroyed by evil. Unlike Pierre or Ahab, he has no divine madness or defiance. He[252] does have the grief which Melville associated with greatness, the melancholy with which he thought all noble things were touched. Delano, a man somewhat like Stubb, cannot understand this sorrowfulness; for Cereno, like other Melville heroes who have met with evil, is cut off from all men except those who share his knowledge of the blackness at the center of life. At the end Delano says:

"I think I understand you; you generalize, Don Benito; and mournfully enough. But the past is passed; why moralize upon it? Forget it. See, yon bright sun has forgotten it all, and the blue sea, and the blue sky; these have turned over new leaves."

"Because they have no memory," he dejectedly replied; "because they are not human."

"But these mild trades that now fan your cheek, Don Benito, do they not come with a human-like healing to you? Warm friends, steadfast friends are the trades."

"With their steadfastness they but waft me to my tomb, Señor," was the foreboding response.

"You are saved, Don Benito," cried Captain Delano, more and more astonished and pained; "you are saved; what has cast such a shadow upon you?"

"The negro."

Since Melville has used Spanish to symbolical effect in other parts of the story, it is not irrelevant to point out that in Spanish *el negro* means not only "the negro," but also "blackness" and "darkness." With the exception of the white whale (whose very whiteness is an aspect of the ambiguity of evil), blackness and darkness are Melville's predominant symbols of evil, and Babo is blackness, not simply a Negro. Something of what is expressed in Hautia and Isabel is in Babo; but he is pure evil, more like Fedallah and Claggart, like them with a character entirely free from minor flaws and vices. There is a trace of nineteenth-century satanism in Babo, with his grim, unyielding fixity of purpose, his refusal even to speak when he can no longer do deeds. Even after death, his head, "that hive of subtlety, fixed on a pole in the Plaza, met, unabashed, the gaze of the whites; and across the Plaza looked toward St. Bartholomew's church, in whose vaults slept the recovered body of Aranda; and across the Rimac bridge looked toward the monastery[253] . . ." where Cereno was dying. Babo is not really exalted, however, and this touch of satanism seems to be for dramatic purposes and to suggest the enduring power of evil.

Primitivism, originally the source of Melville's most optimistic symbols, is completely inverted and ironic in relation to Babo and the slaves. At first they seem to be another set of noble savages, simple, docile, and loyal; but with bitter irony Melville rips away the masks from these kindly exteriors. There is one curious, almost idyllic episode when Delano sees

. . . a slumbering negress, partly disclosed through a lace-work of some rigging, lying with youthful limbs carelessly disposed, under the lee of the bulwarks, like a doe in the shade of a woodland rock. Sprawling at her lapped breasts was her wide-awake fawn, stark naked. . . .

The child wakes its mother; she catches it up and covers it with kisses. "There's naked nature now; pure tenderness and love, thought Captain Delano, well pleased." But this is one of the Negresses who want to torture to death instead of simply killing the Spaniards, who use all their influence to have Cereno murdered, and who sing and dance during the slaughter to urge the men on to greater ferocity.

In *Benito Cereno* Melville's vision of evil at first seems to be expressed with less complexity than in some of his other works. The good and the evil ultimately emerge distinctly; and even though there is ambiguity, it is completely one-sided and then completely removed. Mr. Matthiessen criticizes this sharp contrast, calling it picturesque and theatrical, but "unfortunate in raising unanswered questions." The question he raises is that the Negroes were slaves, "that evil had thus originally been done to them," and that Melville's failure to reckon with this fact within the limits of his narrative makes his tragedy, "for all its prolonged suspense, comparatively superficial." There are two possible answers to this objection. First, the question is irrelevant, since a story must have limits, and also since such a question does not have an answer. Slavery is not the issue here; the focus is upon evil in action in a certain situation. Melville is not investigating the causes but the operations of evil; and were he to explore its origins, he would be[254] led on in a series of infinite regresses. From this fact it by no means follows that Melville was not thinking all that he ever thought. Secondly, there is no reason to suppose that Melville was not thoroughly aware of the slavery question. The question raised in the reader's mind by the fact that the Negroes have been enslaved is inevitable and obvious. Melville must have known that such a question would arise, especially since he was writing when the antislavery movement was at its height, and knew that even as an implication it would add more power to his treatment of the baffling ambiguity of evil. . . .[255]

~~~

THE MONK AND THE BACHELOR: MELVILLE'S
BENITO CERENO

Richard Harter Fogle

. . .

The primary theme of *Benito Cereno,* determined by Melville's emphasis, is in Delano's struggle to comprehend the action. The first part of the story is told entirely from his point of view. Later the emphasis shifts partly to the trial, where the causes of the action are revealed. At the end two conclusions are made about the meaning of the facts: first that reality is a mystery and hard to read, and, second, that evil is real and must be reckoned with. To which should perhaps be added, there are some evils that are cureless, and some mysteries insoluble to man. These propositions are related, for the mystery of *Benito Cereno* is a mystery of evil, contrived by an evil will: [158]

"You were with me all day [says Cereno]; stood with me, sat with me, talked with me, looked at me, ate with me, drank with me; and yet, your last act was to clutch for a monster, not only an innocent man, but the most pitiable of all men. To such a degree may malign machinations and deceptions impose. So far may even the best man err, in judging the conduct of one with the recesses of whose condition he is not acquainted. But you were forced to it; and you were in time undeceived. Would that, in both respects, it was so ever, and with all men."

But Delano is not wholly undeceived. And this speech hints at a corollary: once evil has occurred, it is hard to distinguish between its consequences in the perpetrator and in the victim. So, on the deck of the *San Dominick* Delano comes upon a Spanish sailor, with

a face which would have been a very fine one but for its haggardness. Whether this haggardness had aught to do with criminality, could not be determined; since, as intense heat and cold, though unlike, produce like sensations, so innocence and guilt, when, through casual association with mental pain, stamping any visible impress, use one seal—a hacked one.

Delano, the observer of the action, lacks the sense of evil. Without this key he cannot penetrate the meaning until Cereno forces it upon

---

From Richard Harter Fogle, "The Monk and the Bachelor: Melville's *Benito Cereno,*" *Tulane Studies in English,* III (1952), 155–178. Reprinted by permission of the author and *Tulane Studies in English.*

him, and its deeper implications are permanently closed to him. Consequently the primary theme opposes the appearance, which Delano sees, to the reality, which Delano does not see. *Benito Cereno* is a story of delusion, of a mind wandering in a maze, struggling but failing to find the essential clue. This theme requires that the reader possess the clue withheld from the character, but the final solution must be no more than generally suggested. The reader takes pleasure in his clear superiority to the baffled character, but he must not take the character for a fool. He must sufficiently participate in the bafflement himself to feel suspense. For this purpose ambiguity is useful: a sense of alternative or multiple interpretations and possibilities, keeping us in indecision. Melville makes full[159] use of ambiguity in *Benito Cereno*. Finally, both inward and outward action must have in addition to complexity development and firm design. The maze must have a structure.

The structure of Delano's experience aboard the *San Dominick* is most simply projected in the unities of time, place, and action. The time is twelve hours, the place is the ship, the action moves directly toward the climax. A deeper element is the principle of alternation or rhythm, which relates the definite to the complex. The mind of Delano alternates steadily between mistrust and reassurance. It wanders, but wanders in a pattern. The deck of the *San Dominick* strikes him with wonder, with her noisy crowd of blacks, its oakum-pickers, its wild Ashantis. But this confusion is attributed to abnormal circumstances, in which discipline has naturally slackened. The strangeness of Cereno is explainable from his sufferings. At one point Cereno confers aside with his servant, then asks some highly suspicious questions about the weapons and manning of Delano's ship. But the very crudeness of the questioning disarms suspicion. "To solicit such information openly of the chief person endangered, and so, in effect, setting him on his guard; how unlikely a procedure was that." Delano's misgivings gradually rise in intensity, but until the end are allayed. Thus, finally emerging from the Spaniard's cabin to leave the ship, he has got to the point of fearing to be murdered in the passage-way. But his fears vanish as soon as he reaches the deck.

This alternation of feeling has a corresponding rhythm in Cereno, who moves consistently between opposite moods. "The singular alternations of courtesy and ill-breeding in the Spanish captain were unaccountable, except on one of two suppositions [both wrong]—innocent lunacy, or wicked imposture." In one phase Don Benito is ceremonious, in the other he withdraws into gloomy indifference, regardless of his guest. At some moments he seems overcome; at others he puts on a rigid self-command.

Critics have commented upon the atmosphere of nightmarish unreality with which Melville invests the *San*[160] *Dominick*. This atmosphere is in keeping with the theme. The strangeness of the ship is an element of the soul's delusion. Certain motifs and images, however, recur, suggesting that this nightmare has a structure and a meaning.

The skill which isolates and focusses the scene is directed toward something more crucial than merely theatrical emphasis:

Always upon boarding a large and populous ship at sea, especially a foreign one, with a nondescript crew such as Lascars or Manilla men, the impression varies in a peculiar way from that produced by first entering a strange house with strange inmates in a strange land. Both house and ship—the one by its walls and blinds, the other by its high bulwarks like ramparts—hoard from view their interiors till the last moment: but in the case of the ship there is this addition; that the living spectacle it contains, upon its sudden and complete disclosure, has, in contrast with the blank ocean which zones it, something of the effect of enchantment. The ship seems unreal; these strange costumes, gestures, and faces, but a shadowy tableau just emerged from the deep, which directly must receive back what it gave.

The advantages of this effect are obvious enough, but by emphasizing the strangeness and isolation it also can image the mind which perceives them. Delano is removed from all his customary associations, his supports, his criteria. Some have maintained that his slowness amounts to plain stupidity, seriously damaging the story. Certainly the problem is inherent in the theme, which depends upon a balance of uncertainty and knowledge. The eventual revelation of truth must be inevitable; probably the hero will always seem slow in learning the truth. And if he seems *too* slow the story is ruined. Therefore it is worthwhile reasserting that Melville has dealt with this difficulty. Delano has one vital disability, clearly stated and essential to the meaning of *Benito Cereno*. He is "a person of a singularly undistrustful good nature, not liable except on extraordinary and repeated incentives, and hardly then, to indulge in personal alarms, any way involving the imputation of malign evil in man." He does not understand "of what humanity is[161] capable." Beyond this, the problem is real. It is the creation of a complex and malignant mind, a "hive of subtlety," which has deliberately contrived its confusions.

Benito Cereno has a decorative color scheme of white, black, and gray. As in the isolation of the ship, this use of color-motifs has both an immediate function of design and along with it a deeper significance in theme. In Delano's search for truth the white is good, the black is evil, the gray the ambiguity between them. The first color is quite fittingly gray, for the *San Dominick* is a ship of mystery.

The morning was one peculiar to that coast. Everything was mute and calm; everything was gray. The sea, though undulated into long roods of swells, seemed fixed, and was sleeked at the surface like waved lead that has cooled and set in the smelter's mould. The sky seemed a gray surtout. Flights of troubled gray fowl, kith and kin with troubled gray vapors among which they were mixed, skimmed low and fitfully over the waters, as swallows over meadows before storms. Shadows present, foreshadowing deeper shadows to come.

Out of these vapors comes wandering the fateful *San Dominick*. Against the gray she looks "like a white-washed monastery after a thunder-storm"; peering over the bulwarks are what seem to be "throngs of dark cowls; while, fitfully revealed through the open portholes, other dark moving figures were dimly descried, as of Black Friars pacing the cloisters." The black is evil, the white is good, since we take the side of the whites and accept the verdict of a white court of law. This symbolism of white and black F. O. Matthiessen has called "unfortunate in raising unanswered questions," since the Negroes are the victims of social injustice: the failure to answer which makes the tragedy "for all its prolonged suspense, comparatively superficial."

The charge is a crucial one. It is a true one, if we require that tragedy convey an ideal order. There is none such in *Benito Cereno*. Melville's symbols, however, are[162] complex, and supply a self-criticism of their own. Melville was certainly conscious of the problem. The white is good, but it is also decay and death—a fate deserved from self-neglect and inertia. "As the whale-boat drew more and more nigh, the cause of the peculiar pipe-clayed aspect of the stranger was seen in the slovenly neglect pervading her. The spars, ropes, and great part of the bulwarks, looked woolly, from long unacquaintance with the scraper, tar, and the brush. Her keel seemed laid, her ribs put together, and she launched, from Ezekiel's Valley of Dry Bones." These images are not accidental. They bear a theme, and lead directly to the revelation, the unveiling of the figurehead. At the moment of climax the slaves cut the cable to flee. The end of it whips off a canvas shroud, and reveals a white human skeleton: the skeleton of Don Alexandro Aranda, owner of the slaves and the friend of Cereno.

Upon this theme of whiteness the black makes his comment. Beneath the skeleton is chalked the inscription, "Follow your leader!" This is ironically addressed to the white man, but also to the white ship—white with decay. It is not unimportant that the skeleton has been substituted for "the ship's proper figure-head—the image of Christopher Colon, the discoverer of the New World," with its connotation of energy, freedom, youth, and hope. Aranda was killed by the blacks to assure their liberty, and his skeleton was set up to remind the whites to keep their faith—an oath of assistance of course extorted by force and fear. The Negro Babo has his say on whiteness. At the trial Cereno deposes that "the negro Babo showed him a skeleton ... that the negro Babo asked him whose skeleton that was, and whether, from its whiteness, he should not think it a white's ... that the same morning the negro Babo took by succession each Spaniard forward, and asked him whose skeleton that was, and whether, from its whiteness, he should not think it a white's; that each Spaniard covered his face. . . ." Babo's revenge goes far beyond the provocation. Yet he is partially justified within the theme of whiteness.

Order is important in *Benito Cereno*. "In armies, navies, cities, or families, in nature herself, nothing more relaxes[163] good order than misery." "Wonted to the quiet orderliness of the sealer's comfortable family of a crew, the noisy confusion of the *San Dominick's* suffering host repeatedly challenged his [Delano's] eye." "Events have not been favorable to much order in my arrangements," says Cereno. "The negro Babo appointed the four aged negroes ... to keep what domestic order they could on the decks. ..." "Had such a thing happened on board the *Bachelor's Delight,* instant punishment would have followed," says Captain Delano. The primary order of *Benito Cereno* is the order of Spain, an hierarchical system in which Church and State are one. The *San Dominick* is a symbol of this order, and its fate.

The *San Dominick* is "A very large, and, in its time, a very fine vessel, such as in those days were at intervals encountered along that main; sometimes superseded Acapulco treasure-ships, or retired frigates of the Spanish king's navy, which, like superannuated palaces, still, under a decline of masters, preserved signs of former state." Once a warship, the vessel's teeth have been drawn. "The ship's general model and rig appeared to have undergone no material change from their original warlike and Froissart pattern. However, no guns were seen." "At present neither men nor cannon were seen, though huge ringbolts and other rusty iron fixtures of the woodwork hinted of twenty-four pounders." The *San Dominick* has a state-cabin and state-balconies, once splendid but now abandoned and dead. "His glance fell upon the row of small, round dead-lights—closed like coppered eyes of the coffined —and the state-cabin door, once connecting with the gallery, even as the dead-lights had once looked out upon it, but now calked fast like a sarcophagus-lid. ..." Delano speculates that "that state-cabin and this state-balcony had heard the voices of the Spanish king's officers, and the forms of the Lima viceroy's daughters had perhaps leaned where he stood. ..." Delano looks down to the ship's water-line, leaning upon the balustrade of the balcony. Below him he sees ribbon grass, "straight as a border of green box; and parterres of sea-weed, broad ovals and crescents, floating nigh and far, with what seemed[164] long formal alleys between, crossing the terraces of swells, and sweeping round as if leading to the grottoes below." The balustrade itself seems "the charred ruin of some summer-house in a grand garden long running to waste." Here is the formal grandeur of the old regime, and its decadence. Delano leans too heavily upon the balustrade; it gives way, and nearly pitches him into the sea.

Benito Cereno is dressed with singular but outmoded richness, in small-clothes and stockings. "There was a certain precision in his attire curiously at variance with the unsightly disorder around; especially in the belittered Ghetto, forward of the mainmast, wholly occupied by the blacks." He wears "a slender sword, silver mounted," the emblem of rule. This sword is in reality an empty hilt in an artificially stiffened scabbard. Cereno's cabin is in disorder. "Part of it had formerly been the quarters of the officers; but since their death all the partitionings had been thrown down. ..." It now resembles "the wide, cluttered hall of some eccentric bachelor-squire in the country." Amid the clutter are "four or five old muskets," an old table with a thumbed missal on it, and over it a small crucifix. Under the table is "a dented cutlass or two, with a hacked harpoon, among some melancholy old rigging, like a heap of poor friar's girdles." There are two settees "of Malacca cane, black with age, and uncomfortable to look at as inquisitor's racks," with an armchair which because it is supplied with a barber's crotch "seemed some grotesque engine of torture." There is an open flag-locker which reveals various flags in disorder, and a cumbrous washstand of black mahogany, "with a pedestal like a font." Finally there is Cereno's bed, "a torn hammock of stained grass . . . the sheets tossed, and the pillow wrinkled up like a brow, as if whoever slept here slept but illy." The cabin is a microcosm of the old Spanish order, fallen now in confusion. It figures forth its warlike power, its spiritual strength, its traditional loyalties— and its inquisitorial rigors. It is also the unhappy chaos of the soul of Cereno. This cabin, a place of actual events, is counterpointed against the state-cabin and the balconies, undisturbed relics of the past.[165] Here is the cluttered hall, still occupied; there is the formal palace, dead but unaltered.

The *San Dominick* is massive. Its physical bulk, however, merges with the ambiguities of its meaning. About its great masts are "groves of rigging," which mirror in their complexity the maze in which Delano is wandering. A Spanish sailor seems to gesture to him, "but immediately, as if alarmed by some advancing step along the deck within, vanished into *the recesses of the hempen forest,* like a poacher." This ambiguity can be moral. The corroded main-chains, "Of an ancient style, massy and rusty in link, shackle and bolt . . . seemed even more fit for the ship's present business [slaving] than the one for which she had been built." In the midst of the sternpiece, carved with the arms of Castile and Leon, is a device of mysterious significance: "uppermost and central . . . was a dark satyr in a mask, holding his foot on the prostrate neck of a writhing figure, likewise masked."

The *San Dominick* is the old order of western civilization. This order is solidly grounded in fundamental loyalties and faiths; it is complex and profound. Deeply set in man's spirit, it is worthy of reverence. But in Cereno's cabin the settees are like inquisitor's racks, and the armchair resembles an instrument of torture. These spiritual depths have their dark places, this order its sins. The massive chains are well fitted for slaving.

The old order was made for a "man of war world," in which evil perpetually threatens. Like the organization of a warship's company, its tightly formed hierarchies were framed for emergencies. The successful revolt of the slaves is a sign of the system's decay. It was possible because the Negroes were left unchained, by order of their master Aranda. But as a slave-owner what had he to do with kindness and indulgence? The original sin has been committed: he must either reject it completely, or else adhere strictly to the terms of his tenure. Melville compares the *San Dominick* to a "transatlantic emigrant ship, among whose multitude of living freight are some individuals, doubt-less,[166] as little troublesome as crates and bales; but the friendly remonstrances of such with their ruder companions are of not so much avail as the unfriendly arm of the mate. What the *San Dominick* wanted was, what the emigrant ship has, stern superior officers." What the order has now is the ceremony without the substance of power, and insight without the faculty of action. It has looked too long in the face of evil, and at last grown unnerved. Its proper symbol is now a monk.

Delano's first sight of the *San Dominick* suggests to him "a white-washed monastery after a thunderstorm." The slaves peering over the bulwarks are Black Friars—Dominicans. It has been remarked that "Benito" is a Benedictine's cloak; and "benito" is derived from "benedictus." Shut in his ship's walls, Cereno is like "some hypochon-driac abbot" too long cloistered; his manner is like "his imperial coun-tryman's, Charles V, just previous to the anchoritish retirement of that monarch from the throne." At the end Don Benito retires to the monastery "on Mount Agonia," accompanied by "one special guardian and consoler, by night and by day." This inseparable companion is the monk *Infelez*.

In Melville, the monk, seeing too well that the world is evil, is forced to retire from it. He is not a bachelor, but has wedded reality all too closely—and Benito is a benedict. A bachelor is a man who would keep his freedom; if necessary he will close his eyes and heart in order to avoid entanglement. The bachelor shuns real commitments. Melville has drawn two kinds of bachelors. One kind believes that the world is wholly and simply bad. But since this is so, the bachelor need have no traffic with it; it does not engage him deeply. Such a man is the Missouri Bachelor of *The Confidence-Man,* "A Hard Case," who has "No confidence in boys, no confidence in men, no confidence in nature." St. Augustine on Original Sin is his text-book. His universal pessimism is, however, shallow, since he has not paid the price of wisdom. He is justly dismissed as "less a man-hater[167] than a man-hooter." The other and more frequent type is the merry bachelor who shuts his eyes to evil and pain. He believes that men can be happy at the slight expense of a little commonsense and foresight. This bachelor is com-petent and canny; he often succeeds in leading a pleasant and tranquil life. Now and then, however, he runs into more things than are dreamt of in his philosophy. Such is the narrator of *Bartleby,* who finds through his strange clerk that some ills are cureless. And such is Captain Delano of the *Bachelor's Delight.*[168] . . .

Captain Delano believes in a beneficent Providence. Himself well-disposed, he expects no harm; it would be atheistical to doubt that good men are protected. "I to be murdered here at the ends of the earth, on board a haunted pirate-ship by a horrible Spaniard? Too nonsensical to think of! Who would murder Amasa Delano? His conscience is clean. There is some one above." The order of Delano is the order of the *Bachelor's Delight:* a commonsense order, comfortable and quiet. The crew of the *Bachelor's Delight* is easily governed by its good-natured but decisive captain. One golden rule solves all problems—keep them busy. "I should think, Don Benito [says the American captain] . . . that you woud find it advantageous to keep all your blacks employed, especially the younger ones, no matter at what useless task, and no matter what happens to the ship. Why, even with my little band, I find such a course indispensable."

The practical Delano, believing as he does in his simple Providence, which he is inclined to associate with the order of nature, is able to save alive the body of Cereno, but cannot help his soul. He has little notion of the effect of malignant evil upon the Spaniard's deeper spirit. The world is[170] good, and accidental ills now happily removed; what then remains?

"But the past is passed; why moralize upon it? Forget it. See, yon bright sun has forgotten it all, and the blue sea, and the blue sky; these have turned over new leaves."

"Because they have no memory," he dejectedly replied; "because they are not human."

"But these mild trades that now fan your cheek, do they not come with a human-like healing to you? Warm friends, steadfast friends are the trades."

"With their steadfastness they but waft me to my tomb, Señor," was the foreboding response.

"You are saved," cried Captain Delano, more and more astonished and pained: "you are saved: what has cast such a shadow upon you?"

"The negro."

What is "the negro"? After his rescue Cereno will not board the *Bachelor's Delight* until the Negro Babo has been taken below. "Nor then, nor at any time after, would he look at him." Babo is the symbol of the slaves, one kind of blackness. With a wider reference he is everything untamed and demoniac: the principle of unknown terror. . . .

Babo is not quite, however, the motiveless malignity of Iago, who must invent the reasons for his wickedness.[171] Correspondingly he is not quite Claggart, the master-at-arms of *Billy Budd,* who is a pure evil according to nature. In Babo the evil he is is merged with the evil he suffers. For he has been oppressed by social order, and not only by the white man's. "Poor Babo here, in his own land, was only a poor slave; a black man's slave was Babo, who now is the white's." Therefore, while from one point of view Babo is Satan, an absolute principle of destruction, a pure hatred of all order, he is likewise a sufferer from order, its prober and test, the sign of its weakness. In this aspect he is the vengeance of nature, evoked by the inequities of all orders. When they transgress too far against nature, the vengeance beats them down.

Babo is thus in part the symbol of the slaves, whose blackness is the destructive vigor of the primitive. But he goes beyond their natural savagery; even beyond the fierceness of the untamed Ashantis. They have had their own simpler order, and their revolt is their attempt to return to it. The giant Atufal was a king in his own country, and significantly counterbalances the deeper, more equivocal Babo. The source of the action is Babo's revolt. Thus the *San Dominick* which Delano sees is a malign parody of the original system, in which the real power conceals itself behind animated puppets. Since the truth cannot wholly be hidden, Babo tries to confuse it. Further, going beyond the necessities of the situation, Babo deliberately desecrates the sanctities of the old faith and rule.

He plays the role of the loyal, solicitous servant, the shadow of Cereno, while secretly ruling the ship. One ironic effect of this device is to make Cereno appear an absolute monarch of godlike pride and assumption. "Proud as he was moody, he condescended to no personal mandate. Whatever special orders were necessary, their delivery was delegated to his body-servant. . . ." This equivocal association of master and servant has a more vital result: it diverts the suspicions of Delano always to Cereno, concealing from him their true source. In addition, Babo has arranged the elaborate mockery by which the ex-king Atufal appears before[172] Cereno at stated hours in chains, to which the latter alone has the key. In reality the chains can be instantly thrown aside, but the innocent Delano begs that the punishment be remitted. He is so thoroughly deceived as to say, "for all the license you permit in some things, I fear lest at bottom, you are a bitter hard master." He misinterprets Cereno's response: "Again Don Benito shrank; and this time, as the good sailor thought, from a genuine twinge of his conscience."

The true state of things cannot completely be hidden. A Spanish lad is assaulted by a slave boy; a sailor is trampled by two Negroes; these incidents are difficult to explain. Against the restraining and concealing agency of the four old oakum-pickers, whom Babo has appointed to keep order, are the six Ashantis, who are polishing hatchets. These "sat intent upon their task, except at intervals, when, with the peculiar love in negroes of uniting industry with pastime, two and two they sideways clashed their hatchets together, like cymbals, with a barbarous din." This clashing, which mingles with the action like a chorus, is like a chorus the voice of truth, if Delano could interpret it. At his most suspicious he has some glimmerings. "By a curious coincidence, as each point was recalled, the black wizards of Ashantees would strike up with their hatchets, as in ominous comment on the white stranger's thoughts."

The Spanish sailors try to communicate with Delano by indirection, under surveillance and at deadly risk. Thus he comes upon an old seaman working a knot, with some blacks obligingly holding the strands of the rope. This knot, a most extraordinary artifice, is strangely like Delano's present state of mind, which passes by a not uncongenial transition . . . from its own entanglements to those of the hemp. For intricacy, such a knot he had never seen in an American ship, nor indeed any other. The old man looked like an Egyptian priest, making Gordian knots for the temple of Ammon. The knot seemed a combination of double-blowing-knot, treble-crown-knot, back-handed-well-knot, knot-in-and-out-knot, and jamming-knot. At last, puzzled to comprehend the meaning of such a knot, Captain Delano addressed the knotter:—[173]

> "What are you knotting there, my man?"
> "The knot," was the brief reply, without looking up.
> "So it seems; but what is it for?"
> "For some one else to undo," muttered back the old man.

While Captain Delano stood watching him suddenly the old man threw the knot towards him, saying . . . something to this effect: "Undo it, cut it, quick."

This is the Gordian knot of the *San Dominick,* too complicated to untie. Delano cannot cut it yet, for he is only dimly aware that the knot exists until Cereno enlightens him. To try to cut it now would be suicide, for he himself is a part of it. He cuts it at last, but this practical solution is inadequate, it will not save the Spaniard. Ideally the knot should be unwound, its relationships fathomed, its intricate mazes traced back to their beginnings. It is the real tragedy of *Benito Cereno* that this real solution is impossible. Could a deeper than Delano have found the deep truth? Melville makes us consider this question, but the symbol itself says no; the problem is beyond the human intellect.[174] . . .

SSS

MASQUE AND SYMBOL IN MELVILLE'S *BENITO CERENO*

Robin Magowan

. . .

Before moving on to an examination of masque and symbol in *Benito Cereno* it seems noteworthy that at this juncture of Melville's career, when he was becoming increasingly preoccupied with an emblematic way of writing—one that works through a set of fixed symbols—that he should have turned for his plots to outside sources. In the case of *Benito Cereno* the outside source was Chapter 18 of Amasa Delano's *A Narrative of Voyages and Travels in the Northern*

From Robin Magowan, "Masque and Symbol in Melville's *Benito Cereno*," *College English,* XXIII (February 1962), 346–351. Reprinted with the permission of the National Council of Teachers of English and Professor Robin Magowan.

and Southern Hemispheres.[1] Now the point of the source lies in its set character. The action is fixed, almost fatalistically predetermined—a mold to be filled in. That Melville himself accepted these aesthetic conditions and indeed contrived to incorporate them in the structure of his novella may be seen from the fact that the all-important opening description of the sea in the second paragraph of *Benito Cereno* has an equally "fixed" character:

The sea, though undulated into long roods of swells, seemed fixed, and was sleeked at the surface like waved lead that has cooled and set in the smelter's mould.

And yet the sea, paradoxically, contains in itself, in its sleekly undulated surface, an atmosphere or mood that will govern the whole subsequent rhythm of the novella.

To be brief, then, I feel that Melville's great achievement in *Benito Cereno* lies in the total atmosphere that he evokes and, in particular, in his creation of the world of the slave-ship, or floating coffin as it was then known. For in the *San Dominick* there is portrayed a world mortally corroded by the use to which it has been put, a sham world in which decay has taken on the allure of life and an intriguing counterfeit beauty which is like art. And it is here that we must look for Melville's condemnation of the evil of slavery, rather than in any examination of a color symbolism that cannot help but be ambiguous. There is, moreover, in the presentation of the world of the *San Dominick* a curiously Spenserian quality, somewhat like the dense, elaborately enclosed Bower of Acrasia in the *Faery Queene,* a counterfeit if almost exact replica of the world as we might, in an evil hour, find it to be. And here it may help to see Captain Delano in these terms—as a kind of Spenserian fairy hero, a temporarily becharmed Knight of Civilization owing his survival to nothing less than his continuing faith—in any case, a person other than the Obtuse American of Professor[348] Chase's study, baffled by an international situation of which he is culturally innocent.[2] It is apparent that the world of the *San Dominick,* with its show of good manners and animal spirits on the part of the slaves and its vestiges of a feudal courtesy in the person of Don Benito, exerts a wonderful fascination over Captain Delano. There is something in it, perhaps what psychologists would term his "death wish," to which the American captain feels mysteriously drawn, and it is in this light that the scene in the *San Dominick's* quarter-gallery, where Delano first experiences a sense of loss and isolation, should be read.

As this scene holds perhaps the core of the novella, a brief sum-

---

1 Of Melville's several departures from his source, among the more curious is his substitution of Babo for Muri as captain of the slaves, the name "Babo" being possibly a variant of the Tuscan "Babbo," meaning "Daddy."

2 Richard Chase, *Herman Melville* (New York, 1949), p. 158.

mary may be in order. It will be remembered that the enchantment Captain Delano undergoes has come in the wake of a vision he has had of a Negress, doelike, giving suck, a vision that represents for him all that he understands by natural or animal love—in short, an ideal state of nature. In clambering into the enchanted maze of the starboard quarter-gallery Delano beholds first death, tricked out in moss and assigned a kind of Venetian splendor, and then, presented in even more loving detail, the garden of romance receding into the image of a deserted country château in which he sees himself held prisoner while before him the roads blur. Abruptly then the scene shifts and we next see him peering down into a confusion of chains and rigging. Yet as he gazes, the benign, grovelike aspect that he has read into this confusion of chains and rigging suddenly changes and transforms itself into a "hempen forest," and the Captain realizes for the first time that he is lost, truly in the woods, and unable there to read the necessary signs. Whereupon looking wildly about for a familiar image (in this case his longboat, Rover), he loses his balance, topples from his perch, and with the ensuing crash comes in effect to his senses. It is immediately after this nightmare-like episode that he is presented with the answer to the riddle of the *San Dominick:* first in the form of the enigmatic five-knotted rope handed him by a Spanish sailor, and then, with more éclat, in the silent figure of the towering African king, Atufal, whose chains must seemingly contain the key to the mystery. We can thus understand why the ritual progress of the novella should require that this evilly enchanted quarter-gallery be swept away with the first salvo fired from the gun of the *Bachelor's Delight*—an action which fails to make sense except in terms of that total canvas we have been describing.

Now the spectacle that first greets Captain Delano upon his boarding the distressed *San Dominick* is a saturnalia or "black masque" in which Don Benito, in his exaggerated white finery, has been called upon to enact the role, perhaps sacrificial, of lord of "misrule." And it makes sense to see in Don Benito, with his husky whisper and nervous puppetlike gestures, a figure out of the Italian *commedia dell'arte;* while it is the presence of this same world that explains the "dark satyr in a mask" of the ship's figure-head, and possibly even the occasional Venetian imagery. It is a world of masquerade that has been present, moreover, from the very first page—from that initial description of the sun showing "not unlike a Lima intriguante's one sinister eye peering across the Plaza from the loop-hole of her dusk *saya-y-manta*" which precedes our first glimpse of the slave-ship and its crew of black-cloaked friars. Now, in the spirit of a true saturnalia the Negroes have staged for the benefit of their distinguished American visitor *The Play of Atufal,* which play represents a mock opposite or parody of the real state of things aboard the *San Dominick.* And in the costumes and minor detail there is surely great wit, from the stage point of[349] view. The play, however, turns on the dumb-show performance of the mute Atufal, the key to whose mock chains hangs ironically suspended on a slender silken cord attached to Don Benito's neck. It is a gratuitous performance, if you will, but for that reason all the more essential to the ritual action of the novella. And it is this quality of a "performance" that Captain Delano is finally, in the incident of the five-knotted rope, compelled to recognize. Yet the one element with which he might sever the knot of the *San Dominick*—the missing sword in Don Benito's stiffened scabbard—is precisely the one withheld from him. Without it no intervention on the captain's part is possible.

Of the three main strands of symbolism in *Benito Cereno*—color, religion, animal imagery—the last may prove most readily accessible. For the further the action advances the wilder this imagery becomes, reaching in the final "bat" and "wolf" metaphors a savage intensity illustrative of the danger Captain Delano runs while lost in these woods. As this imagery characterizes both Spanish sailors and Negro slaves alike, extending even to Don Benito who in his white somnambulism is compared to a white noddy spied earlier in the *San Dominick's* top rigging, we may identify it with a Hobbesian state of nature in which man, deprived of sovereign authority, finds himself reduced to a bestial condition. This wild imagery, however, is also to be seen against such infrequent domestic imagery as that of Captain Delano's longboat, Rover, and his memories of Newfoundland dogs. As the action draws toward its climax this Hobbesian imagery becomes transmuted and assumes an underwater character that effectively renders the full horror involved in this death-struggle between black and white—"there was a vague, muffled, inner sound as of submerged sword-fish rushing hither and thither through shoals of black-fish."

The color symbolism poses more difficulty, perhaps because one senses that it was Melville's perception of the black-and-white or painterly possibilities inherent in his theme that first drew him to Captain Delano's *Narrative*. The problem here is that one may read too much into the symbolism and thus be forced into F. O. Matthiessen's position of condemning Melville for having equated the Negroes with evil, whereas the great body of evidence, both textual and biographical, seemingly points the other way. Thus rather than emphasize the black-and-white imagery which is pervasive in *Benito Cereno*, it makes better sense to show how both black and white are subsumed, resolved by that greater gray which is, in effect, the atmosphere enshrouding the tale from its beginning:[3]

Everything was mute and calm; everything gray. The sea, though undulated into long roods of swells, seemed fixed, and was sleeked at the surface like waved lead that has cooled and set in the smelter's mould.

---

[3] See Guy A. Cardwell's excellent study [pp. 99–104 in this book].

Like the painter Albert Ryder, Melville's concern is with the density of his canvas, with building up the various coloristic surfaces, layer on layer, until the desired level of opacity has been achieved, where-upon the several aspects of the Slave Question, political, economic,[350] ethical, can reverberate in those blacks and whites which prose fiction can handle—the whole perceived through that gray medium posed by the perfectly understandable obtuseness of Captain Delano, and in him finally reconciled. . . .

In my view Don Benito is more the creature of pathos, and of a pathos at that not far removed from saturnalian comedy, a penitent such as one might expect to find placed among the Self-Violent in an upper circle of Dante's *Inferno*. It seems in this case significant that none of the personages in *Benito Cereno* undergoes a substantial change. If for the sake of an action they have been compelled to assume a role, it is no less true that in the course of that action they have become that role, as if born to it and always destined to have played it. The only change possible, therefore, is a ceremonial change, of a rite successfully undergone. Thus, for Captain Delano the action is a testing of his faith. He only becomes endangered through his occasional lapses of taste, those moments when he forgets himself and treats the Negroes not as fellow human beings but as the slaves they nominally are, and thus departs from that standard of good taste and human decency which it is his role as Knight of Civilization to up-hold.[351]

✿✿✿

THE SOURCE AND THE SYMBOLS OF MELVILLE'S *BENITO CERENO*

Max Putzel

I

The unfathomable ambiguity Melville is probing [in *Benito Cereno*] concerns man and nature in their temporal–historic, their atemporal–cyclical, and their perhaps moral, ontological relations. It

From Max Putzel, "The Source and the Symbols of Melville's *Benito Cereno*," *American Literature*, XXXIV (May 1962), 191–206. Reprinted by permission of *American Literature* and the author.

deals with the appearance and the reality of human experience—both individual and collective—in this aspect raising the problem of knowledge. It treats of problems of freedom and law which accompany man in his evolution from primitive barbarity to civilized and organized barbarity. Like Conrad, Melville explores the problem of force as an evil rather than the problem of abstract evil: not so much why evil exists in a world where benevolence is ostensibly omnipotent, but how moral values can survive at all in a universe where both man and nature are subject to blind, amoral forces essential to their very being.

In his book Captain Delano, too, dealt with moral problems,[192] though in a fairly crude and naïve way. Melville is not simply trying to refine his moralizing. He is revising what Delano himself had experienced, elucidating what baffled Delano, and going on to shadow forth a higher, more lucid reality, which baffles himself. What establishes the greatness of the work is that Melville sees a universe like Shakespeare's or Sophocles', where seeming and being interreflect in an endless series, where suggestive ambiguities are as close as man can come to truth, and where the wisest man must admit he sees only a little more than the fool. To some extent Melville makes Delano his tragic hero, who catches a glint of reality like a jewel mysteriously sparkling on the bosom of a Spanish sailor and sees nothing more.

The plot Melville took from Delano's short chapter is based on the interplay between three characters. In the forefront is Delano himself, through whose eyes we see the event. The captain of a Yankee sealer and general trader lying in a lonely island harbor off the coast of Chile, he comes to the aid of a Spanish ship in a shocking state of decay, seemingly about to run on a reef as she blunders shoreward on a gray morning, desperately short of rations. In the center of the stage is the Spanish captain Benito Cereno, whose hardships seem to have unhinged his mind as they have emaciated his richly clad frame. Don Benito knows what Captain Delano cannot know: that the hundred and sixty Negro slaves who were his principal cargo have risen in mutiny, killed his officers and most of his Spanish crew, and hung the corpse of their owner (his closest friend) below the ship's figurehead, where it is hidden by canvas. Hovering in the background is Babo, the leader of the mutiny, disguised as captain of the slaves and a faithful body servant of the ship captain's, desperately intent on forcing the captain and surviving crew to carry him and his Negro rebels back to Africa.

Each of the three sees the reality in a different light—the narrator giving it a subtle twist whose irony is alien to all of them. Delano is the credulous, good-natured, optimistic commander of a ship redolent of newness, prosperiy, and order. The Spaniard is the victim of illness, disorder, disillusionment, and malign force. The Negro is a sinister and primitive conundrum.

Each also represents a stage of human development. Delano is the

Revolutionary American, a spokesman for New-World innocence, vigor, and promise. Born to command, he accepts the[193] republican state of affairs a little condescendingly. Don Benito stands for the old order, a feudal structure of caste and fealty fast losing its hold. He is ready to withdraw from life and contemplate in tragic passivity the ruins of a faith that has all but slipped from his grasp. Babo is harder to categorize, for he seems one thing to Delano, another to Don Benito, and first the one, then the other, to us. But that he represents primitive man in a cyclical world where time and history do not exist, of this there can be no doubt. Close to nature, he is remote from both the worlds that dominate history, yet he has made an art of pretending to serve them. This gives him at first the appearance of fidelity, solicitude, and obedience, but these mask a vengeful fury which when released goes to barbaric lengths outside the law.

Finally we are forced to reconsider Babo in the light of a larger vision of justice. After Captain Delano has subdued him and the law has judged him, we see his head stuck on a pole with a barbarity that matches his own—a detail Melville found in his source. And that head stares inscrutably down the whole vista of Christian civilization, medieval and American, in implacable accusation.

II

What Melville borrowed from Delano and what he rejected partly reveal his purpose, if we can read the pattern. The most important loan is Delano himself, a most engaging figure, though he serves as a foil for Melville's irony rather than the central character he at first seems. As Professor Morison has characterized him, unmindful of Melville, the benevolence he attributes to himself is not salient:

Amasa Delano, of Duxbury (private, U. S. A., at fourteen, privateersman at sixteen, master shipbuilder at twenty-one, second mate of the ship *Massachusetts*), with his brother built the sealers *Perseverance* and *Pilgrim,* and sailed as far as Tasmania, where they matched rascalities and exchanged brutalities with one of the British convict colonies.[1]

Hard to fit into any nutshell, he has also had a varied career as[194] explorer and master, suffered every species of hardship and misfortune, and lived to write a tolerable account of his career as a manual for other seamen. He hopes it will be "valuable to the cause of morality and humanity, and ... stimulate others to do the same things for their fellow men which are recommended here."[2]

An orderly man adventuring in a violently disordered world, he has seen the American Revolution cost him the chance of a formal education, the French Revolution cost him his ship. Yet he has com-

1 Samuel Eliot Morison, *Maritime History of Massachusetts* (Boston, 1941), p. 62.
2 Amasa Delano, *Narrative of Voyages* (Boston, 1817), p. 20.

pensated for lack of schooling by much reading and, despite hardships and losses, he retains an optimistic view of human nature and a balanced, disinterested tolerance of its vagaries. Of the French Revolution he says,

It was mortifying to see very low men, without talents or integrity, in possession of power, and using it for the worst purposes. ... But we are not to go to the opposite extreme, under the idea that whatever is hostile to error in one of its forms, is of course truth. There is such a thing as civil and religious liberty. ...[3]

And of philanthropy, he remarks that

A man, who finds it hard to conceive of real benevolence in the motives of his fellow creatures, gives no very favourable testimony to the public in regard to the state of his own heart, or the elevation of his moral sentiments.[4]

What baffles Captain Delano beyond measure is the ingratitude of those he has aided and saved. Benito Cereno is one of the ingrates—though Melville suppresses all that phase of the incident for reasons I shall take up in concluding this essay. Melville's narrator simply remarks that Delano seems to him "a person of singularly undistrustful good nature, not liable ... to indulge in personal alarms, any way involving the imputation of malign evil in man." He goes on to wonder "Whether, in view of what humanity is capable, such a trait implies, along with a benevolent heart, more than ordinary quickness and accuracy of intellectual perception. ..."

While this may be gently satiric as applied to Delano, it becomes devastating as we follow the plot to its conclusion and realize[195] that the slur on Delano's intelligence applies to the American people he represents—or at least to their leaders. Melville seems to question whether this nation's benevolent optimism is more than a form of self-satisfaction based on blindness to the figure we cut with other peoples—especially primitive ones we exploit. The real Delano believed, at least, that "Virtue and vice, happiness and misery, are much more equally distributed to nations than those are permitted to suppose who have never been from home. ..."[5]

To Melville the American dream of philanthropic idealism was sure to increase the evil in the world unless it were armed with sharper insight than Delano's. He could concur in Delano's belief that his altruism was responsible for saving his life when he went on board the Spanish ship and unknowingly put himself in the power of the mutineers. At the same time Melville selected the episode, of the many he might have chosen, largely, I think, because it revealed the dangers inherent in such pious naïveté as he detected in his source. The man's

---

[3] *Ibid.*, pp. 200–201.
[4] *Ibid.*, p. 73.
[5] *Ibid.*, p. 256.

courage so far outran his perception that he seemed to symbolize a national destiny over which clouds were rapidly gathering.

Another thing that must have struck Melville was Delano's appearance. The atmosphere of bland confidence which emanates from his broad face as seen in the frontispiece of his book is indescribable. He stares out at the world through eyes that are pale yet piercing, slightly squinting as from long familiarity with the sea yet strangely lacking in depth. His face is firm though well-fleshed, and there is a well-fed fold above the high, white linen cravat into which his strong chin is tucked. He holds himself stiffly upright, his head tilted slightly back; and his hair, which has receded, is trimmed very short, ending in sideburns just below the ears, in one of which he wears a small jewel. Not only does he seem still youthful in his early fifties: he has the look of a tow-headed boy, almost albino in the preternatural whiteness of his complexion.

Melville's imagination could not but magnify that whiteness as he read Benito Cereno's deposition telling of the uprising led by the Negro Mure and his son Babo, who could write and therefore (like Atufal) signed the agreement under which Don Benito was forced to carry them to Senegal on condition that there would be[196] no more murders. In that deposition and another given by Delano's midshipman Melville read how Delano remained aboard the Spanish ship all day, and how Don Benito spoke to him continually about his pretended misfortunes, "not having had it in his power to tell a single word, nor giving [Delano] the least hint, that he might know the truth, and state of things; because the negro Mure, who is a man of capacity and talents, performing the office of an officious servant, with all the appearance of a humble slave, did not leave the deponent [Don Benito] one moment, in order to observe his actions and words. . . ."[6]

The picture of Delano's whiteness and Don Benito's pallor beside the dusky, hovering ever-present Negro must have worked on Melville as strongly as the tale of the slave leader's graceless plot to capture the American ship that night, on learning from the two captains' overheard conversation that she would have only ten men on board.

---

6 *Ibid.*, p. 338, translated from the deposition of Don Benito Cereno. The documents Delano prints in translation are as follows: (1) notary's certification; decree of commencement of process; (2) declaration of first witness, Don Benito Cereno; ratification of same; (3) declaration of Don Amasa Delano; ratification; (4) declaration of Don Nathaniel Luther, midshipman; ratification; (5) sentence pronounced by Dr. Juan Martinez de Rozas; confirmation and acknowledgment of the sentence by the Royal Audience; (6) a resolution by the Royal Audience commending Captain Delano for "the generous and benevolent conduct" he displayed in aiding the Spanish captain; (7) correspondence between Delano and the Spanish minister plenipotentiary at Washington, who presented him with a gold medal on behalf of the king of Spain for his "noble and generous conduct" in rescuing his subjects. Melville in his recension pretends to quote only from (1) and (2), but actually makes fairly basic revisions while trying to keep the tone intact.

III

In expanding Delano's chapter from about 14,000 to about 34,000 words, Melville rejects elements prominent in his source, admits others which might seem to have sprung from the process of his own poetic symbol-making, and builds his essential structure on a few trifling hints greatly elaborated. The pattern is Captain Delano's imagined vacillation between his mistrust of some sinister threat and his recurrent, common-sense self-assurance. Apart from the tale of a slave mutiny and the Negro ringleader's plan to make a piratical raid on the American benefactor's ship, Melville takes from the *Narrative* two central and vital symbolic elements. The stranger when she made her first appearance showed no colors, and when approached her deck swarmed with a distressed horde in [197] which blacks greatly outnumbered whites. Then her movements, first almost running on the rocks, veering away, approaching the anchored sealer, then drifting off out of sight, and finally sailing up to her anchorage under the American captain's direction—all follow precisely the account in the *Narrative.* The ship entering a strange port without showing her colors was regarded with suspicion aboard the *Perseverance,* in Delano's recollection. And the meanderings of the Spanish ship, which seem to parallel the vagaries of Captain Delano's mental process—approaching an ominous truth, veering off, drifting all day, and at last coming swiftly to an anchorage instantly abandoned under fire—are not Melville's invention. But he traced these cloudy figures as "with the magic hand of chance."

The inward and psychological structure Melville developed by enlarging and paralleling small incidents in the *Narrative.* Out of a few instances of insubordination and disorder aboard the slaver, which annoyed the real Delano rather than arousing his suspicion, Melville creates the two dozen or more actions which make up the body of his plot, its complication, if you will. And they serve like knots in a bowstring to give the structure its taut suspension, as the arrow is drawn with maddening deliberation. There is reason to question the artistic effectiveness of introducing so many delaying actions, each conforming to the same scheme. One almost wonders whether Melville, who was writing at space rates in a time of financial embarrassment, did not prolong the agony of suspense beyond the bounds of artistic good judgment. Two arguments militate against this crass aspersion. Melville was borrowing from Poe a literary method acceptable to contemporary readers, and he was building on details of symbolic value with a deliberateness also characteristic of *Moby-Dick, Pierre,* and *Mardi*— works where such a low motive cannot have been a consideration.

What Melville eliminates in reworking his source is as revealing as what he admits or expands. The real Delano was daring to the point of bravado, for he went aboard the stranger and stayed there all day, leaving a disaffected crew, some seventeen of whom had deserted in Botany Bay and been replaced by convict stowaways, at least three of them desperate outlaws. (Five jumped ship in that very harbor.) Far from having been prosperous, the historic voyage had earned the *Perseverance's* crew less than $20 per man,[198] and she had been away from home a year and a half. Melville's purpose in altering these facts is clear. In general he is making Captain Delano's ship and voyage typical of the man's career and of the kind of figure Melville sees him to be. He is also heightening the contrast between the New-World sealer and the Old-World slaver. He is improving the credibility of the tale in its salient features in order to add exotic symbolic details that detract from its realism but add to its psychological and poetic weight.

Melville likewise adopted from his source the device of appending legal depositions attesting the truth of occurrences so unlikely that Captain Delano himself seems to have felt the need of proving them to his readers. It was necessary to alter the documents considerably to accord with changes of date and detail. The Spanish ship had been made far grander in scale, for example, so her complement of crew and slaves was greatly enlarged. The time of action was moved back to put it in the eighteenth century (a period associated with the two great revolutions) rather than the nineteenth century (a time associated with the rising controversy over the slavery question). But the appendix had another function in Melville's recension—as in Delano's original. While apparently destroying the unity of the work, it served to emphasize the unifying theme of law. It threw into contrast the value of legal evidence as against psychological factors which such evidence cannot take into account, and suggested that legal justice is often at odds with absolute justice. Such a case as Melville adduced had an etiology reaching back far beyond the chain of evidence, reaching indeed into the farthest recesses of depravity in their primordial dusky beginnings.

IV

It is noteworthy that while Melville took the names of all his characters from Delano and thought seriously of identifying his source, he changed the names of the two ships. The *Perseverance* became the *Bachelor's Delight,* the *Tryal* (odd name for a Spanish ship) became the *San Dominick.* We are all familiar with the sexual associations bachelorhood had for Melville, whose "Paradise of Bachelors and Tartarus of Maids" appeared in *Harper's Monthly* the very month he submitted *Benito Cereno* to *Putnam's.*[7] Bachelorhood[199] seems to have connoted the innocence of a life free from those sexual fears and

---

[7] Jay Leyda, *The Melville Log* (New York, 1951), II, 500–501. See also M. M. Sealts, Jr., "The Publication of Melville's *Piazza Tales,*" *Modern Language Notes,* LIX (January 1944), 56.

revulsions emblemed in "Tartarus of Maids" and in "The Bell-Tower," which went to *Putnam's* the following month, terrors which I am convinced are for Melville also associated with whiteness. As others have pointed out, the *Bachelor* (overflowing with sperm) and the *Delight* ("most miserably misnamed") were two of the last ships spoken by the *Pequod* as she rushed to her fatal rendezvous. The *Bachelor's* captain did not believe in the existence of the malignant whale. The *Delight* had just lost five of her crew to such a monster, probably Moby-Dick himself.

But the monkish retreat of Don Benito in his Dominican ship warrants closer scrutiny than even Mr. Fogle has given it. After all, while we are speaking of nomenclature, it should be recalled that the work takes its title not from Delano or Babo and his insurrection, but from Benito Cereno. His name connotes the blessed serenity of the Benedictine or perhaps the serenity of lifeless withdrawal.[8] And Don Benito *is* the central character, for all the difficulty one has in dissociating oneself from Amasa Delano. Considered in the light of the depth psychology Melville's symbolism invites, both Babo and Delano are mistrusted by Don Benito as father figures, the one malicious, the other benign. Saved from the one, he retires to a monastery far from home, as if still fleeing the other, though the name of his retreat is agony and his companion there is grief. And there he dies, at twenty-nine.

Melville had to alter his source fundamentally to achieve such an ending and a symbolism compact of so many meanings. Its closing dialogue may be read in the reflected light of the Adamic myth: "the ritualistic trials of the young innocent, liberated from family and social history or bereft of them; advancing hopefully into a complex world he knows not of; . . . defeated, perhaps even destroyed . . . but leaving his mark upon the world, and a sign in which conquest may later become possible for the survivors." The myth does not quite fit. Amasa Delano is no Adam for all his innocence. Don Benito is not an American.[9]

He is rather the Poe-esque exemplar of the decadent son of a [200] decayed noble family, the sensitive, the congenitally weakened and diseased heir of empty and horrific grandeur. His fainting spells, his readiness to throw himself into the arms of the hypocritical body servant he knows to be his deadliest enemy, his unwillingness to retaliate when he has the opportunity—all these traits somehow spell a death wish even beyond the limits of Don Benito's withdrawal. They

---

[8] Thomas E. Connolly, "A Note on Name-Symbolism in Melville," *American Literature*, XXV (January 1954), 489.

[9] R. W. B. Lewis, *The American Adam* (Chicago, 1955), p. 127. It is worth noting that Mr. Lewis does not discuss *Benito Cereno* in his valuable chapter, "Melville: The Apotheosis of Adam."

are not in the least explained by his no doubt traumatic experience in the uprising and thereafter. They reflect an earlier, deeper-buried trauma.

In that final conversation between the two captains each states his trust in a divine Providence, the Spaniard's based on faith, the American's on belief in good works; the American voices his hope in the future, the Spaniard his fear that the past will have its revenge on him and his kind. The American revels in the beneficence of nature; the Spaniard says that for him it holds only the promise of death. While this poses the essential Adamic problem, confronting the Old World's guilt with the stubborn optimism of a young nation eager to cast off the past with its load of incurable hate and injustice; and while it poses also the existentialist dilemma of individual responsibility laboring under anxiety as it confronts the void of non-being, these are not the only themes. For just beyond this exchange we come on a most enigmatic paragraph:

> But if the Spaniard's melancholy sometimes ended in muteness upon topics like the above, there were others upon which he never spoke at all; on which, indeed, all his old reserves were piled. Pass over the worst, and, only to lucidate, let an item or two be cited. The dress, so precise and costly, worn by him on the day whose events have been narrated, had not willingly been put on. And that silver-mounted sword, apparent symbol of despotic command, was not, indeed, a sword, but the ghost of one. The scabbard, artificially stiffened was empty.

There is no rational link between this dark passage and the foregoing. Whatever the secret causes of Don Benito's melancholy, they are tinged with shame. Whether the dress he was reluctant to put on was reluctantly worn because it was fine, because it bespoke nobility and command, because it was gay and he was in mourning for his closest friend, or simply because it was male attire, is not made clear. All we know is that Don Benito's mourning has an exaggerated abundance like Hamlet's, though in Don Benito it is[201] unmanly. Earlier, at the mere mention of his friend's name, "his air was heart-broken; his knees shook; his servant supported him." Captain Delano's misinterpretation of his grief—his assuming that it would be less crushing if Don Benito's friend had not been buried at sea—sends Don Benito into a faint. He falls unconscious "into the ready arms of his attendant."

Taken with the undoubtedly phallic implication of the artificially stiffened scabbard, which is empty, the whole spells a failure of vital drive and virility. The Spaniard alienates us. Even the hardships he has suffered cannot explain his withdrawal from life, which is in line with his effort to prevent Captain Delano from recovering his ship. It is what forces Captain Delano to exclaim, "How unlike we are made!" —as if he were speaking of a woman.

To explain these enigmas we must re-examine two other incidents Melville has interpolated into Delano's narrative.

V

The skeleton that replaces Christopher Columbus below the monkish vessel's bowsprit, the slaveowner whom Don Benito follows in dying, the ship that had reversed herself to point toward dark Africa and show the New World a stern-piece whereon a dark satyr in a mask tramples "a writhing figure, likewise masked"—these symbolic devices of Melville's allude to the sinister fact of slavery, something the historic Delano also regarded as an evil.[10] The fictitious Delano was no symbol-hunting critic either, yet he saw in the padlock that chained the African king and the key to it worn round Don Benito's throat "significant symbols, truly."

But slavery itself is symbolic. The key Don Benito wears is as galling a bond as the chain Melville gave King Atufal—a mere name in the source. The debilitated weakling who wears the key is more pitiable than the giant African, whose chains prove to be a mere figment, a disguise, and a warning. Don Benito is enslaved by memories, by history, by the sins of medieval Spain and modern Spanish America—by the iniquity of the fathers that is visited upon the children. But as we accompany Captain Delano into the *San Dominick's* cuddy we get the eerie feelings of a conscious mind penetrating into the black depths of the totally subconscious world. We cling to Delano's reassuring common sense as Dante to Virgil,[202] and are shaken when he entertains some of those "antic conceits, appearing and vanishing in a breath, from which, perhaps, the best regulated mind is not always free." With Captain Delano we are permitted to walk out again into the light, but we are darkly aware that Don Benito does not enjoy our freedom. He must stay behind with the pertinacious black servant who is in fact his master. Babo is the real *"jefe"* whom Benito must follow in death.

I have spoken of a pattern of vacillation between suspicion and sensible reassurance which makes up the body of Melville's narrative. Two incidents conforming to that pattern most strongly suggest the intuitive process by which the mind of awareness catches the dumb signals of the unconscious mind it can read no better than Captain Delano can decipher the messages of the frantic Spanish seaman evading the watchful eyes of their dark captors. The incidents are those two unforgettable scenes wherein Captain Delano watches Babo shave Don Benito, and wherein he himself passes in panic through the dark corridor whose exit is guarded by the chained Atufal.

The shaving scene is a nest of ironic duplicity that bristles with concealed meanings. It is climactic no matter on what level it is read. In the seascape of grays and blacks and whites it is the scene that is splashed with color. Having noted that the Spanish ship on entering

---

10 Delano, *Narrative*, p. 204.

the harbor showed no colors, Melville's imagination conceived the flag locker where Babo keeps the ensigns and pennants and out of which he takes the colors of the king of Spain to wrap around Don Benito while he shaves him. Melville goes on to endow Captain Delano with the typical American's indulgent attitude toward Negroes, especially Negro servants. Being on "chatty and half-gamesome terms" with all darkies the captain joshes Babo about taking such liberties with the royal arms—"black, blue, and yellow—a closed castle in a blood-red field diagonal with a lion rampant in a white."

" 'It's all one, I suppose,' " he says, condescending to the Negro's love of garish show, " 'so the colors be gay,' which playful remark did not fail somewhat to tickle the negro."

It is ironic that the American should be reflecting on the Negro's "easy cheerfulness, harmonious in every glance and gesture; as though God had set the whole negro to some pleasant tune," just as Babo is menacing Don Benito with a razor that will soon draw[203] blood. It is ironic that the narrator should speak of the "docility arising from the unaspiring contentment of a limited mind," while Babo bends to his task, as sly, as quick-witted, as ferine and desperately intransigent a man as one has met since Iago. It is ironic that Captain Delano should mistake for an amenity what is in fact a scene of torment and third-degree compulsion. It is doubly ironic that something in this supposedly tranquil scene suggests to Delano that "in the black he saw a headsman, and in the white a man at the block."

The situation has in it the classic components of nightmare. One is in the hands of a lethal enemy disguised as the soul of gentleness and tender consideration. One is held down in a chair of black Malacca cane that is "like some grotesque engine of torment." One watches paralyzed as the razor is drawn and honed and brought with deadly menace to a delicate spot "low down under the throat." And the stupid bystander imagines that what he is seeing is all commonplace, indifferent, everyday domestic ritual. One wants to cry out and cannot utter a sound. One longs to spring up and is motionless, bound like a slave. One watches the spots of blood stain the creamy lather at the throat, as Babo holds up the razor trickling with one's own blood. And one hears the impenitent murderer of one's best friend declare with infinite ambiguity, "Babo's first blood."

The scene has connotations of ritual murder and human sacrifice and the unspeakable horrors of the torture chamber. It is edged with the threat, nay the promise, of castration. For Don Benito, screening his morbid memories under his heavy dark beard, it holds threats more fearsome than death. It echoes with the reiteration of ancient torment that has no words, of secret fears deep as the womb. Don Benito's passivity, his reserve, his muteness ("pass over the worst") seem a little clearer in the light of that horrible scene.

And it is here that Melville has taken the greatest liberties with his source. The real Don Benito (whom Delano calls "Don Bonito") proved to be a malicious ingrate as well as a coward. Under stress he promised Delano half the worth of his ship and cargo as rightful salvage dues. He would not join the boarding party to recover the ship but was barely prevented from stabbing a slave once the Negroes[204] were bound. He expressed gratitude to his rescuer while testifying at the trial of the slaves, but went around to the jailed Botany Bay convicts who had deserted Delano's ship, and persuaded them to give affidavits that Delano was a pirate.

How are we to explain the impulse that led Melville to turn this repulsive creature into one who could honestly call himself "not only an innocent man, but the most pitiable of all men?" The other two figures in the plot are drawn from life. Don Benito is cut from the whole cloth. One feels Melville is seeking to excuse him, to plead for him, to expiate his sins, to be his attorney in the face of universal calumny. The Don Benito of Melville's fiction has many of the elements of Bartleby in him. Is he also an Ishmael in the embrace of some dark cannibal?

To get even a tentative answer to these questions and those they in turn raise we must look at the other scene. It is the most gripping of all the incidents in which terror is succeeded by easy reassurance that all is well—reassurances that we later know to be all illusory. Delano has left the cabin annoyed at Don Benito's aloofness and reserve:

He was hardly midway in the narrow corridor, dim as a tunnel, leading from the cabin to the stairs, when a sound, as of the tolling for execution in some jail-yard fell on his ears. Instantly . . . his mind, responsive to the portent, swarmed with superstitious suspicions.

At this moment Captain Delano apprehends what turns out to be the truth—the existence of a plot to seize his ship and destroy him. For once it is not the Spaniard he suspects, but the Negroes. And for once he gives in to helpless panic, as he rushes past Atufal, the chained king lurking just beyond the threshold. Then, unwisely but fortunately as it turns out, Captain Delano has another one of his accesses of good common sense.

The next moment, with clenched jaw and hand, he passed Atufal, and stood unharmed in the light. As he saw his trim ship lying peacefully at anchor, . . . his household boat, with familiar faces in it, patiently rising and falling on the short waves . . . and more than all, as he saw the benign aspect of nature, taking her innocent repose in the evening; . . . as charmed eye and ear took in all these, with the chained figure of the black, clenched jaw and hand relaxed.[205]

Captain Delano has had a momentary flash of the kind of terror Don Benito constantly lives under. He feels himself menaced in fancy as Don Benito is in fact. He fears the hate of the blacks as an omen of some cataclysmic disaster, and his fear echoes deeper existential anxiety and perhaps a trace of that secret guilt that cannot penetrate the thick sludge of his native stupidity. For an instant he knows the black men as his ancient and injured enemy, his primitive brother and forefather, threatening him at the verge of a dark tunnel that throbs with the pulsing sexual rhythms of war drums.

The real Delano tells us that the Negro women were not content with murdering Don Benito's men, but wanted to torture them as well. He recalls that "in the act of murder, and before that of the engagement of the ship [by Delano's boat crews], they began to sing, and were singing a very melancholy song during the action, to excite the courage of the negroes."

The fictitious Delano has a moment's experience of the perpetual anxiety that is Don Benito's life. The healthy, practical mind has a flashing intuition of what the neurotic suffers in his tormented imagination. But Captain Delano is no shivering Spaniard and is menaced by no threatening father image, black or white. Emerging into the light he sees the "screened sun in the quiet camp of the west shining out like the mild light from Abraham's tent." He is the son of a line of strong yet kindly patriarchs like Abraham. And the black slave king is to his blind vision still safely and tamely chained.[206]

𝔊𝔊𝔊

BENITO CERENO: MELVILLE'S VISION AND RE-VISION OF THE SOURCE

Marjorie Dew

The theme that Melville develops in altering Delano's *Narrative* is this: the exceptional man inevitably comes before a wall. He inquires and he perceives; and what he perceives is that whatever-there-may-be behind life is incomprehensible and indifferent. The knowledge destroys him—or, what is the same thing, he destroys himself because he chooses to continue the confrontation. He will inquire; and "the dead, blind wall butts all *inquiring* heads at last." The dead, blind wall— unseeing men, unfeeling men, uncaring nature. Benito Cereno confronts Amasa Delano, Babo, and exterior nature.

This paper was presented to the Melville Society at the 1964 meeting of the Modern Language Association, and is here published for the first time.

To accomplish his artistic purpose, to give to the characters and events of Delano's narrative the symbolic meaning of this view of life, Melville does three things to his source story: he enlarges Amasa Delano, he creates Babo,[1] and he transforms Benito Cereno.

Under Melville's pen, Cereno becomes man knowing, knowing the world and knowing nature, and therefore man alone. His re-characterization is accomplished largely through Delano's reactions to him. A sense of Cereno's isolation grows, for the reader, with both the ebb and the flow of Delano's suspicions and with Delano's special obtuseness at the moments of Cereno's greatest need, when Cereno's life is in greatest danger at the hand of the slave Babo. One is struck by the ironic contrasts between Delano's assumptions and reality in the cabin scene passages, where the man who assumes confronts the man who knows. Here Melville's Delano is blithe, gurgling and merry, and reproachful like the waters; at a loss to account but resolved to regulate, well satisfied, well-bred, rebukeful, chilled (frozen in feeling). Cereno is feverish, longing with an ague of cold (cold unto death), far beyond mere unsociability or sourness, silent, tremulous, agitated. But Melville's Delano *sees* Cereno as sullen, glaring, impatient, with dark spleen, sulky, cold (unfeeling). Delano *sees* Babo as mutely concerned. Compare the spareness of Captain Delano's narrative:

...in parting [Captain Delano] asked the Spanish captain to come on board his ship to take coffee, tea, and other refreshments; but he answered him with *coldness* and indifference; that he could not go then, but that he would in two or three days. (My italics.)

Here, and in the passage quoted below, Captain Delano barely suggests an image of coldness in Cereno, an image Melville's creative imagination runs away with.

After the Spanish ship was anchored, I invited the captain to go on board my ship and take tea or coffee with me. His answer was short and seemingly reserved; and his air very different from that with which he had received my assistance. As I was at a loss to account for this change in his demeanour, and knew he had seen nothing in my conduct to justify it, and as I felt certain that he treated me with intentional neglect; in return I became less sociable, and said little to him.

The real-life Delano's obtusely innocent suggestion of self-righteousness is expanded, spread on canvas, in Melville's painting: Delano—sunny-faced, cheerful—moves blithely across the portholes through which blows a bracing wind and through which can be seen the approaching *Bachelor's Delight* ("all a-taunt-o!") and heard the gurgling and merry

---

[1] The Mure of Delano's *Narrative*, who becomes Melville's Babo, is little more than a shadow at Cereno's elbow. Babo in Delano is nothing but a name.

waters. Nature obliges the "good-natured" man, reinforces his all's-well-with-the-world view.

Near the conclusion of Melville's narrative, Cereno says to Delano:

... You were with me all day; stood with me, sat with me, talked with me, looked at me, ate with me, drank with me; and yet, your last act was to clutch for a monster, not only an innocent man, but the most pitiable of all men.

Now become the man of sorrows, Cereno has become a character far other than Captain Delano's Cereno. According to Delano, Captain Cereno *was* a monstrous man. According to Melville, he is the type of sensitive and, hence, suffering humanity—the figure in the garden saying, Why do you sleep? The type of the meek of the Sermon on the Mount, and, hence, "ridiculous to men." Melville must omit two sections, important to the story as Delano tells it, to transform Cereno from a monster into his suffering-savior figure. The morning-after passage of Captain Delano's story would be wholly inconsistent. Delano describes the atrocities perpetrated upon the Negro captives by the members of Cereno's crew and by Cereno himself, who is seen in the act of stabbing one of the slaves. Melville omits it. His Cereno could not so behave.

The other important omission—the entire last half of the source story—is Delano's recital of Cereno's machinations to deprive Delano of his rights of salvage. It does not suit Melville's purpose. Cereno could be interested in no such matters.

His transformation perfected, Melville's Cereno is the savior paradox, a figure of strength in weakness and fear. He is strong enough to refuse to deny the abominations he has seen under the surface of things, strong enough to refuse illusion, although his refusal bring him weakness unto death. In his strength, he extends the light of grace to Delano: he would release Delano from his windowless world, would reveal to him what life really is. Things are not so easily ordered, not so easily explained as Delano would have it. Delano almost sees, but his unwelcome "start" of understanding does not stay. No, the weak cannot be thought to save the strong; the disordered mind has nothing to offer the ordered, as any good citizen of Duxbury, Massachusetts, knows. Try as he will, Cereno cannot, of course, communicate with Delano.

Babo, as Melville creates him, symbolizes unreason—highly sensitive, highly intelligent unreason. Like Claggart in *Billy Budd,* he has "apparently little to do with reason further than to employ it as an ambidexter implement for effecting the irrational." Seeming to be perfectly rational, he is Irrational Man. In Delano's account, it was Captain Cereno who proposed *to the Negroes* the whole plan of deception, everything that was to be said and done when the American captain boarded the Spanish ship—

with which they were tranquilized, warning him that if he varied in the least, or uttered any word that should give the least intimation of the past occurrences, they would instantly kill him and all his companions.

But Cereno as source of the deception plot would not suit Melville's purpose. He changed Cereno's deposition: it is Babo who "cast[s] about what to do" when the American ship appears. Babo does the plotting.

Many of Melville's Gothic additions are organic to his creation of Babo. The luncheon and shaving passages, for example. Inexplicably, during the luncheon—

[Don Benito's] hand shook, his face became hueless, broken words escaped; but directly the sane memory of the past seemed replaced by insane terrors of the present. With starting eyes he stared before him at vacancy. For nothing was to be seen but the hand of his servant pushing the Canary over towards him.

And during the shaving scene, in a quickly-put-down "fancy," Delano sees Babo as executioner.

Essentially Cereno and Babo are alike, as Billy Budd and Claggart are alike, and as all four are like Conrad's Nigger of the *Narcissus*. They are exceptional men, not able to be understood by ordinary men like Delano, possessing that quality, sometimes masked by a seeming weakness, that mystifies and overwhelms ordinary men: a disdain, Melville often calls it,[2] an I-won't-stir, I-won't-extend-myself, I-should-prefer-not-to decisiveness. Although Delano has no understanding cf it, it is this quality in Cereno that will not allow the American captain to explain away Cereno's behavior as weakness. Time after time, Melville's Delano turns away from Cereno in disgust—and yet . . . there is something about the man. He has "that wondrous ascendancy" over Delano that Bartleby, "the inscrutable scrivener," has over the attorney. Babo also holds such an ascendancy over ordinary men, so long as he lives, and thereafter; his power, in fact, increases where Melville makes him "weakest." Like Cereno, the slave Babo has been a victim of men's insensitivity to other men. Like Cereno he has been able to face the facts of the universe, choosing not to whine that men do thus behave and that the universe does not care, choosing to reject entreaty. To the end, Babo refuses to submit; he dies without speaking, cannot be forced to speak. And, after he is burned, his head on the pole meets "unabashed, the gaze of the whites."

Only Captain Delano remains essentially the same character in

---

2 See, for example, Melville's "Bartleby," "The Paradise of Bachelors," and "The Fiddler."

Melville that he reveals himself to be in his own narrative; Melville's great expansion of Delano's character does not basically change it. The real-life Delano is the man of assumptions: his "regulated" mind, his everything-can-be-accounted-for world view, his insistence on a world in which one can feel at home[3]—everything about the real Delano fits Melville's concept of the average mind. Unconsciously, somewhat stupidly, the sea captain-author has provided Melville with an effigy from which grows Melville's Delano, symbol of self-righteous unseeingness.

Life is not what it seems to such men of assumptions, says Melville. Melville's Starbuck will not and Melville's Delano cannot look under the surface and see the sharks. Neither has accepted with Ishmael that, between sharks and spades (foes and "friends"), "you are in a sad pickle" in this life. Delano's suspicions—the nearest he comes to a kind of awareness—are repeatedly lulled by his regulating assumptions: Could Don Benito be in complicity with the blacks? No, whites were the superior race; the blacks were too stupid. Stupid and docile, the blacks—"Captain Delano took to negroes, not philanthropically, but genially, just as other men to Newfoundland dogs." Does Captain Cereno behave strangely? Well—

As a nation . . . Spaniards are all an odd set; the very word Spaniard has a curious, conspirator, Guy-Fawkish twang to it. And yet, I dare say, Spaniards in the main are as good folks as any in Duxbury, Mass.

The world is Duxbury to Delano. His boat Rover (Melville plays upon the word) is, ironically, as familiar as a Newfoundland dog (as filled with "trustful associations" as the "delightfully" subservient Babo):

What, I . . . little Jack of the Beach, that used to go berrying with cousin Nat and the rest; I to be murdered here at the ends of the earth, on board a haunted pirate-ship by a horrible Spaniard? Too nonsensical to think of!

Melville's nausea for the man who can see only joy and not woe, who has no real communication with the sufferer is further drawn by his changing the names of the ships. Captain Delano's *Perseverance* becomes Melville's *Bachelor's Delight*—the ship of a "sunny-faced" bachelor. We know what Melville thinks of sunny-faced bachelors, one of whom says in "The Paradise of Bachelors": "Pain! Trouble! As well talk of Catholic miracles. No such thing. . . ." The insensitive proprietor of the Devil's Dungeon paper mill in "The Tartarus of Maids," Melville points out, is a bachelor. The captain of the *Bachelor* encountered by the *Pequod* in *Moby-Dick* was "too damned jolly"—

---

[3] Such a world view held by a laborer once dismayed Martin Buber: "It came to me that I must shatter the security of his Weltanschauung, through which he thought of a 'world' in which one 'felt at home'." (*Eclipse of God* [New York, 1952], p. 5.)

the White Whale?—"Don't believe in him at all." Compare Delano's: Murder?—Too nonsensical to think of!

In the name of the Negro-dominated ship, *San Dominick* (the *Tryal* of the original story), Melville ironically symbolizes the abode of saintly men, a "ship-load of monks" it *appears* to Delano at first sight; and it well may be the abode of saintly men—only any facile lining up of saints and sinners by a bachelor is repellent and bound to be mistaken. The carving on the stern-piece insists on the ambiguity; the dark satyr is masked as is the writhing figure he steps on; and the death's head, under its canvas wrapping, the figure-head labelled, "Follow your leader," is followed by the whole ship and all aboard.

Perhaps most ironic in the characterization of Delano and most illustrative of Melville's artistic freedom with his source is his great expansion of the brief reference to the Negresses in the original Benito Cereno's deposition, which reads:

... the negresses of age, were *knowing* to the revolt, and influenced the death of their master; who also used their influence to kill the deponent; ... in the act of murder, and before that of the engagement of the ship, they began to sing, and were singing a very melancholy song during the action, to excite the courage of the negroes. (My italics.)

From the word *knowing*, Melville's image grows: the chilling contrast between the knowing of the Negresses ("loving as doves") and the un-knowing of the "well-pleased" Captain Delano. The artist unfolds the truth that, for him, lies in the knowing-Negresses Captain Delano encounters: "There's naked nature, now; pure tenderness and love, thought Captain Delano, well pleased." How ironically true! For Melville, the "pure tenderness and love" of nature is exactly like the tenderness and love of the Negresses, an aiding and abetting to de-ception.

Sights and sounds of nature other than the Negresses also "deepen the confidence and ease" of Melville's Delano. One is in the passage already referred to in which the merry, gurgling water shows that "nature cared not a jot; since, whose fault was it, pray?" However, it was *not* Cereno's fault; Delano's assumption is false. Then where is God's loving care that Delano counts on, pray? Again, in another passage, nature assures Delano that all is what it seems, that Atufal is nothing more than the chained rebel he pretends to be:

... [Delano] saw the benign aspect of nature, taking her innocent repose in the evening; the screened sun in the quiet camp of the west shining out like the mild light from Abraham's tent; as charmed eye and ear took in all these, with the chained figure of the black, clenched jaw and hand relaxed. Once again he smiled at the phantoms which had mocked him, and felt something like a tinge of remorse, that, by harboring them even for a moment, he should, by implication, have betrayed an atheist doubt of the ever-watchful Providence above.

Notice that it is "an atheist doubt" that would have led Delano to truth; a trust in a God who cares and whose care is manifest in nature (lo, from the time of Abraham) encourages evasion or delusion.

In his concluding narrative passage, Melville again raises the question of cosmic indifference: "the yon bright sky has forgotten it all, and the blue sea, and the blue sky; these have turned over new leaves," says Delano. They are not human, replies Cereno; they can forget—and so can Delano. For Cereno, illusion is gone. A man must see the black, feel the chill in even the warm, "steadfast" trade winds.

The court depositions of *Benito Cereno*, borrowed (only slightly altered) from Delano's work, "tacked-on" to pad Melville's, and, therefore, some critics say, a defect aesthetically, is surely nothing of the sort. Melville the artist, not Melville the family man in a financial hole and in a hurry, used the deposition: structure and statement mesh in this novel. The language and the content of the court deposition undergird what Melville is trying to make the reader see, ingeniously, subtly. The irony is supremely artistic. With its use, he says, in effect: Have things seemed chaotic? Has the universe seemed unfriendly? Have evil men seemed to run rampant over good? Well, we ordinary men (the author would include himself) can tidy up. What more in the interest of order and regulation than legal documents, depositions and subsequent depositions? Is there some doubt as to causes and effects? Then take another deposition to "give credence to the rest"; finally everything will be accounted for by order of the court, and the last deposition will serve "as the key to fit into the lock of the complications which precede it." This method, according to the original Captain Delano, will "be the most correct course, ... give the reader a better view of the subject than any other method that could be adopted." Things can be seen to be "perfectly consistent," says Delano, every man's view seen to fit with every other man's view, belying appearances to the contrary. And now the story is complete, ambiguity removed, for all us good-natured, practical, ordinary people.

The opposition in Melville's *Benito Cereno* is not between good and evil but rather between average sensibilities and uncommon sensibilities. The question of the book is—Can an ordinary man see? The suspense lies in—When will Delano see? Will he see? Can he see?

Melville says—the well-being of one's fellow man cannot be left to a benevolent providence; no benevolence exists except perhaps in the hearts of men. Unfortunately, only a few, only the exceptional, realize this. The rest, like Amasa Delano, too willingly leave things to a Father-God. "Cannot you see"—Cereno cries out to Delano, Melville cries out to the world, a few men cry out to the rest, "cannot you see that there is no understanding unless we can understand each other, no help unless we help each other!" And the possibility lurks barely beneath the surface in Melville's world (the diver always reaches it) that men cannot, perhaps, communicate even with each other.

Note: The questions under each heading are divided into two groups: those that can be treated in relatively short papers (A) and those that require a relatively longer treatment (B).

I. Textual Problems

A

1. Discuss any essay in this book whose critical position would have been strengthened (or weakened) by taking into account the revisions.

2. Are all of the revisions improvements, or is it possible to argue that some affect the story adversely?

B

1. Not all the variants are of the same order—some are clearly revisions, some merely corrections. Catalogue the variants so as to distinguish between them, paying special attention to those that do not readily fall into one category or the other. Defend the validity of your lists.

2. Using what you demonstrate to be bona fide revisions, write a paper on Melville's changes in the story.

3. Four of the other five pieces which appeared with *Benito Cereno* in *The Piazza Tales* were also first published in *Putnam's*. The Hendricks House edition of the volume (1948) lists (pp. 251–256) the variants in these stories. Do the variants in these other stories shed any light on the variants in *Benito Cereno?*

II. Point of View

A

1. To what extent are Miller's and Cardwell's defences of Delano alike or unalike? Which seems more convincing? Why?

2. How convincing is Canaday's explanation for Delano's misconstruing the story's central situation?

3. Miller and Phillips both use the term "masks" in their essays. Do they use them in essentially the same way?

4. In what ways does Miller's interpretation of Delano depend on his interpretation of Cereno and Babo?

5. Discuss: "[Delano] is not a dialectician, but his silences carry meaning" (Cardwell).

6. Write a critique of Canaday's use of the depositions in support of his thesis.

7. Write a critique of Miller's assertion that *Benito Cereno*, "As always in Melville, . . . revolves about the balance of *heart* and *mind.*"

8. Discuss: "Babo obviously enjoys evil for itself alone" (Miller).

9. Discuss: "Cereno's faithful servant never transcends the implied confines of an historical context and a personal rationale which render him impure and susceptible" (Phillips).

10. Does Phillips's description of Cereno as "sad, mad, wise" strike you as convincing?

B

1. Write a critique of the following statement: "Delano as a character is not a problem; the problem is, what did Melville intend him to represent?"

2. What are some of the problems involved in trying to assess what Delano is meant to symbolize? The student may wish to consult the relevant sections on point of view in Wayne C. Booth's *The Rhetoric of Fiction* (Chicago, 1961) as a means of structuring his answer.

3. Canaday asserts that the theme of authority appears in each of Melville's novels dealing with the sea. On the basis of your reading of *Billy Budd* (or *Moby-Dick* or *White-Jacket*) defend or attack Canaday's contention.

4. By analyzing the evidence that each critic in this section employs in support of his position, and the ways in which he employs it, account for the disagreement as to what Delano is meant to represent.

5. Write an essay on Delano's function in the story.

III. The Negro Problem

A

1. Analyze Glicksberg's method of demonstrating that Melville is not anti-Negro in the story.

2. How convincing is Glicksberg's assertion that the story arouses "mixed emotions"?

3. Do you agree with Schiffman that Melville could not felicitously discuss the slavery issue within the compass of a short story?

4. In the twelve years between his two published views of the slavery issue in *Benito Cereno*, Schiffman has changed his mind. On the basis of the two essays, document the shift and try to explain why.

5. What is the function of Kaplan's account of the slave revolts on the *Creole* and *Amistad*? Do you consider this a valid means of supporting his argument?

6. Kaplan interprets Delano's silence after Cereno says "the negro" as a sign of agreement—he too now knows malign evil and where it exists. Do you agree?

7. What view of the function of literature underlies Kaplan's last paragraph?

8. Analyze D'Azevedo's method of defending Melville from the charge of being anti-Negro.

9. Discuss: "Melville wisely did not presume . . . to know a Negro slave's innermost mind or the complex structure of his personality" (D'Azevedo).

10. Discuss: "With its legalistic pretensions of objectivity, the deposition misses the truth as widely as did Delano in his completest innocence" (Guttmann).

11. Analyze Guttman's method of demonstrating that Melville is not anti-Negro.

12. Which of the "pro-Negro" interpretations is most convincing? Why?

13. Which of the "anti-Negro" interpretations is most convincing? Why?

14. Compare Putzel's interpretation of the function of the Negro (in the section on Source, Symbol, and Theme) with Kaplan's.

15. Write a critique of Feltenstein's handling of the slavery issue in her final paragraph (in the section on Source, Symbol, and Theme).

B

1. Compare Delano's attitude toward Negroes in the source with his attitude toward them in the story.

2. Analyze the use made of Melville's other works in the essays in this section.

3. Select one essay in this section which in your opinion most satis-factorily deals with the Negro problem and explain why. Make

certain to demonstrate the weaknesses or inadequacies of the other treatments.

4. Write an essay in which you argue that the Negro as a social issue is *not* an intended element in the story but rather is a product of our present-day preoccupation with the problem.

5. Write an essay in which you demonstrate that the slavery issue *is* an intended element in the story.

IV. Source, Symbol, and Theme

Source

A

1. Write a critique of any essay in this section which is substantially concerned with Melville's use of his source.

2. Which of the essays on Delano as point of view (Cardwell, Canaday, Miller, Phillips) interprets Melville's Delano in a manner most consistent with the source? Is this a critically valid method of getting at Melville's intention?

3. Discuss: ". . . the man who penned the journal on which *Benito Cereno* is based is almost precisely the smug buffoon who appears in Melville's fictional amplification" (Phillips in the section on Point of View).

4. Discuss: "That the name Babo had any special symbolic meaning for Melville is unlikely. He found the name in Delano's *Narrative* . . ." (Schiffman in the section on The Negro Problem).

5. Discuss: "Melville *did* rewrite the deposition, and the changes he made serve to increase the stature of Babo" (Guttmann in the section on The Negro Problem).

6. Discuss: "Everywhere Melville pruned the Cereno of Delano's *Narrative* to vein and flesh him with altruism and goodness" (Kaplan in the section on The Negro Problem).

7. Discuss: "Although the moral meaning of the source is comparable to the moral meaning of the story, the source is too crassly candid and too naively pessimistic to suit Melville" (Cardwell in the section on Point of View).

8. Discuss: "The whole point of the original tale seems to be that Americans should be very cautious in their dealings with foreigners" (Feltenstein).

9. On the basis of your reading of Chapter XVIII of Delano's *Narrative,* write a critique of Putzel's analysis of the historical Delano.

10. Discuss: "Now the point of the source lies in its set character. The action is fixed, almost fatalistically predetermined—a mold to be filled in" (Magowan).

11. Compare Feltenstein, Putzel, and Dew on the changes in the ships' names.

12. Discuss: "Melville is not simply trying to refine [Delano's] moralizing. He is revising what Delano himself had experienced, elucidating what baffled Delano, and going on to shadow forth a higher, more lucid reality, which baffles himself" (Putzel).

13. Do you agree with Dew's assertion that the Delano in the source and the Delano in Melville's story are essentially the same?

B

1. Walter Teller in his *Five Sea Captains* (New York, 1960) states that "the underlying difference between the fiction and the fact is that in [Melville's story] the reader's sympathy finally lies with neither protagonist but with the author. Reading Melville, you admire the author; reading Delano, you admire the man" (p. 22). Discuss.

2. Write an essay on the critical value of knowing the source for *Benito Cereno*.

3. Franklin H. Bruce (see Bibliography) finds a source for *Benito Cereno* in William Stirling's *Cloister Life of the Emperor Charles the Fifth*. Read Bruce's essay (and, if possible, Stirling's book) and then write an essay comparing the value of Delano and Stirling as source materials.

4. On the basis of your reading of the source and those essays that deal fully with Melville's use of Delano, discuss the ways the source has been used and the pitfalls a source-study is prone to.

Symbol and Theme

A

1. Write a critique of Feltenstein's analysis of the monastic imagery.

2. Compare the treatments of Babo in Feltenstein and Putzel.

3. Compare Putzel, Feltenstein, and Dew on the "evil" in *Benito Cereno*.

4. Several critics in this section compare Don Benito to Bartleby. On the basis of your reading of "Bartleby the Scrivener," write a critique of the values of such a comparison.

5. How does Fogle handle the social implications in the story? In what ways does his treatment differ from the treatment of the slavery issue in the Negro Problem essays?

6. How does Fogle differ from Canaday (in the section on Point of View) in his interpretation of "order"?

7. Discuss: ". . . ideally the knot should be unwound" (Fogle).

8. Write a critique of Fogle's interpretation of the Old World symbolism.

9. Compare Fogle and Putzel on Babo.

10. Discuss: ". . . the problem [in *Benito Cereno*] is beyond the human intellect" (Fogle).

11. Is Magowan's handling of the slavery issue convincing?

12. Discuss: "Delano [is] a temporarily becharmed Knight of Civilization" (Magowan).

13. How convincing is Magowan's use of color symbolism in support of his thesis?

14. Analyze the final paragraph of Magowan's essay.

15. Compare Putzel's handling of the Negro with the treatments in the Negro Problem essays.

16. Putzel asserts that all three characters see reality in a different light; Dew says Cereno and Babo are fundamentally the same. Which is more convincing? Why?

17. Write a critique of Putzel's assertion that the three main characters represent different stages in human development.

18. Do you agree with Putzel that Don Benito is the central character?

19. Write a critique of that part of Putzel's essay which handles the story from the point of view of depth psychology.

20. On the basis of your reading of some of Poe's stories (e.g., "The Fall of the House of Usher," "Ligeia," "The Tell-Tale Heart," "The Black Cat"), discuss the validity of Putzel's statement that Don Benito is a Poe-esque character.

21. Compare Putzel and Dew on Don Benito.

22. Discuss: "Slavery itself is symbolic" (Dew).

23. How convincing is Dew's assertion that the issue in the story is not between good and evil but between "average sensibilities and uncommon sensibilities"?

B

1. Analyze the use of color symbolism in the story.

2. Discuss the symbolic implications of names in *Benito Cereno*.

3. Write a paper on Melville's use of animal imagery.

4. The Depositions: Dreary Documents or Artistic Triumph?

5. Masks: Appearance and Reality in *Benito Cereno.*
6. *Benito Cereno:* The Old World and the New.
7. Write a paper on the function of nature in *Benito Cereno.*
8. Discuss Melville's use of religious symbolism in the story.

V. Additional Topics

1. In his essay on Hawthorne's fiction, *Hawthorne and His Mosses* (1850), Melville singles out "Young Goodman Brown" as a particularly powerful treatment of the evil in human history. The two stories are alike in that in both a young, hopeful man confronts life's negative capabilities and responds despairingly. Write a comparative analysis of the two stories.

2. Feltenstein asserts that Melville's use of symbolism is superior to Hawthorne's. On the basis of your reading of *The Scarlet Letter* (or a representative group of Hawthorne's short stories) assess the validity of her statement.

3. Compare Melville's *Benito Cereno* and Robert Lowell's *Benito Cereno,* a verse-drama adaptation of Melville's story, which virtually constitutes an interpretation (*Show,* August 1964).

4. Write a paper on Melville's depiction of the Negro in his fiction prior to *Benito Cereno.*

5. Compare *Benito Cereno* and Conrad's *Heart of Darkness* (or *The Nigger of the "Narcissus"*). (Cf. Green in the Bibliography.)

6. Write a paper on the image of the Negro in *Benito Cereno,* Poe's *The Narrative of Arthur Gordon Pym,* and Mrs. Stowe's *Uncle Tom's Cabin.*

PART FIVE
A SELECTED BIBLIOGRAPHY
OF *BENITO CERENO* CRITICISM

Note: Items preceded by an asterisk (*) are included in this book and therefore carry no annotation.

Arvin, Newton. *Herman Melville* (New York, 1950), pp. 238–240. A negative view of the story's artistry: tired use of a prosaic source, tediously built up atmosphere, poorly imagined narrative details, clichéd language. Delano borders on weak-wittedness; Babo is a monster out of Gothic fiction at its worst; Cereno, at most, is the object of a half-reluctant compassion. The moral significance of the story is just about nonexistent.

Bernstein, John Albert. " 'Benito Cereno' and the Spanish Inquisition," *Nineteenth Century Fiction*, XVI (March 1962), 345–350. It is through the use of the Spanish Inquisition that Melville destroys any simple distinctions between good and evil, appearance and reality, past and present. On board the *San Dominick* there is going forth a modern Inquisition, "an Inquisition which the colored races of the world are holding for the white race, an Inquisition which is brought about as a direct result of the white man's maltreatment of the darker races."

Berthoff, Warner. *The Example of Melville* (Princeton, 1962), pp. 149–158. Centers on Melville's narrative procedure in *Benito Cereno*, the "logic and fascination" of its storytelling, rather than on its allegorical significance. The moral gravity, psychological intensity, shadowy atmosphere, ironic realization of the stain of slavery "is built directly upon . . . the mechanism of mystification." The "dreary documents" at the end are a mistake if we take the story as a fable; but as a stylized solution to the riddle they are exactly right.

Bowen, Merlin. *The Long Encounter: Self and Experience in the Writings of Herman Melville* (Chicago, 1960), pp. 66–68, 203–204. Delano's blindness is not the result of a simple mind but of sentimental prejudices arising from a too benevolent heart, which does not deny the existence of evil but sees it as held in check by an ever watchful Providence. Cereno is powerless to withstand the spiritual terror, which is embodied for him in the "fiendlike Babo."

Brown, Sterling. *The Negro in American Fiction* (Washington, D.C., 1937), pp. 12–13. Though opposed to slavery, Melville does not make *Benito Cereno* into an abolitionist tract; the slaves revolt as man has always revolted—they are not villains.

Bruce, Franklin H. " 'Apparent Symbol of Despotic Command': Melville's 'Benito Cereno,' " *New England Quarterly*, XXXIV (December 1961), 462–477. Reprinted in *The Wake of the Gods: Melville's Mythology* (Stanford, 1963), pp. 136–152. An elaborate and detailed study of the similarities (arguing influence) between *Benito Cereno* and William Stirling's *Cloister Life of the Emperor Charles the Fifth.* "As the metaphorical ghost of Charles the Fifth, [Cereno] re-enacts the emperor's abdication and servitude to the church. When he follows the teaching of that church's leader, he, too, is betrayed by the men in whom he has confidence."

*Canaday, Nicholas, Jr. "A New Reading of Melville's 'Benito Cereno,' " *Studies in American Literature,* Waldo McNeir and Leo B. Levy, eds. (Baton Rouge, 1960), pp. 49–57.

*Cardwell, Guy. "Melville's Gray Story: Symbols and Meaning in 'Benito Cereno,' " *Bucknell Review*, VIII (May 1959), 154–167.

Chase, Richard. *Herman Melville: A Critical Study* (New York, 1949), pp. 148–159. Delano is that familiar fictional American—the man of energy and good will who is bewildered by the coiled complexities of the Old World. Committed to pragmatic virtues, Delano can save Cereno's body but not his soul. "Melville is guessing that the accomplishment of the New World will be abortive if the American remains ignorant of the Old World's spiritual depths."

Connolly, Thomas E. "A Note on Name-Symbolism in Melville," *American Literature*, XXV (May 1954), 489–490. Speculates cn the name change from source to story. In Delano's *Narrative* the Spanish captain is called Bonito Sereno (which could mean "the handsome, shameless fellow"). But in the story because Cereno "i· the representative of pure goodness," Melville opts for Benito Cereno ("Blessed Serenity").

*D'Azevedo, Warren. "Revolt on the *San Dominick*," *Phylon*, XVII (June 1956), 129–140.

Ensslen, Klaus. "Melville's 'Benito Cereno,' " *Kleine Beitrage zur Amerikanischen Literaturgeschichte,* Hans Galinsky and Hans-Joachim Lang, eds. (Heidelberg, 1961), 27–33. *Benito Cereno* is not a story of evil destroying good, but of the manifestation of evil in human nature in general. The change of Cereno's character from the source was to take away the accidental character of the mutiny. The Negroes do not commit gratuitous atrocities; they are simply trying to escape to Africa. The "story is . . . a revelation of an abyss in human nature, . . . of mutual degradation, hatred and oppression, of which white and black equally partake."

*Feltenstein, Rosalie. "Melville's 'Benito Cereno,' " *American Literature*, XIX (November 1947), 245–255.

Fiedler, Leslie. *Love and Death in the American Novel* (New York, 1960), pp. 382–383. *Benito Cereno* is related to the history of the minstrel show in which a "grotesque semblance of the archetypal nigger" attempts to exorcise with high-jinks and ritualistic jokes the threat of "black rebellion and the sense of guilt which secretly demands it as penance." Melville, like Delano, finds the problem of slavery and the Negro "a little exotic, a Gothic horror in an almost theatrical sense of the word."

*Fogle, Richard Harter. "The Monk and the Bachelor: Melville's *Benito Cereno*," *Tulane Studies in English*, III (1952), 155–178. Reprinted in *Melville's Shorter Tales* (Norman, 1960), 116–147.

Forrey, Robert. "Herman Melville and the Negro Question," *Mainstream*, XV (February 1962), 28–29. The story is not anti-Negro—Babo is a refutation of the stereotype of the docile, stupid Negro. Melville has sympathy neither for Delano (shallow commercial mind) nor for Cereno (decaying feudal order).

Freeman, John. *Herman Melville* (London, 1926), pp. 145–149. The story is a "flaming instance of the author's pure genius"; through our knowledge of Conrad we can now appreciate Melville's use of oblique narration and the horrific use of the Negro.

Galván, Enrique Tierno. "Benito Cereno o el mito de Europa," *Cuadernos Hispanoamericanos*, XXXVI (December, 1952), 215–233 (in Spanish). In its prediction of the fate of modern Europe *Benito Cereno* is elevated to the status of a myth. Like Don Benito, Europe finds itself in a series of false realities; order and authority have broken down. Cereno as the conscience of the elite can only watch and suffer—he cannot flee. Caught in the grip of historical circumstance (Babo) and terror (Atufal), Cereno substitutes tired dignity for rebellion. Delano as the man free of history offers the strength of the new, a release from the barnacled Spanish ship of state.

Gibson, William M. "Herman Melville's 'Bartleby the Scrivener' and 'Benito Cereno,' " *The American Renaissance*, George Hendricks, ed. (Frankfort, 1961), pp. 112–116. If Don Benito saved Delano's life by his terrified imposture, Delano equally saved Benito's by his good-natured innocence. The story is "a drama of the 'ugly passions' inevitable in slavery, perhaps as a contrast of the old world (Spain) and the new (America), and certainly as an exploration of the 'mystery of iniquity.' "

*Glicksberg, Charles I. "Melville and the Negro Problem," *Phylon*, XI (Autumn 1950), 207–215.

Green, Jesse D. "Diabolism, Pessimism, and Democracy: Notes on Melville and Conrad," *Modern Fiction Studies*, VIII (Autumn 1962), 287–305. Granting the obvious similarities between *Benito Cereno* and *Heart of Darkness* (and some other Conrad works), this essay emphasizes important differences. Conrad's "controlled skepticism" in contrast to Melville's shifting ambiguous responses makes for a different relationship between author and narrator and for a different quality attaching to the symbol of blackness.

*Guttmann, Allen. "The Enduring Innocence of Captain Amasa Delano," *Boston University Studies in English*, V (Spring 1961), 35–45.

Haber, Tom Burns. "A Note on Melville's 'Benito Cereno,'" *Nineteenth Century Fiction*, VI (September 1951), 146–147. Argues that the cut on Babo's cheek (after the shaving scene) was inflicted by Cereno, thus endangering not only his own but Delano's life as well. Babo's allowing Cereno to live shows that he, unlike the civilized Cereno, is capable of restraint. (See Pafford and Watkins for rebuttal.)

Hagopian, John V., et al. *Insight I: Analyses of American Literature* (Frankfurt Am Main, 1962), pp. 150–155. Explicates the Christian symbolism in the story. Negroes do not symbolize evil—their revolt is purely retaliatory and their motives are as praiseworthy as Jefferson's. "In fact, the Negroes are in revolt against evil; but because Melville is working in cosmic-religious, rather than political-social terms, the revolt cannot ultimately succeed. . . . evil in the universe cannot be overcome, and it is inextricably linked with Christianity."

Hillway, Tyrus. *Herman Helville* (New York, 1963), pp. 117–118. The story presents the case of a "passive resister" who is so appalled by the world's evil that he withdraws from it in fear.

Hoffman, Charles G. "The Shorter Fiction of Herman Melville," *South Atlantic Quarterly*, LII (July 1953), 425–430. The key to Melville's achievement is the portrayal of Delano: brave, resourceful, yet prone to doubts and suspicions; his is the "innocent eye."

Howard, Leon. *Herman Melville: A Biography* (Berkeley, 1951), pp. 218–223. Biographical details and an account of the publication of the story help fill in something of Melville's state of mind during the composition and revision of the story.

Jackson, Margaret Y. "Melville's Use of a Real Slave Mutiny in 'Benito Cereno,'" *CLA Journal*, IV (December 1960), 79–93. Melville is censured for allowing a possible pro-slavery interpretation of his story. "Nevertheless, despite his unpleasant handling of the story, one cannot fail to observe that the author's chief concern . . . is not with the slavery question per se, but rather with the problem of good and evil; and that . . . in his search for one more symbol, [he] seized upon the Negro to represent in his tale the formidable force against which good could offer no substantial resistance."

*Kaplan, Sidney. "Herman Melville and the American National Sin: The Meaning of 'Benito Cereno,' " *Journal of Negro History,* XLI (October 1956), 311–338; XLII (January 1957), 11–37.

Knox, George. "Lost Command: 'Benito Cereno' Reconsidered," *Personalist,* XL (Summer 1959), 280–291. The story does not enforce a hopeless and cynical abandonment of faith in the power of decision and command. Cereno follows his leader, Aranda, to death, but he also follows the leader he created—Babo. "Evil has apparently triumphed, but it need not."

Lawson, John Howard. *The Hidden Heritage* (New York, 1950), pp. 430–431. The story is cheap melodrama and a distortion of human and moral values. The pro-slavery sentiment in the tale is a result of Melville's wanting to cater to the ready market for such things.

Levin, Harry. *The Power of Blackness* (New York, 1958), pp. 189–190. Melville's most forthright confrontation of blackness. The innocent American is drawn into the evils of the old world. Slavery is an outrage against nature, which "authorizes the vengeance of the enslaved." Yet the interracial antagonism is recognized and Melville "seems ready to concede that life is a bloodfeud."

Leyda, Jay, ed. *The Complete Stories of Herman Melville* (New York, 1949), pp. xxi–xxiii. The story offers what is perhaps the most rewarding study of Melville's imagination and craftsmanship, especially as it relates to Melville's "policy of concealment" behind an "I" narrator.

*Magowan, Robin. "Masque and Symbol in Melville's 'Benito Cereno,' " *College English,* XXIII (February 1962), 346–351.

Mason, Ronald. *The Spirit above the Dust* (London, 1951), pp. 184–188. One of Melville's best sustained "allegorical essays," *Benito Cereno* symbolizes the conflict between the primitive and civilized and the dreadful uncertainty in which a man of good will can find himself when he sets out to determine which is in control. "Innocence, exploring experience, found the way hopelessly divided."

Matthiessen, F. O. *American Renaissance* (New York, 1941), p. 508. In *Benito Cereno* "the embodiment of good in the pale Spanish Captain and of evil in the mutinied African crew, though pictorially and theatrically effective, was unfortunate in raising unanswered questions. Although the Negroes were savagely vindictive . . . , the fact remains that they were slaves and that evil had thus originally been done to them."

*Miller, James E., Jr. *A Reader's Guide to Herman Melville* (New York, 1962), pp. 152–159.

Mumford, Lewis. *Herman Melville: A Study of His Life and Vision,* rev. ed. (New York, 1962), pp. 168–170. The moral point of the tale is the ease with which good and evil can be confounded, and the presence of inscrutable evil in the world as a constant torture to "fine souls."

Neider, Charles, ed. *Short Novels of the Masters* (New York, 1948), pp. 7–11. The story perhaps has an autobiographical element: Cereno is a personification of the author's "dark literary fate." The bulky mass of depositions is anticlimactic. The story suggests the theme of the decay of the old order's "monasticism, feudalism, and fanaticism." In contrast to Cereno's over-refinement there is Delano's healthy practicality. Preoccupied by the theme of masquerade, Melville inadvertently glosses over the circumstances that extenuate the Negroes' actions and turns them into "poetic images of pure evil."

Núñez, Estuardo. "Herman Melville en El Peru," *Panorama,* III, 11 (1954), 12–22 (in Spanish). Babo is perhaps the exteriorizing of Cereno's guilt for his part in slavery. Don Benito's career in the story follows something of the spiritual testing of the monk. The historical Delano was a pioneer in establishing inter-American ties, an early and forgotten bearer of international understanding.

Pafford, Ward, and Floyd Watkins. " 'Benito Cereno': A Note in Rebuttal," *Nineteenth Century Fiction,* VII (June 1952), 68–71. Rebuts Haber's view that Cereno cuts Babo: nowhere does Melville indicate that Cereno is capable of such a move; Babo's self-inflicted injury is artistically consistent with the rest of the narrative.

Phelps, Leland R. "The Reaction to *Benito Cereno* and *Billy Budd* in Germany," *Symposium,* XIII (Fall 1959), 294–299. In 1938 (when *Benito Cereno* was first translated into German) the story was read in Germany as a sublime treatment of the horror and ambiguity of existence. In the post-World War II period, critics tended to see the plight of Cereno as an analogue to the German intellectual under Hitler, who was forced to follow his leader or be destroyed.

*Phillips, Barry. " 'The Good Captain': A Reading of 'Benito Cereno,' " *Texas Studies in Literature and Language,* IV (Summer 1962), 188–197.

*Putzel, Max. "The Source and the Symbols of Melville's 'Benito Cereno,' " *American Literature,* XXXIV (May 1962), 191–206.

Ridge, George Ross, and Davy S. Ridge. "A Bird and a Motto: Source for 'Benito Cereno,' " *Mississippi Quarterly,* XII (Winter 1959–1960), 22–29. Points out "obviously parallel themes and thematic development" in *Benito Cereno* and Coleridge's *Ancient Mariner.* "Cosmic love is of course the theme in both works."

*Schiffman, Joseph. "Critical Problems in Melville's 'Benito Cereno,' " *Modern Language Quarterly,* XI (September 1950), 317–324.

*Schiffman, Joseph, ed. *Three Shorter Novels of Herman Melville* (New York, 1962), pp. 230–235.

Scudder, Harold H. "Melville's 'Benito Cereno' and Captain Delano's *Voyages,*" *PMLA,* XLIII (June 1928), 502–532. Reprints source, and comments on some of the changes Melville made. Extreme autobiographical interpretation: Cereno is Melville and Babo is the spirit of malicious criticism, which caused Melville to be unappreciated as an artist.

Stein, William Bysshe. "The Moral Axis of 'Benito Cereno,' " *Accent,* XV (Summer 1955), 221–233. Using the Christian symbolism and Biblical allusions in the story, argues that Cereno is the "mock host," Babo the "devil nonpareil [who] usurps the position cf Christ," Delano the "rootlessness of Protestant iconoclasm," and Aranda the true Christ.

Stewart, Randall, and Dorothy Betherum, eds. *Classic American Fiction* (Chicago, 1954), pp. 180–183. Defends the use of extracts as proper to the built-up tension and as a splendid symbolic contrast to the preceding mystery. The principal characters are allegorical embodiments in a drama of evil vs. innocence.

Stone, Geoffrey. *Melville* (New York, 1949), pp. 217–221. The documents, "coiling along like a wounded snake," dissipate the story's power. "Energy, taste, or technical resources here failed Melville. . . ."

Turner, Darwin T. "A View of Melville's 'Piazza,' " *CLA Journal,* VII (September 1963), 61–62. Relates *Benito Cereno* to the allegorical meaning of "The Piazza": man must accept the ambivalence of life without recourse to either naive daydreaming or human isolation.

Vogelback, Arthur L. "Shakespeare and Melville's 'Benito Cereno,' " *Modern Language Notes,* LXVII (February 1952), 113–116. Melville decided on the name Babo (rather than Mure) for his slave ring-leader because of its similarity to Iago. Parallels between Babo and Iago are pointed out.

Weaver, Raymond, ed. *The Shorter Novels of Herman Melville* (London, 1925, 1956), pp. xxxvii–xl. "In *Benito Cereno,* for once, at least, he saved his soul as an artist by losing it in something outside of himself. . . . For once he composed in the spirit of true beauty: a work devotedly finished, simple, and truly just."

Williams, Stanley T. " 'Follow Your Leader': Melville's 'Benito Cereno,' " *Virginia Quarterly Review,* XXII (Winter 1947), 65–76. Indicates, rather than analyzes, the wealth of symbolic material in the story. Cereno typifies the fading glories of the church and state in the Old World; Babo represents the elemental side of primitivism; Delano stands (remotely) for the energy of a new civilization, which is, however, philosophically immature.

Winters, Yvor. *In Defense of Reason* (New York, 1947), pp. 221–222. "The morality of slavery is not an issue in this story; the issue is this, that through a series of acts of performance and of negligence, the fundamental evil of a group of men, evil which normally should have been kept in abeyance, was freed to act."